UNFINISHED BUSINESS

UNFINISHED BUSINESS

Social Policy for
Social Care Students in Ireland

Joe Moran

ORPEN PRESS

Published by
Orpen Press
Lonsdale House
Avoca Avenue
Blackrock
Co. Dublin
Ireland

e-mail: info@orpenpress.com
www.orpenpress.com

Paperback ISBN 978-1-909895-01-0
Kindle ISBN 978-1-909895-08-9
ePub ISBN 978-1-909895-09-6

Printed in Dublin by SPRINT-print Ltd

This book is dedicated to my deceased parents, Joe and Anna Moran, of Lower William Street, New Ross, County Wexford, where it all began.

Contents

Contents

Contents

Contents

Contents

Boxes

Tables

Key Concepts

Capitalism
Capitalism is a socio-economic system based on profit-making from the private ownership of goods and services.

Catholic social teaching
This is teaching on social issues from a Catholic Church perspective. One of its fundamental principles is that the state should not involve itself in the affairs of family life.

'Celtic Tiger'
The 'Celtic Tiger' was the name given to Ireland and its economy during the period of unprecedented prosperity and boom, which lasted from the mid-1990s until the economy collapsed in 2008. Ireland's rapid economic growth and success were similar to those of the so-called East Asian 'Tiger' economies in the late 1980s and early 1990s, hence the term 'Tiger'.

Deliberate self-harm (DSH)
'The various methods by which people deliberately harm themselves, including self-cutting and taking overdoses. Varying degrees of suicide intent can be present and sometimes there may not be any suicidal intent, although an increased risk of further suicidal behaviour is associated with all DSH' (HSE 2005: 9).

Familialisation
Familialisation or 'family-centred ideology' refers to the fusion of childhood into the institution of the family and definition of children only as an extension of their parents, thus leaving children without rights as individuals.

Fiscal crisis
A fiscal crisis occurs when government expenditure is greater than its revenues (income from taxation) and it cannot borrow from the money markets to pay for its day-to-day commitments.

Mandatory reporting of child abuse
This is a requirement in law for those who work with children to report suspicions of child abuse to the appropriate authorities. Failure to report can result in legal sanctions against the mandated individual (Buckley 2009).

Marketplace
The marketplace is where all goods and services are exchanged in a capitalist system. Capitalism holds that the marketplace should be free of government interference and believes that rational individuals will make informed choices about their own needs which are served in the marketplace.

Median income
The median income is the middle value of incomes in Ireland (half of incomes are below and half are above), and is different from the average income (where all incomes are added together then divided by the number of people who have incomes to give an average value).

Neoliberalism
Neoliberalism is the dominant economic philosophy of our time, which promotes the marketplace as the answer to all human need. It believes in rational individuals who are motivated by self-interest, a very limited role for government and minimum welfare provision.

Poverty
'People are living in poverty if their income and resources (material, cultural and social) are so inadequate as to preclude them from having a standard of living that is regarded as acceptable by Irish society generally. As a result of inadequate income and resources, people may be excluded and marginalised from

participating in activities that are considered the norm for other people' (Government of Ireland 1997: 3).

Poverty – 'At risk of poverty'
'At risk of poverty' is a measurement indicator which identifies all those households that fall below a certain income level. In the European Union this has been set at 60 per cent of the median income. Ireland as a member state of the European Union uses the 60 per cent income level for the determination of at risk of poverty.

Poverty – Consistent poverty
Consistent poverty is defined by two elements, income and deprivation. People are deemed to be in consistent poverty if their income is less than 60 per cent of median income and if they are deprived of two or more goods or services considered essential for a basic standard of living. This is the measurement used by the Irish government in its anti-poverty strategies.

Social democracy
The traditional form of social democracy believes in the state's obligation to control the marketplace, collective support for individual freedom and the provision of welfare for all of its citizens.

Social exclusion
Social exclusion is the '[c]umulative marginalisation: from production (unemployment), from consumption (income poverty), from social networks (community, family and neighbours), from decision making and from an adequate quality of life' (Government of Ireland 1997: 3).

Suicide
Suicide is a 'conscious or deliberate act that ends one's life when an individual is attempting to solve a problem that is perceived as unsolvable by any other means' (HSE 2005: 9).

Abbreviations

ABFI	Alcohol Beverage Federation of Ireland
CERD	Convention for the Elimination of All Forms of Racial Discrimination
CMEDP	Committee to Monitor the Effectiveness of the Diversion Programme
CPD	continuing professional development
CSO	Central Statistics Office
DCYA	Department of Children and Youth Affairs
DECLG	Department of Environment, Community and Local Government
DEHLG	Department of Environment, Heritage and Local Government
DES	Department of Education and Science
DHC	Department of Health and Children
DJELR	Department of Justice, Equality and Law Reform
DRHE	Dublin Regional Homeless Executive
DSH	deliberate self-harm
EBP	evidence-based practice
ECB	European Central Bank
EMCDDA	European Monitoring Centre for Drugs and Drug Addiction
EMN	European Migration Network
EPSEN	Education for Persons with Special Educational Needs
ESPAD	European School Survey Project on Alcohol and Other Drugs
ESRI	Economic and Social Research Institute
EU	European Union
FESET	Formation d'Educateurs Sociaux Européens / European Social Educator Training
FLAC	Free Legal Advice Centres
GAA	Gaelic Athletic Association

HBSC	Health Behaviour in School-Aged Children
HETAC	Higher Education and Training Awards Council
HIQA	Health Information and Quality Authority
HRB	Health Research Board
HSCPC	Health and Social Care Professionals Council
HSE	Health Service Executive
IASCE	Irish Association of Social Care Educators
IASCW	Irish Association of Social Care Workers
ICF	International Classification of Functioning
ICI	Immigrant Council of Ireland
ICIDH	International Classification of Impairments, Disabilities and Handicap
IFSW	International Federation of Social Workers
IMF	International Monetary Fund
ISPCC	Irish Society for the Prevention of Cruelty to Children
ITM	Irish Traveller Movement
JCCAC	Joint Committee on the Constitutional Amendment on Children
LGBT	lesbian, gay, bisexual and transgender
LIS	Living in Ireland Survey
MEAS	Mature Enjoyment of Alcohol in Society
MRCI	Migrants Rights Centre Ireland
NACD	National Advisory Committee on Drugs
NAI	Non-Accidental Injury
NAPincl	National Action Programme on Social Inclusion
NAPinclusion	National Action Plan for Social Inclusion
NAPS	National Anti-Poverty Strategy
NCCA	National Council for Curriculum and Assessment
NCS	National Children's Strategy
n.d.	no date
NDA	National Disability Authority
NESF	National Economic and Social Forum
NFQ	National Framework of Qualifications
NIDD	National Intellectual Disability Database
NPSDD	National Physical and Sensory Disability Database

NSMSSG	National Substance Misuse Strategy Steering Group
NSPCC	National Society for the Prevention of Cruelty to Children
NSRF	National Suicide Research Foundation
NYC	National Youth Council
NYCI	National Youth Council of Ireland
NYWDP	National Youth Work Development Plan
OCO	Ombudsman for Children's Office
OECD	Organisation for Economic Co-Operation and Development
OMCYA	Office of the Minister for Children and Youth Affairs
ORAC	Office of the Refugee Applications Commissioner
PHIRB	Public Health Information and Research Branch
RAS	Rental Accommodation Scheme
RIA	Reception and Integration Agency
RMA	Resident Managers Association
SCI	Social Care Ireland
SCWRB	Social Care Workers Registration Board
SILC	Survey on Income and Living Conditions
SJI	Social Justice Ireland
UK	United Kingdom
UNCRC	United Nations Convention on the Rights of the Child
UNHCR	United Nations High Commissioner for Refugees
UPIAS	Union of the Physically Impaired Against Segregation
US	United States
VAT	value-added tax
VEC	Vocational Education Committee
WHO	World Health Organization
WIT	Waterford Institute of Technology

Preface

The idea for this textbook came from social care students I taught some years ago. Excellent social policy books were available for Irish undergraduates at the time, including the wonderful UCD Press social policy series and John Curry's enduring *Irish Social Services* (2003, 2011). Mairéad Considine and Fiona Dukelow's superb work, *Irish Social Policy: A Critical Introduction* (2009) had yet to be published. The social care students were of the opinion that these social policy texts did not meet their specific needs. In response I decided to write a social policy book for social care students, and this is the end result.

As this is a social policy text for students studying social care, the topics chosen represent policy areas of relevance to the practice of social care. Unfortunately, necessary limitations mean there has not been enough space to include chapters on all relevant policy issues. It is regrettable therefore that a number of very important policy areas have been omitted, such as chapters on older people, the family and domestic violence, to name but a few. However, the chapters included were prioritised as representing the crucial issues that need to be considered by social care students at this time.

I do not believe in the notion of objectivity in social policy, a political activity. Social policy is informed by values, and values are not neutral. Of course there is informed argument to be made, but it is not possible to be objective on the major issues of poverty, inequality and social exclusion, whatever form these may take and to whatever social grouping they may apply. All of the chapters in this book question policy decisions, point to ideological positions which dictate the thrust of policy, and attempt to show up inconsistencies in policy direction. It is my hope that this book will foster this critical perspective in the social care students who use it.

Thanks

Over the past two and a half years I have spent an inordinate amount of time on my own, researching and writing this book. While the actual act of writing was completed in isolation, the production of the book is much more collaborative. Many people played an active part in that collaboration, and no words can adequately thank them for their contribution. They include a number of then social care students who read early chapters of the book, and whose feedback not only gave me comfort that the approach I was taking met their needs but also pointed to some gaps that required plugging – Seamus Anderson, Lia Barron, Katrina Barry, Rebecca Beegan, Michelle Collins, Brendan Deighan, Brenda McGinn and Jean Yves Mwzerwa. Some former students with experience in social care practice also gave willingly of their time to read chapters, and gave me feedback that was both constructive and reassuring – David Dwyer, Catherine Kiersey, Domeneca Mac Rory and Kenny Mahony Quinn.

I extend my sincere gratitude to colleagues at the Waterford Institute of Technology (WIT) – Katie Cagney, Danielle Douglas, Hazel Finlay, Jane McGrath, John O'Brien, Máire O'Reilly, Méabh Savage, Cathy Wells and John Wells – for their collegiality and generosity, which was shown in a number of ways: by reading chapters, offering insights and pointing out important issues that I had missed, directing me to materials I had overlooked and loaning me books and articles. I also thank WIT's College Street library staff for their assistance, especially Neill Darbey, Brian Madigan and Diarmuid McElhinney.

I also offer my thanks to three peer reviewers, one reviewer who read an early draft of a chapter and two others who read a draft of the completed book. My thanks go to them for their helpful and encouraging comments. This work was shaped by all of those who commented on chapters, but of course I take full responsibility for all that I have written in this book.

At Orpen Press I am most grateful for the support of Elizabeth Brennan, Eileen O'Brien, Jennifer Thompson, Elizabeth O'Shaughnessy, and in particular Ailbhe O'Reilly, commissioning editor. From my first meeting with Ailbhe and throughout the whole process she has been extremely positive, helpful and so calm. I offer sincere thanks also to Susan Curran for the time she spent editing the book. Finally, I thank the cover designer, Clifford Hayes, for his interpretation of the ideas generated in my work.

Closer to home I thank my extended family for their love and concern for me and their interest in this project. In the early stages of writing this book my father became ill and died; he would have been very proud of my achievement. And finally thank you Anne, Anna, Mairéad and Róisín, for your extraordinary love and patience.

Joe Moran
January 2013

1

Introduction:
Irish Social Policy in a Neoliberal World

Area of Social Care for which this Chapter Is Relevant

This chapter sets the context for all that follows in this book on social policy for social care students.

Key Words in this Chapter

Social policy, social care, politics, neoliberalism

Key Themes in this Chapter

- Social policy and social care students
- Defining social policy
- Irish social policy in a neoliberal world
- Chapter outlines

Introduction

This introductory chapter sets out the context for this textbook, the aim of which is to address social policy with the social care student in mind. It is my contention that a good understanding of social policy is essential for social care students, if they are to give a holistic service to the people they work with. Social policy is quite simply the politics of welfare, and social care is itself a political act. Let me explain: the fact that a particular social service exists at all, the nature of the service, the funding for that service, the policy and legal frameworks around the service and even the lack of all or any of these elements stem from policy decisions made, or indeed not made, at a political level. This may not always be apparent in the day-to-day work of social care, but if that work is traced from the individual act back up the policy line, a link to political decision-making or the neglect of such decision-making is always evident. The political is part of the everyday social care job as much as the welcoming smile, the listening ear, the piece of advice, a therapeutic intervention or the formal well-planned activity. It is the underlying contention of this chapter and this textbook that social care workers who understand the politics of welfare are ultimately in a better position to support and advocate for their clients and their service.

In this chapter a number of different issues are discussed. The first is the relationship between social care students and social policy as a field of academic study. This is followed by an effort to define social policy and the way it is viewed from key ideological positions: social democratic, critical and neoliberal. The dominant political discourse in our world is neoliberalism, and a longer discussion on this is presented to provide a context for the recent development of Irish social policy. Aspects of social policy that are particularly relevant to social care students are presented in the subsequent chapters, and a brief synopsis of each of these is outlined in the final section of this chapter.

Social Policy and Social Care Students

Social policy is as much an integral part of social care as psychology, for example, but while the latter is accepted by students without a second thought, social policy is not. Why is this so? In the absence of any research (to my knowledge) on the views of Irish social care students on social policy, we can only examine research carried out on the closely related profession of social work. Henman (2012: 1) says that 'generating an interest and passion for social policy' among social work students can be quite 'challenging'. Henman quotes Weiss and colleagues (2006: 791), who explain that '[n]ot only do [social work] students display little desire to be involved in politics or policy formulation and view social policy as irrelevant to social work practice, but they often reach the end of their studies with an uncritical acceptance of existing policies and the dominant political discourse'.

Henman (2012: 2) suggests a number of reasons for a lack of interest in social policy:

- Students do not see social policy as having personal and professional relevance.
- Students do not believe they have the ability to bring about change in social policy.
- Students cannot make sense of social policy.
- Students may 'conceptualise professional practice from an individualised perspective'.
- Teachers may be the cause of a lack of interest because they are boring or do not show an interest in the topic themselves (although he says this cannot fully explain the lack of interest 'given the repeated observation of a lack of student interest').

Henman's (2012) concluding speculation that a more political stance by the teacher which identifies with the poor and oppressed would increase student interest coincides with the findings of Gibbons and Gray (2005). They found that students are motivated by a sense of social justice, and this contradicts the often-held view that social work students have little or no interest in politics or policy. They say that '[s]tudents with a motivation to work towards social justice are likely to be much more interested in the processes of policy' (Gibbons and Gray 2005: 58). The challenge for social work, then, according to these authors, is to make the connection between the commitment to social justice and everyday practice, rather than treating policy and practice as separate entities which run along parallel tracks. The findings of these two pieces of research pose challenges for social work education which can equally be applied to social care education, for as Henman (2012: 13) says, '[h]elping [students] to be capable to engage in social policy processes for the benefit of their clients is indeed an important professional and educational goal'. But what is social policy?

Defining Social Policy

There are many definitions or explanations of social policy, a term not easily defined. These are some samples from well-established scholars in this field:

> The term 'social policy' is not only used to refer to academic study . . . it is also used to refer to social actions taken by policy-makers in the real world. So social policy refers both to the activity of policy-making to promote well-being and to the academic study of such actions. (Alcock 2003: 3)

> The study of social policy is concerned with those aspects of public policies, market operations, personal consumption and inter-personal relationships which contribute to, or detract from, the well-being or welfare of groups. Social policy explores the social, political, ideological and institutional context within which welfare is explored. (Erskine 2003: 15)

> Those actions of government which deliberately or accidentally affect the distribution of resources, status, opportunities and life chances among social groups and categories of people within the country and thus help to shape the general character and equity of its social relations. (Donnison 1975: 30 cited in Curry 2011: 1)

Alcock's (2003) description of social policy as 'actions aimed at promoting well-being' may be accurate in certain circumstances, maybe even in many circumstances, but it is uncritically optimistic. Erskine's (2003) description of social policy as contributing to or detracting from the well-being or welfare of groups demonstrates the conflictual nature of social policy. Furthermore, Erskine's final sentence indicates that social policy is not just a matter of personal welfare; it is far broader than the individual, and reaches into the political structures and value systems of society. Donnison's (1975) definition of social policy is also close to encompassing the full breadth of its meaning, and indicates the political nature of social policy and the extent of its impact on society.

Box 1.1

Political Ideology and Views on Social Policy

Traditional social democracy

- Believes in a welfare state to support those who cannot care for themselves in a capitalist economic system
- Supports ideas of advancing equality
- Believes the state should redistribute wealth and incomes to ensure greater equality
- Believes the state should involve itself in all areas of life, such as education and health, to maximise life chances
- Supports the idea that the state is responsible for its citizens from the 'cradle to the grave'

Critical perspective (Marxist/socialist)

- Rejects the welfare state as it has a political role in supporting capitalism
- Believes social policy and welfare states are in place to give legitimacy to the capitalist system
- Believes the welfare state fails to lift people out of poverty
- Believes the welfare state fails to bring about equality
- Believes the welfare state helps to maintain the existing structures in society

Neoliberalism

- Is dismissive of large welfare states
- Supports small government
- Regards individuals as consumers
- Believes individuals make their own rational choices about their needs, including welfare
- Believes the state should not interfere with choices of individuals
- Believes the state should only provide a basic welfare system for those who cannot protect themselves

The definitions of social policy by Donnison (1975), Alcock (2003) and Erskine (2003) stem from a social democratic perspective on social policy and welfare, which held sway from the mid-1940s until the 1970s. This perspective was the dominant political philosophy in the Western world during this period, and is based on the idea of personal well-being promoted through a welfare state system in a capitalist world. The historical origins of the social democratic perspective stem from classical liberalism, and thus social democracy accepts the capitalism system. However, social democrats believe that capitalism should be managed properly by the state, and that those who do not benefit from the capitalist system should be supported by a welfare state (Kearns 1997).

An alternative and more critical left-wing perspective, informed by a Marxist analysis of the role of social policy in society, views social policy as a means of supporting capitalism. This means that rather than promoting the well-being of the majority, social policy supports the wealthy and powerful minority who benefit from the capitalist system (Lavalette 1997). Social policy and the provision of welfare through the welfare state are, according to this view, primarily tools that legitimise the capitalist system and the social relations that underline it. This critical perspective on social policy therefore rejects the concept of the welfare state, as it is perceived to be a political activity to support capitalism (Lavalette 1997).

At the other end of the political ideological continuum sit the neoliberal right. They, like the critical left wing, are also dismissive of the welfare state but for entirely different reasons. Neoliberals believe in what they call 'small government', where individuals should be allowed to shape their own lives with as little interference from the state as possible. If left alone individuals will make rational choices in their own interest, and will do so in what is regarded as the best and most neutral of environments, the marketplace, where goods and services are bought and sold (Pratt 1997). Following the logic of this argument there is little room for state interference in the welfare of individuals. Thus, individuals are the best judges of their welfare needs and should be allowed to make their own choices in this regard just as they do about all other aspects of their lives. Therefore individuals should be left to buy all services, including all welfare services such as health and education, in the marketplace for the best price they can find, rather than rely on state provision. The belief is that if the state intervenes it will encourage individuals to become dependent on the state. Neoliberals thus insist that there should be only a minimal (also called residual) welfare state, to provide basic welfare for people when all else has failed (Pratt 1997).

Irish Social Policy in a Neoliberal World

The aim of this section is to provide a political and economic analysis of the context of Irish social policy in order to aid social care students gain a better understanding of the place of their profession in a social and political world, which according to Garrett (2010) is being restructured by neoliberal values. The Irish state's approach to social policy has been portrayed as conservative and informed by the social teaching of the Catholic Church (Fanning 1999), and this led to a delay in devising a modern welfare system to meet the needs of the population (see also Burke 1999, Conroy 1999). However, with the emergence of the so-called 'Celtic Tiger' period all this was to change. The characteristics of the new Ireland were economic growth at rates previously unknown, the virtual elimination of unemployment – for so long one of the state's most deeply embedded problems – and a shift from a country of emigration to one of immigration (Kirby 2010). As a result of these developments the second half of the 1990s saw the beginnings of an enormous expansion in social policy commitment and provision in Ireland. These changes may have given the appearance of Ireland catching up on other European states in its welfare obligations, and so it did to a point.

In keeping with trends in other Anglo-Saxon countries, Ireland's welfare system followed the path of the neoliberal model of the new era, which emerged from the early 1980s onwards. Hyslop (2011: 405) describes this as 'an era which privileges modernization at the expense of tradition, individual over collective interests, and places economic value before social development'. Neoliberalism cannot be regarded as a coherent model across all states though, as it is subject to national variations which lead to substantial differences in policy outcomes

(Clarke 2004). Kirby links 'neoliberalism Irish style' to a 'highly market-friendly state' and the favouring of large global corporate players (Kirby 2010: 147), thus strongly making the connection between Irish neoliberalism and globalisation. The policy of encouraging these global corporate players to establish businesses in Ireland has long been a feature of Irish economic and industrial policy, beginning in the late 1950s, with the publication of the influential government White Paper (that is, policy paper) *The Programme for Economic Expansion* (Government of Ireland 1958). This policy of encouraging foreign direct investment, particularly by American capital, and offering tax incentives to investors, was to give Ireland an advantageous position with the 'completion of the European single market in 1992' (Dellepiane and Hardiman 2012: 84).

Other factors would also contribute to Ireland's economic miracle. O'Donnell and O'Reardon summarise the features of Ireland's developmental strategy which underpinned what was to become known as the 'Celtic Tiger':

> These included a young, well-educated, English-speaking workforce, improved infrastructure (funded by both the EU and the Irish state), an inflow of leading US enterprises (attracted by both Irish conditions and the deepening European market), a new population of Irish enterprises (free of the debilitating weaknesses of the past and open to new organisational patterns), and de-regulation of the service sectors. (O'Donnell and O'Reardon 2000: 4)

Another development closely associated with this period of success in Ireland's economic fortunes was social partnership. Social partnership was born in the late 1980s of the economic necessity to overcome an indebted and stagnant economy (Baccaro 2003). The social partnership model used in Ireland provided structures for policy engagement between government and the major economic and social interest groups in the state. Social partnership has been 'credited with facilitating fiscal policy adjustment out of the depression of the 1980s and stable management of the rapid growth of the 1990s and 2000s' (Dellepiane and Hardiman 2012: 85). Social partnership was also used as a vehicle for addressing social policy issues as the economy began to improve in the 1990s. Over the following decade and a half it brought about strategic plans to deal with pressing needs in health care provision, poverty eradication, homelessness, children's services, and services for disabled people, to name but some of the areas targeted by government. Ireland's social spending in real terms more than doubled in the period 1990–2004, the highest increase in the European Union (Callan et al. 2008). Yet the proportion of the overall wealth generated by the Irish economy during that period spent on social protection actually deteriorated (see Eurostat 2007). By the time the boom period came to an end in 2008, inequality had increased (Dellepiane and Hardiman 2012, Nolan 2009, Ó Riain 2008) and there remained many other intractable problems, in for instance housing (Healy et al. 2012) and health care (Burke 2009).

Kirby and Murphy (2011) divide the Celtic Tiger period into three phases. The first, 1987–1992, identified as the *growth phase*, saw what is described as a right-of-centre coalition (Fianna Fáil–Progressive Democrats) bring the fiscal problems of the state under control, and positioned Ireland to benefit from international developments, such as the completion of the European single market and expansion by US companies in the 1990s. The second phase, 1992–1997, known as the *developmental phase*, had a centre-left coalition government (Fianna Fáil–Labour) followed by a Fine Gael–Labour–Democratic Left government, which 'brought a focus on equality and on the development of a dynamic indigenous software sector'(Kirby and Murphy 2011: 72, emphasis in original). The final phase, 1997–2007, Kirby and Murphy (2011: 72, emphasis in original) call the *competition phase*, overseen by a centre-right coalition government (Fianna Fáil–Progressive Democrats), with a focus 'on reducing taxes and stimulated a property boom through state subsidies and tax breaks'.

In their analysis Dellepiane and Hardiman draw a similar conclusion about the nature of growth in the Irish economy in this latter period: it was 'based on the domestic sector, particularly on an unsustainable reliance on construction' (2012: 104). They note the strong association between the key beneficiaries from the boom – 'property-owners, developers, builders and bankers', who enjoyed favourable tax incentives – and the major governing party Fianna Fáil. They conclude that this association ultimately led to 'fatally flawed policies: a form of "crony capitalism" Irish-style' (2012: 104). Unfortunately for Ireland and its people, these policies led to a banking and economic crisis. Of the former, Honahon says, '[i]n short, although international pressures contributed to the timing, intensity and depth of the Irish banking crisis, the essential characteristic of the problem was domestic and classic' (2010: 22).

According to Healy and colleagues (2012), the origins of this national and global financial crisis were long in the making. They argue that it stemmed from the era of Thatcher (in the United Kingdom) and Reagan (in the United States) in the 1980s, who were the political initiators of the central elements of neoliberal capitalism: competition, unregulated markets, privatisation of public goods, reduction in taxation, and the rolling-back of state welfare provision. This policy mix was adopted throughout the advanced economies of the English-speaking world, and in time it also became the dominant model of the European Union (Kirby and Murphy 2011; see also Gray 2004). The very lightly regulated banking and financial sector was the immediate cause of the Irish economic collapse (Allen 2012), but the consequences of this calamity showed up deeper problems in the values and structure of the globally established economic model of neoliberalism, and nowhere more so than Ireland. According to Allen:

> Ireland could, therefore, be presented as a textbook case for the failures of neoliberalism. The open embrace of light regulation in finance and tax breaks to stimulate a housing market led directly to the crash. Yet far from producing a re-think, the crash has led to an intensification of neoliberal policies. In fact, Ireland has led the way in Europe in promoting such a response. (Allen 2012: 425)

The collapse of the Irish banking system and its 'rescue' by the Irish state were to cost Ireland dearly (Honahon 2010). The move by the Irish government in 2008 to guarantee the (as then unknown in size) huge losses of the Irish banks by taking on the full extent of their debt, and in effect to prop up a local version of capitalism, has been characterised as 'socialism for the rich – neoliberalism for the poor' (Allen 2009: 76).

The Irish crisis was not only a financial one; another dimension to the crisis was fiscal (Dellepiane and Hardiman 2012, Honahon 2010). Ireland did not have a debt problem prior to the financial crisis. In fact through most of the 'Celtic Tiger' period there were substantial fiscal surpluses (that is, the state's income was greater than its expenditure) (Dellepiane and Hardiman 2012). However, Ireland's tax base was structurally very weak, as Honahon (2010) points out. He says that 'stable and reliable sources' of revenue, such as personal income tax, value-added tax (VAT) and excise duties were removed systematically over two decades and replaced by what he terms '"fair weather" taxes': corporation tax, stamp duties and capital gains taxes (Honahon 2010: 29).

Ireland's model of low taxation and a narrow tax base was not in a position to cope with the shock of the new economic realities (Healy et al. 2012). Once the bubble burst and the sources of government revenue collapsed, the state found it impossible to meet its day-to-day spending commitments because of falling revenues. The response by government was 'to implement its fiscal adjustment entirely through spending cuts' (Commission on Taxation 2009, cited in Dellapiane and Hardiman 2012: 97). The gains that were made during the boom times, including low unemployment and an end to emigration, were to be reversed. Austerity and so-called structural reform were to follow.

By the end of 2008 the first of a series of austerity budgets was introduced, beginning the row-back in social policy expenditure. The Budget 2009 (presented in October 2008) and subsequent budgets began a policy of welfare cuts; reductions in public services across health, education and housing; increasing taxes, both personal and indirect; the introduction of levies and a range of new charges; and reductions in public sector pay and pensions. The social and economic consequences of these policies were an economy that is stagnant, with high unemployment at over 14 per cent, increasing poverty (see Chapter 3 in this volume), and as Allen (2012) points out, greater inequality. Increasingly austerity as a policy is being questioned by economists and political leaders across Europe (Sweeney 2012). As early as 2010 Krugman commented:

Both textbook economics and experience say that slashing spending when you're still suffering from high unemployment is a really bad idea – not only does it deepen the slump, but it does little to improve the budget outlook, because much of what governments save by spending less they lose as a weaker economy depresses tax receipts. (Krugman 2010a)

Less than a month later Krugman wrote again about austerity, giving Ireland a special mention:

For the last few months, I and others have watched, with amazement and horror, the emergence of a consensus in policy circles in favor [sic] of immediate fiscal austerity. … Ireland has been a good soldier in this crisis, grimly implementing savage spending cuts. Its reward has been a Depression-level slump — and financial markets continue to treat it as a serious default risk. (Krugman 2010b)

Things were to get worse when the imposition of 'austerity measures' became 'structural reform'. This is explained by Healy and colleagues as involving 'the introduction of measures to ensure that national budgets are balanced and economic growth promoted' (2012: 10). In November 2010 Ireland sought, and in early December 2010 it entered into, a European Union (EU)/ European Central Bank (ECB)/International Monetary Fund (IMF) bailout programme in order to secure credit to cover the day-to-day running costs of the state and to support the banking system (Government of Ireland 2010a). At this time credit was becoming increasingly expensive for the Irish government to obtain. This bailout was conditional on certain public expenditure targets being met by the Irish government.

The Irish government had already introduced *The National Recovery Plan 2011–2014* (Government of Ireland 2010b), and this was integrated into the bailout programme. Central to the *National Recovery Plan* were targets which coincided with the requirements of the EU/ECB/IMF programme. These included commitments to reduce welfare spending, reduce public sector pay and pensions, and reduce public services 'including student supports, free or subsidised medical care and treatment'

(Government of Ireland 2010b: 11). In its strategy for competitiveness, growth and employment, the government's policy is
to 'support the private sector by removing potential structural
impediments to competitiveness and employment creation'
(Government of Ireland 2010b: 10). Removing 'structural impediments' refers to cuts in pay in both public and private sectors,
a more flexible workforce, greater use of employment activation
programmes and reduced welfare rates to incentivise work and
training rather than welfare dependency (see Allen 2012, Healy
et al. 2012). The election of a new government in 2011 did not
change the substance of the overall approach to dealing with
Ireland's economic and fiscal predicament, and the policy path
of structural reform continues.

The economic and fiscal crisis was not just an Irish problem,
as a number of European countries faced economic meltdown,
threatening the existence of the euro and monetary union. In
response a new treaty on Stability, Coordination and Governance in the Economic and Monetary Union was introduced by the
European Union in early 2012. This treaty gives the institutions
of the European Union an unprecedented say in the management of the economic affairs of member states. The treaty, unlike
the EU/ECB/IMF bailout, is not a temporary arrangement from
which Ireland and other EU member states in a similar position
can hope eventually to escape. According to Beesley, this new
treaty will enforce strict limits on public debt and public expenditure indefinitely:

> Thanks to the EU–IMF bailout, Ireland is no stranger to the
> hazards of intrusive external oversight of its internal affairs.
> There will be more of the same forever in the new dispensa-
> tion, with considerably less national discretion over fiscal
> policy, and heavy-handed treatment for any government
> which flouts the pact. (Beesley 2012)

For a people who have lost faith in the ability of their politicians
to manage their affairs, this new treaty may seem like a welcome
step. However, it ties the hands of governments in the future
even if economic circumstances become more positive (Beesley
2012). Healy and colleagues argue that if this new treaty had

been in place for the decade before the bust, 'it would have made no difference to Ireland', as it would 'not have forced the Government or the banks to do anything differently' (2012: 11). The treaty does not address the underlying causes of the difficulties being experienced, and '[i]t also ignores social context, containing no reference to social policy, poverty, inequality or social inclusion' (Healy et al. 2012: 11).

For social policy in Ireland these are not good times. The economic model pursued by the Irish government and the European Union demands that economic growth be the priority. Where spending on social policy is deemed to hinder that growth, then social programmes are cut back irrespective of the consequences for vulnerable citizens. Furthermore there is apparently no questioning of the view that economic growth in and of itself is a good thing, or that it can or should be sustained at previous levels (see Kirby and Murphy 2011). The consequences of this policy path are enormous for those who need the support of the state to be treated fairly and equally in Irish society, as well as for those who depend on the state for financial and practical assistance. For the foreseeable future the path ahead is likely to create a society more unequal than before, and a society in which many of those in need will inevitably have to depend on family, neighbours and community to share ever scarcer resources. The remainder of this book probes the challenges (many of which were well entrenched long before the boom and bust of recent years) for social policy, for social care workers and for those who have an expectation of support from the Irish state in their time of need.

Chapter Outlines

Each chapter in this text follows a similar pattern. First it states the area of social care to which it is relevant, followed by key words and the key themes to be addressed. Then there is an introduction, and some background to the topic under discussion, followed by a description of legislation and policy, a discussion on the policy approach, and a conclusion. Recommendations for further reading and web links to important documents are provided at the end of each chapter, as are some useful web addresses.

Chapter 2 – 'The "Political": Social Care Beyond the Individual' – aims to introduce the student to the policy context for social care. While recognising the difficulties in defining social care (admittedly not an easy task), the chapter acknowledges development and growth in the field over the past decade and a half, in both practice and the provision of social care education. A significant part of the chapter is given over to the Health and Social Care Professionals Act 2005, the most important piece of legislation directed at the social care profession and other allied professions in the health and social services sector in Ireland. This legislation when fully implemented has the potential to affect social care practice and education very significantly. The central discussion in the chapter concerns the political nature of social care as an activity, and argues for a greater emphasis on this dimension of social care, which is very much neglected in education and practice. It also highlights the impact of the lack of an international dimension to the profession of social care.

Chapter 3 – 'Poverty in Ireland: "the poor will always be with us"' – addresses the complex area of poverty, and the closely related issues of social exclusion and inequality. Poverty is one of the areas in Irish social policy that has received a lot of attention over a number of decades. Although the level of poverty in Ireland has declined, the targets to reduce poverty that were set during the first decade of this century were not met, and the current targets are also unlikely to be met given the social policy path being followed by the government. Definitions of poverty are explored, as is the extent of poverty, and policies to combat poverty and the relationship between poverty, social exclusion and inequality are discussed.

Chapter 4 – 'Shame of it: child protection in Ireland' – reviews Irish child protection policies. The Irish state has failed vulnerable children in need of protection through the years. Over the past twenty years positive initiatives such as the watershed Child Care Act 1991, Children First, the National Children's Strategy and a range of other policy, administrative and regulatory initiatives have all been extremely valuable, and yet fundamental failings in the system of child protection have continued. Much hope has been placed in the change to the Irish Constitution to improve the rights of children, and in the restructuring of child and family services.

Young people are the subject of Chapter 5 – 'It could only be youth: hoodies and "folk devils"'. The concept of young people or youth in Irish public policy covers a wide range of ages from children to young adults. Policy in this area tends to focus on youth work (particularly with young people deemed to be at risk) and youth justice work. These aspects receive the bulk of public funding too. There is a lack of a policy base to meet the broader needs of young people. The chapter concludes with a discussion on the ambivalent nature of Irish policy on young people.

Chapter 6 – 'Whither disability policy?' – argues that despite improvement in the landscape of disability policy over the past twenty years, disabled people remain marginal in Irish society. The past decade saw the introduction of important disability legislation, a National Disability Strategy and the promise of large-scale investment in disability services. The hope gener-ated by these policy developments has yet to be fulfilled. Some elements of these plans have been implemented and increased funding was made available, but they fall far short of what was promised. The result has been a continued exclusion of disabled people from Irish society. It is argued in the chapter that the most recent direction in disability policy towards individualised care, while it may seem appealing, is not without potential pitfalls.

In Chapter 7 – 'Travellers: the most excluded of all?' – much evidence is outlined that suggests Travellers are the most excluded of all social groups in Irish society. In relation to issues of health, mortality, education, employment, accommodation, poverty and social exclusion, Travellers fare extremely badly. Research has also found much hostility and racism towards Trav-ellers from the general population, and that this is manifested in policies concerning Travellers. Policies based on absorption and assimilation of Travellers into the majority community have not succeeded. The alternative, the recognition of Travellers as a minority ethnic group, has yet to be tried, but may provide the most realistic basis for improving the lives of Travellers.

Homelessness seems to be an intractable problem, as is discussed in Chapter 8 – 'Will we ever see the end of homelessness?' A number of policies and strategies have been developed to tackle homelessness, yet the problem persists. A definition of homelessness is provided in the Homeless Act 1988, but not all those interested in the issue agree with it. The definition of homelessness determines the number of people judged to be homeless at any given point, a highly contentious and emotive matter. Aside from these important matters, it is argued that the historical thrust of government housing policy, with its emphasis on home ownership as a central policy plank, contributes to the problems of homelessness.

Policies regarding a still relatively new social group in Irish society are explored in Chapter 9 – 'Lest we forget the *céad míle fáilte*: immigrants, refugees and asylum seekers'. While we are all only too aware of the history of emigration from Ireland, there is less recognition that immigration into the country also has a long history. It is only since the mid-1990s that the issue of immigration has entered the public consciousness and begun to be addressed politically through the development of legislation and policy. This chapter examines the policies of the Irish state on economic immigrants, refugees and asylum seekers, and questions the nature of these policies and whether they meet the welfare needs of these groups.

Chapter 10 – 'The ambiguity of Ireland's alcohol and drugs policies' – explores the less than coherent policy approaches to alcohol and drugs in Ireland. Although alcohol is technically a drug, its consumption in Ireland is legal. There are major differences therefore between the policy approaches to alcohol and illegal drugs use. Even within these policy areas ambivalence is evident, especially in relation to alcohol. The current government is committed to developing a unified alcohol and drugs strategy, but the question remains how the new policy direction will deal with the existing deeply embedded ambiguities.

Finally, Chapter 11 – 'The neglected? Suicide and mental health in Ireland' – turns to an area of policy which poses many challenges to Irish society and to policy-makers. In recent years the issue of suicide has gained greater public recognition, leading to more openness and debate. But stigma still remains. When it comes to mental health there has been less progress in the awakening of a positive public consciousness, as there are still serious problems of stigma and denial. Mental health policy has been and continues to be a marginal area of health policy in Ireland, with very limited budgetary resources and inadequately executed policy strategies. Progress in mental health occurs very slowly, as the Irish state has never shown any great urgency or commitment to this area. This in turn adversely impacts on those who experience mental health problems, and can also have an influence on those who consider committing suicide.

Conclusion

The title of this book, *Unfinished Business: Social Policy for Social Care Students in Ireland,* might lead some to observe – rightly – that due to its nature social policy is never finished business. Social policy is always changing, as it did while I was writing this book: I had to revise many passages because a new policy document had been published, a new set of data had become available, or a new policy decision had been made. But this continuous movement in social policy is not what I had in mind in choosing the title. There are three particularly relevant aspects of 'unfinished business' which I would like to highlight for readers. First, policy for social care is unfinished business, as it has yet to become a core, intrinsically connected element of social care education and practice. Furthermore the field of social care, as an object of policy, is still in its infancy. To date social care, as an educational and professional activity, has received limited attention in government policy and in academic research, which means there is surely unfinished business.

The second point is that time and again worthwhile social policies are developed but are not implemented. They are not given specific timeframes, they lack sufficient resources and infrastructure, targets are sometimes not set and often not met when they are set, and the political and administrative will to implement social policy is often missing. Much of social policy in Ireland does not achieve what was originally intended.

The third point is that I believe social progress based on social justice and equality is impossible to achieve within the ideologically dominant framework of neoliberalism. This assessment may seem unduly pessimistic, but that is not my intention. The intention is to point to the social policy context in which social care functions in Ireland. If that context is to be challenged, I suggest that the most important first step to achieving change is to develop a critical awareness of the accepted social policy approach pursued by the state. I hope this book will contribute to the awakening of this critical awareness, and in so doing help to make the case for finishing the business.

2

The 'Political': Social Care Beyond the Individual

Area of Social Care for which this Chapter Is Relevant

Knowledge of the political dimensions of social care is essential for all social care students and social care workers.

Key Words in this Chapter

Social care, politics, ethics, values, education, practice, neoliberalism, social work, social pedagogy, professional registration

Key Themes in this Chapter

- Defining social care
- Health and Social Care Professionals Act 2005
- Politics and social care work
- Where to for Irish social care?

Introduction

The field of social care in Ireland has grown enormously over the past decade and a half, coinciding with the more general expansion of welfare-related activity during the period of economic growth referred to in Chapter 1 (Christie 2005, Lalor and Share 2009). The consequences of this growth for social care have been a proliferation of policy developments, new service areas, increased job opportunities and more educational programmes. The qualification status of social care has also improved, with the basic qualification in social care moving from certificate and diploma levels to degree level. The groups representing professional interests in social care, the long-established Resident Managers Association (RMA) established in 1932 (Resident Managers Association n.d.), the Irish Association of Social Care Workers (IASCW) formed in 1972 (Howard n.d.), and the Irish Association of Social Care Educators (IASCE) set up in 1998 (IASCE n.d.), united as a constituent representative body known as Social Care Ireland (SCI) which was formally launched in 2011. Social Care Ireland aims to bring about greater cohesion between the representative bodies and provide a common voice in the development of social care in Ireland. The academic literature related to social care has grown too, with valuable contributions across a range of publications becoming available in recent years.

It is the intention of this chapter to describe and interrogate these advances in more detail in the context of social policy development, just as the following chapters do with other policy areas. This is not an easy task, since in spite of all of the developments that have taken place in social care, there has been limited research into or theoretical analysis of social care as a social policy and political issue. Academics in the field of social care (I include myself here) have added to the knowledge base of a diverse range of social-care-related issues and activities, but there has been little academic focus on the political or policy relevance of social care itself. There are some exceptions (for example see O'Connor 2006, 2009; Hanlon 2009), and I hope this chapter will add to that literature.

The chapter addresses a number of issues. It begins by examining the definition of social care used by the social care representative bodies in Ireland. This is followed by an extensive outline of the main piece of legislation related to social care, the Health and Social Care Professionals Act 2005 (Government of Ireland 2005a), and policy developments emanating from that legislation. A large section of the chapter then explores the nature of the politics of social care in Ireland. It is argued that the political nature and potential of social care is lost in social care education and practice in Ireland because of the concentration on individual pathology models of practice, the lack of a thought-through value base, and weak international connections. Finally, this debate leads to a 'where to?' discussion about Irish social care.

Defining Social Care

'It is difficult to define social care for a number of reasons' (Lalor and Share 2009). The first of two reasons given by Lalor and Share is that it suits 'government and some agencies *not* to have a standard definition' (2009: 5, emphasis in original). They do not state why this suits these bodies, but instead list the consequences for social care workers: vagueness of salary and career structures, and foot-dragging on defining social care practice because of the lack of implementation of the Health and Social Care Professionals Act 2005. Lalor and Share's second reason is the 'contested notion of social care as a profession' (2009: 5), which they argue is a result of 'the lack of a clear professional grouping we can point to as "practising social care"'. This undoubtedly arises because social care is connected to a range of related and overlapping fields: social work, community work and youth work (Christie 2005). This is not only a problem and challenge for social care in Ireland, as similar situations exist in other countries (see the chapters by Hallstedt and Högström, Charles and Garfa, and Cameron, in Share and Lalor (2009) for examples of these challenges in Europe, North America and the United Kingdom) and for the other related professions such as social work (Staniforth, Fouché and O'Brien 2011), youth work (Jenkinson 2000), and community work (Meade 2009).

A number of variations on the definition of social care are available, but mostly they are nuanced presentations of the same themes. Three of the definitions are presented here. The first is a working definition used by the Health Service Executive (HSE) (2009: 38), which was adopted in the Report of the Joint Committee on Social Care Professionals in 2003 (a report on the profession of social care):

> Social Care is the professional provision of care, protection, support, welfare and advocacy for vulnerable or dependent clients, individually or in groups. This is achieved through the planning and evaluation of individualised and group programmes of care which are based on needs, identified in consultation with the client and delivered through day-to-day shared life experiences. All interventions are based

on established best practice and in-depth knowledge of life-span development. (HSE 2009: 38)

Second is the IASCE agreed definition from 2005, used by Lalor and Share (2009: 5) and McCann James, de Róiste and McHugh (2009: 15). Social care is described as 'a profession committed to the planning and delivery of quality care and other support services for individuals and groups with identified needs'. Lalor and Share expanded on this, quoting an IASCE brochure 'What is social care?':

> Social care is an (emerging) profession characterised by working in partnership with people who experience margin-alisation or disadvantage or who have 'special needs'. Social care practitioners may work, for example, with children and adolescents in residential care; people with learning or physical disabilities; people who are homeless; people with alcohol/drug dependency; families in the community; older people; recent immigrants to Ireland; and others. Typically, though not always, social care practitioners work with children, youth and their families. (Lalor and Share 2009: 7)

The third definition is from the SCI website. Because the SCI was set up recently and is broadly representative of the sector, this is the most up-to-date and widely endorsed definition of social care:

> Social care workers plan and provide professional, individual or group care to clients with personal and social needs. Client groups are varied and include children and adolescents in residential care; young people in detention schools; people with intellectual or physical disabilities; people who are homeless; people with alcohol/drug dependency; families in the community; or older people. Social care workers strive to support, protect, guide and advocate on behalf of clients. Social care work is based on interpersonal relationships which require empathy, strong communication skills, self awareness and an ability to use critical reflection.

Teamwork and interdisciplinary work are also important in social care practice.

The core principles underpinning social care work are similar to those of other helping professions, and they include respect for the dignity of clients; social justice; and empowerment of clients to achieve their full potential.

Social care workers are trained, inter alia, in life span development, parenting, attachment & loss, interpersonal communication and behaviour management. Their training equips them to optimise the personal and social development of those with whom they work. (SCI 2011)

A feature of these definitions is the focus on what social care workers do rather than on what their work is about. Of the three definitions given here, the IASCE is rather vague, and becomes precise only when it lists the clients of social care workers. Lavan, in a review of the book on social care practice in Ireland by McCann James and colleagues (2009), suggests that although these authors endorse the IASCE definition, it 'is not entirely satisfactory' (2010: 149) (but she does not state in what way it is unsatisfactory). The Joint Committee on Social Care Professionals' definition used by the HSE is similarly framed but somewhat more expansive, although its reference to 'day-to-day shared experiences' suggest it is concerned primarily with social care work based in residential services. The SCI definition is the most comprehensive, although it has some limiting features.

Let me highlight two points about the SCI definition. First, it is good that it includes the core principles underpinning social care work, which are missing from the other definitions. Among these principles is 'social justice', which is related to the political context for social care. Social justice, according to Banks (2008: 31) (writing about the concept in social work), challenges negative discrimination and unjust policies and practices, recognises diversity, seeks the distribution of resources fairly according to need, and requires working in solidarity. The second point about the SCI definition is that it contains little by way of commitment to social justice. The final paragraph describes the type of training that social care workers have: it is training for individual change.

There is no reference to training in social justice, an approach that goes beyond the individual and implies broader transformational change (Banks 2008). Lalor and Share note that the 'goal of empowerment and liberation of service users' in social care work 'is perhaps less explicitly stated in definitions of social care work (notwithstanding references to advocacy), compared to social work, where the definition also contains a commitment to principles of human rights and social justice' (2009: 10).

Of the websites of the three representative bodies and the SCI, I could only find a reference to ethical guidelines for social care work on the IASCW site. The IASCW drew up its ethical guidelines in 1988, and revised them in 1996 and 2006 (IASCW n.d.). They claim to reflect 'best practice, professional performance and accountability' and the declarations and principles of the United Nations (although it is not clear which UN declarations and principles this refers to). They mention the principles of professionalism, responsibility, conscientiousness and non-discrimination, in the name of 'the best interests of those with and for whom Social Care Workers carry out their professional duties' (IASCW n.d.). Social care workers 'Must contribute to the physical, intellectual, emotional, social and moral welfare of service users in a context where every effort is made to ensure that the nature and purpose of any care and treatment given is understood by the service user' (IASCW n.d.).

The guidelines list ten things social care workers must do to achieve these ends, all of them related to the professionalism of the social care worker: by showing respect for each person as an individual; by being honest; by being fit for work; by respecting the rights of service users; by promoting the best interests of the service user; by following established policies; by ensuring transparency in procedures for making complaints; by recording information on service users in an accurate and objective way; by not using information obtained in a professional capacity for other purposes; by accepting that exemption from professional confidentiality can only be breached in rare circumstances, in the interests of the service user and in a court of law; and by acting in such a way as to uphold the dignity of social care work (IASCW n.d.). These ethical guidelines are very valuable, and give an indication of the high standards expected of social care workers in carrying out their professional duties. Yet the ethical guidelines, like the definitions discussed earlier, reflect a narrow view of the nature of social care work, which is tellingly described in terms of 'care and treatment given'.

You might ask what is the point of this focus on definitions of social care and ethical principles. My aim is to ascertain the central concern of social care work in Ireland, to essentially seek out its value base. This is extremely important as it informs us of the philosophical approach that underlines social care work in Ireland. All this material suggests it is primarily cemented in an individual model within the narrow confines of 'care and treatment'. This is not an either/or argument (for an individual or a transformational approach), though. Understanding individual need is an essential element of what social care work has to offer, but in responding to that need all options should be considered. The thrust of Irish social care values to date, judging by the publicly available documentation, is predominantly based on an adaptive model of social care. This model reflects a value base informed by the belief that individuals must change to meet the expectations of broader societal norms and structures. Social care education and practice have generally failed to broaden the theoretical base to take into account issues that might become manifest as personal troubles, but the resolution of which goes beyond the world of the personal and reaches into the political world (Mulkeen 2009a, O'Connor 2006, O'Toole 2009). In other words the expectation that underlies Irish social care practice is that service users should adapt to their circumstances rather than social care workers working alongside them to challenge the social structures that may be at the root of their problems.

The Health and Social Care Professionals Act 2005

One piece of legislation is of the utmost importance to social care in Ireland: the Health and Social Care Professionals Act 2005. The implementation of this Act will quite possibly transform social care practice, education, and the meaning of social care as a profession. As this chapter was being written the legislation, which is partially in force, did not yet apply to social care work, so the profession and social care education remain unregulated. This section gives a brief outline of the key provisions of the Health and Social Care Professionals Act 2005, followed by a comment on policy developments since the introduction of the legislation.

In a section on human resources, Action 105 of the national *Health Strategy* commits to statutory registration of professionals who work within the health and social care system, when it says that '[p]rovisions for the statutory registration of health professionals will be strengthened and expanded' (Department of Health and Children (DHC) 2001: 119). The rationale for this was given by the then Minister for Health and Children during a debate on the Bill. She told the Seanad in 2004 that the proposed legally binding registration 'will ensure that members of the public are guided, protected and informed' (Harney 2004: 6). According to the Minister, the legislation would bring about greater quality in care, improved professional standards in the designated professions, and greater accountability, with 'a stronger framework for questioning and investigating clinical decisions in specific circumstances' (Harney 2004: 6). A number of health and social professions are named in the *Health Strategy*, including social workers and child care workers, but it does not refer specifically to social care workers. The Health and Social Care Professionals Act 2005 is a comprehensive document, with ten parts, 97 sections and three schedules, setting out the detail of the law on professional registration for twelve health and social care professions – see Box 2.1 for the complete list of professions included.

Box 2.1

Health and Social Care Professionals Act 2005 – Designated Professions

- Clinical biochemist
- Dietician
- Medical scientist
- Occupational therapist
- Orthoptist
- Physiotherapist
- Podiatrist
- Psychologist

- Radiographer
- Social care worker
- Social worker
- Speech and language therapist

(*Source*: Government of Ireland 2005a: S.4(1))

The legislation provides for the establishment of the Health and Social Care Professionals Council (HSCPC), the object of which is 'to protect the public by promoting high standards of professional conduct and professional education, training and competence among registrants of the designated professions' (Government of Ireland 2005a: S.7). The HSCPC is responsible for overseeing and coordinating registration boards for each of the twelve designated professions. Among a number of other duties the HSCPC is responsible for enforcing standards of practice and codes of professional conduct and ethics adopted by the registration boards, establishing committees of inquiry to investigate complaints made against a registered professional, and making decisions and giving directions regarding disciplinary actions to be taken against a registered professional. Membership of the Council includes representatives of the designated professions, management and the third-level education sector. Six people are to represent the general public (which may include members of advocacy groups or users of services) and there are three appointees who should have expertise of value to the Council (Government of Ireland 2005a). The HSCPC appoints its own chief executive officer (who also acts as registrar for the registration boards) and may appoint other staff to carry out duties relevant to the functioning of the Council and registration boards.

Each of the designated professions will have its own registration board, and the registration board for social care is to be called the Social Care Workers Registration Board (SCWRB). Under Section 27 of the Act the object, functions and powers of the registration boards are set out. The object of each registration board is 'to protect the public by fostering high standards of professional conduct and professional education, training and competence among registrants of that profession' (Government of Ireland 2005a: S.27(1)). The functions of the registration boards are outlined in Box 2.2. The registration board will consist of thirteen members. Six members are to be elected: three social care workers, two managers and one from social care education. Seven members are to be appointed by the Minister: one from management of the health and social care sector, one from the voluntary or private sector, one from the third-level establishments where education and training of the profession occurs, and four to represent the general public (Government of Ireland 2005a: S.28(1)). The registration boards are given the power to make bye-laws on the election of members to their respective boards, on aspects of registration, on education and training, and on codes of ethics.

Box 2.2

Functions of the Social Care Workers Registration Board (When It Becomes Operational)

- Establish and maintain the register of members for the profession
- Issue certificates of registration
- Give guidance to members concerning ethical conduct
- Give guidance to members on practice and continuing professional development
- Monitor the continuing suitability of educational programmes approved for the education and training of applicants who wish to apply for registration
- Make recommendations to the HSCPC on sanctions to be imposed on registered professionals

(*Source*: Government of Ireland 2005a: S.27(3))

With the implementation of the legislation all social care workers will be required under law to register with the SCWRB. Part 4 of the Act outlines the rules and regulations around professional registration. These include the establishment of a register of members' names and other details. It also specifies how to apply to register and the rules of registration, which include having an approved qualification, being a fit person to engage in the practice of the profession, having the requisite language proficiency and paying the required fee (Government of Ireland 2005a: SS.36–38). The registration board may also remove the name of the professional from the register, in circumstances outlined by the legislation. In Part 5 the Act details the role of registration boards in relation to the education and training of the designated professionals. Education providers must seek approval from the appropriate registration board to provide education and training of candidates for registration. All education and training programmes must be reviewed at least every five years by the relevant registration board to monitor their continuing suitability.

In Part 6 the difficult issues of 'complaints, inquiries and discipline' are dealt with in great detail to ensure that due process is available to any professional who becomes the subject of a complaint. Adverse findings under Part 6 could have serious implications for the professional career of a social care worker. Under the legislation these matters are primarily the responsibility of the HSCPC, which is given the authority to establish disciplinary committees to inquire into complaints made about a registered professional. However, registration boards also have a function in complaints and disciplinary procedures. Section 52 sets out the grounds on which complaints can be made – see Box 2.3. Complaints can be made against a social care worker on grounds of professional misconduct or poor professional performance even if the matter occurs outside of the state.

Box 2.3

Grounds on which Complaints Can Be Made against a Social Care Worker under the Health and Social Care Professionals Act 2005

- Professional misconduct
- Poor professional performance
- Impairment of the social care worker's ability to practice because of a physical or mental ailment, an emotional disturbance or an addiction to alcohol or drugs
- Failure to comply with certain parts of the legislation
- A contravention of the Act, the rules or bye-laws

- A conviction in the state for an offence triable on indictment or a conviction outside the state for an offence consisting of acts or omissions that, if done or made in the state, would constitute an offence triable on indictment

(*Source*: Government of Ireland 2005a: S.52(1))

Other important provisions in the legislation of interest to social care workers are Part 7, 'Professional Titles and Offences', Sections 79–81, which deal with the use of professional titles. Only those designated professions who meet the requirements of the legislation and are registered with their registration board can use the title of their profession. Under the legislation it is an offence to use a professional title if the appropriate legal requirements are not fulfilled, and this may result on conviction in a fine or imprisonment. Finally, Part 9 of the Act gives details of transition arrangements for professionals already working in the areas for which they wish to seek registration. Transition arrangements for social care workers are given specific mention in Section 91 – see Box 2.4 for details.

Box 2.4

Transitional Arrangements for the Registration of Social Care Workers

The Social Care Workers Registration Board shall grant registration to a person who, at any time during the period of five years ending on the relevant date, was engaged in the practice of the profession of social care worker and who:

- Applies during the transitional period to that board for registration
- Applies in the form and contains the information required by the bye-laws of the registration board
- Satisfies the board that he or she is a fit and proper person to engage in the practice of that profession
- Has been engaged in the continuous practice of that profession for a period of not less than two years immediately preceding the date of application

> - Is, in the written opinion of the person's employer, competent in the practice of that profession
> - Pays the required fee to the Council
>
> (*Source*: Government of Ireland 2005a: S.91 (1 and 2) and S.37(2))

The implementation of the Health and Social Care Professionals Act 2005 has proceeded at a snail's pace since it was passed (see Farrelly and O'Doherty 2011). The HSCPC was launched in March 2007, and its first staff took up their posts in 2008. The name given to the new agency is CORU, which has origins in 'an Irish word, "cóir" meaning fair, just and proper', and is not an acronym (CORU n.d.a). The Social Workers Registration Board was the first to be established, and its register opened in 2011. Social work already had a registration body in place, the National Social Work Qualification Board, which was wound down and closed in the process of establishing the new board. Subsequently the Radiographers Registration Board has been appointed (CORU, n.d.b). As this chapter is being written in mid-2012 the SCWRB has yet to be set up, although there have been discussions between CORU and social care representative organisations (IASCE 2011). One further development of note is the publication of a *Framework for a Common Code of Professional Conduct and Ethics* (CORU 2010), adopted as guidelines under the 2005 legislation. Included in this framework is an obligation for all designated professionals to engage in continuous professional development.

One of the interesting aspects of the process of social care registration, signalling a step towards professionalisation (Share 2009), is the apparent uncritical acceptance of this move. In fact Lalor and Share voice the hope that registration will address the many problems social care encounters when they write of its difficulties: '[w]ith increasing professionalisation and regulation of the field, there is a hope that many of these issues will be addressed in the future' (2009: 20; see also Williams and Lalor 2001). Similarly, O'Doherty writes with hope about statutory registration when he says that it 'will act as a green light in this process of realising the potential of social care work to finally set its own practice agenda' (2003: 59). Farrelly and O'Doherty enthusiastically endorsed registration, stating that 'the promise of official and public definition and acceptance of social care work has become a reality. We believe that this document provides a landmark in the development of the professional enterprise for all stake-holders involved with social care work in the Republic of Ireland' (2005: 81). In a later article these authors' optimism abated somewhat as they acknowledged delay and the changing 'landscape' in which social care operates (2011: 75). IMPACT, a major trade union representing social care workers, said of registration, 'IMPACT strongly supports the introduction of statutory registration, which can help deliver best practice, high quality health services, outstanding professional standards, and protection for service users' (2012). The only adverse comment that IMPACT had to make was about the fee for registration at €295 per annum, which it said was too high compared with other professions such as nurses and teachers. The union also expressed concern about ensuring the fair implementation of the fitness to practice procedures (IMPACT 2012).

Experience in other countries where social care workers are registered suggests that social care should be cautious in what it wishes for. Jones (1999), in anticipation of social work regulation in the United Kingdom, highlighted the pros and cons, which are equally relevant to social care in Ireland – see Box 2.5. Van Heugten (2011), writing on social work registration in New Zealand, argues that the benefits of improved status for social work are just by-products if they occur at all. She also pointed to the individualisation of risk in the registration process. It is the individual worker who will be penalised for professional and personal inadequacies, and no risk applies to 'employing agencies or the state and its policies for the distribution of resources' (Van Heugten 2011: 181). For some, professional registration has a much more ominous function, as it gives the state 'unprecedented regulation over the workforce' (McLaughlin 2007: 1274, cited in Garrett 2010: 342).

Box 2.5

The Pros and Cons of the Regulation of Social Care

Jones (1999) outlines a number of advantages and disadvantages of social work and social care regulation in the United Kingdom.
  In favour:

- Duty to publish a code of conduct based on explicit ethical values
- Influence from service users
- Potential for setting and enforcing knowledge-based standards of conduct and practice
- Explicit expectation that it will raise standards of education and training and qualifications
- Mechanism to improve service delivery through regulation and training of staff

Adverse factors:

- Loss of public confidence in professions and regulation
- Lack of public/political consensus on ethical principles
- Historic weakness of institutions of social care work and personal social services
- Structural disempowerment of service users
- Inconsistent political support for people undertaking caring roles
- Poor history of workforce investment

(*Source*: Jones 1999: 61)

Politics and Social Care Work

In this section, building on the earlier discussions on definition and the legislation on social care, an argument is made for a broader understanding of the nature of social care work (see Mulkeen 2009a, 2009b; O'Connor 2006, 2009; O'Toole 2009). The everyday practice of social care work tends to operate in a political vacuum. O'Connor observes 'that for the majority of educators and practitioners, social care is all about helping the client on a day-to-day basis – but no more' (2009: 99). He continues, 'the major task for the social care practitioner is to promote the personal development of the client in a broadly therapeutic way' (2009: 99). It is my contention that social care work is about more than therapeutic work with individuals and families, or psycho-social models aimed at social groups and communities. This dominant approach to social care work is deeply rooted in the structures of the political system, and is influenced by prevailing values and ideologies (O'Connor 2006, O'Toole 2009). The impor-tant question is, what is the relevance of this for social care work? The answer to that question will be teased out by exploring the common values of social care and social work, and by examining the role of neoliberalism and its influence on social care.

Social Care Work and Social Work

To begin let us step back in time. Historically social care has had two defining relationships, one with residential care and the other with social work (Christie 2005, Lalor and Share 2009). These relationships are not at all straightforward. Christie says the 'lack of common history' between social work and social care (as well as youth and community work) is used to 'explain and/or justify' differences between these professions (2005: 113). Lalor and Share write that 'social care practice and social work have developed on parallel yet separate paths' (2009: 10). That may well be the case in the sense of professional advance-ment and status (Lalor and Share 2009), but there continue to be 'overlapping areas of professional knowledge, skills and values' (Christie 2005: 112) between these professions.

Both social work and residential care emerged from philan-thropic organisations in Ireland, just as occurred in Britain, and at the forefront of these developments in Ireland were the churches. The roots of Irish social work and residential care in some instances sprung from the same source, for example the Society of St Vincent de Paul and the Sisters of Charity (Chris-tie 2005). The need for these services came about because of widespread poverty in nineteenth-century Ireland, although the first residential care unit, the Dublin Foundling Hospital, was established in 1703 (Powell 1981). Nineteenth-century Catholic Church attitudes towards the poor were based on differentiating between the deserving and undeserving, and both the Catholic and Protestant 'approaches to philanthropy and welfare shared many important characteristics in the modern period, including an emphasis on entitlement, work and self-discipline' (Crossman and Gray 2011: 11). Some commentators have concluded that because of these attitudes, social work and residential care developed not only to alleviate poverty but also to control the poor (Christie 2005). Poverty was judged to be an individual and moral failing, and one which could be 'cured' with appropriate levels of discipline (Squires 1990). Writing about the impact of the nineteenth-century Poor Law in Britain, Squires (1990: 63) argues that two complementary views on relief of the poor emerged, underpinned by discipline. The twin approaches of deterrence were the workhouse, a form of residential care, and 'a system of individual supervision', a form of social case work. Squires locates this approach to poverty in the new social, political and economic order which was emerging in the nineteenth century.

Contemporary social work and social care do not necessarily uphold the philosophy of 'curing poverty', but there are continuities with this early work of religious and charitable organisations. The practice model of individual treatment still dominates the education and practice of social professions, and the characteristics of the people who use social work and social care services are similar. The term 'poverty' is less used in political and policy discourse, and is increasingly being replaced with the terms social exclusion, marginalisation and vulnerability (Lister 2004; see Chapter 3 on poverty in this volume). But however it is dressed up, in essence those individuals, families and communities who need and avail themselves of the support offered by the social professionals are still, by and large, the poorest and suffer the greatest inequalities in society. Social work in Ireland, notwithstanding its limitations, and unlike social care, recognises that the causes of the problems of service users extend beyond the individual to the political, social and economic organisation of society. This recognition is to be found in the *Code of Professional Conduct and Ethics for Social Workers Bye-Law 2011* (Government of Ireland 2011a). In the Foreword to the *Code for Social Workers*, the Chairperson of the Social Workers Registration Board sets out the principles on which social work is based:

Social Work is a profession based on principles of human rights and social justice that work to empower individuals, groups and communities to develop their full potential and wellbeing. The focus of intervention in social work is the relationship between the individual and their immediate and wider social environment. (Government of Ireland 2011a: 6)

The Code outlines the principles in more detail. It requires social workers to uphold human rights in practice. By this it means they should respect the right to self-determination, promote the right to participation, and treat everyone in a caring and respectful way. Under a heading 'pursuit of social justice', the Code requires social workers in their practice to:

- Challenge negative discrimination and unjust policies and practices
- Recognise and respect diversity
- Demonstrate cultural competence
- Advocate for the fair distribution of resources based on identified levels of risk/need
- Work towards social inclusion

(Government of Ireland 2011a: 8–9)

The Code takes advantage of the full scope allowed by CORU to set out its own ethical principles. While the CORU framework includes a requirement to respect the rights and dignity of all individuals, human rights and social justice are not mentioned (CORU 2010). The ethical principles espoused by the *Code of Professional Conduct and Ethics for Social Workers* reflect the ethical standards of the International Federation of Social Workers (IFSW), even though the Code does not expand on some crucial elements. It is worth quoting from the IFSW *Statement of Ethical Principles*, which defines social work as:

The social work profession promotes social change, problem solving in human relationships and the empowerment and liberation of people to enhance well-being. Utilising theories of human behaviour and social systems, social work intervenes at the points where people interact with their environments. Principles of human rights and social justice are fundamental to social work. (IFSW 2012)

One of the IFSW's points on social justice, which is also found in the *Code of Ethics* for Irish social workers, 'challenging unjust policies and practices', says that social workers have 'a duty to bring to the attention of their employers, policy makers, politicians and the general public situations where resources are inadequate or where distribution of resources, policies and practices are oppressive, unfair or harmful' (IFSW 2011). The definition and ethical requirements of social workers do not in any way diminish individual work, but they clearly advocate and demand a broader and more integrated perspective, which addresses political, social and economic issues beyond the individual. This does not imply that Irish social work is preoccupied with the broader issues understood in the discourse of social justice, for it is arguably conservative and less concerned with emancipatory practice (Garrett 2009; see also Hyslop 2011).

In contrast to social work, definitions of social care used by the representative organisations of the social care sector barely use the language of human rights or mention a social justice perspective (see the discussion above). That is not to say that the issue is not a concern for social care, since for example Charleton includes a chapter on social justice in *Ethics for Social Care in Ireland: Philosophy and Practice* (2007). It is argued here that this is urgently required both in the interests of the users of social care services and for the social care profession itself, because as we shall see, the poor, the professions who work with them and even the notion of the 'social' itself are under an unrelenting attack from the proponents of neoliberalism (Squires 1990, Lorenz 2008).

Social Care and Neoliberalism

Chapter 1 presented a picture of the world in which social policy operates, one dominated by a particular ideological viewpoint, neoliberalism (see also Lorenz 2005). The value base of neoliberalism has become the ideological norm for decision-making not just in Ireland but across all institutions of power at a European and global level (see Scholte 2005). The social professions are not exempt from these influences; in fact some argue that they have become another tool in the ideological reshaping of the world that has assumed a generalised neoliberal value system (Garrett 2010, Van Heugten 2011). Here are some examples of how the philosophy of neoliberalism influences and interacts with social care in education and work.

Social care education in Ireland has to date developed in an ad hoc and unplanned way, and in such an unregulated environment Williams and Lalor's observation from over a decade ago remains true: '[t]here is no doubt that the quality of training varies from institution to institution' (2001: 82). Social care education takes place in sixteen institutions across Ireland, a number that has more than doubled since 2002 when there were seven providers of social care education (Lalor 2009). The majority of degree-level social care programmes are provided in institutes of technology, but they are also available in one university and two private educational institutions (Lalor 2009). An accurate number of the jobs in Ireland for these graduates is not available. Lalor made enquiries in 2009, in which the trade union IMPACT estimated that the number of posts was 3,000–5,000 and the HSCPC estimated 8,000. Lalor reported that in 2009 there were 1,303 social care graduates, an output which he judged to be unsustainable since there were not sufficient jobs for them. The lack of regulation allowed the colleges to embark on this 'market'-driven growth path without any real consideration for the needs of social care (see Farrelly and O'Doherty 2011). Those in the profession, social care educators and practitioners, have had negligible influence on these developments in social care education or in the development of the profession (Share 2009). The major impetus in social care development has come from the state itself and its agencies (including education providers), and in a more limited way from the trade unions representing social care staff (Share 2009) in the state sector and the bigger, longer-established voluntary sector organisations.

'Neoliberal approaches to social care not only constrain the delivery of services, but attempt to shape the perspectives of the social care workforce. Education is a potentially powerful tool for achieving that shaping' (Van Heugten 2011). Lolich (2011) argues that the National Framework of Qualifications (NFQ) used by the Higher Education and Training Awards Council (HETAC) to review and validate higher education programmes is an ingredient in neoliberal educational governance in Ireland. These 'nationally agreed standards of knowledge, skill and competence' are 'designed around learning outcomes', a development which shifts education from a 'cognitive to a behavioural approach' (Lolich 2011: 281). According to Lolich, this is part of a broader higher educational policy which ultimately 'reconfigures students as neo-liberal subjects' (2011: 283).

The *Awards Standards – Social Care Work* (HETAC 2010) provides an example of the NFQ in practice. What is especially interesting about this document in light of our earlier discussion on social justice is that it includes issues of human rights and social justice as areas of knowledge that should be acquired by social care students. It requires that by the end of a level 8 degree programme, graduates in social care be able to '[e]xpress a comprehensive internalised, personal world view manifesting solidarity with others, e.g. internalise human rights and social justice discourses' (HETAC 2010: 7). Yet in the skills and application of knowledge sections of the Standards, there is no reference to human rights and social justice. In effect this suggests that these issues should be thought about in a theoretical way but in the real business of practice they are not significant. Whatever the inclinations of HETAC, the social care professions contributed significantly to the process of devising the NFQ standards for social care through a formal consultation process (Share 2009, HETAC 2010). We can only wonder whether social care professionals have shown a normalised acceptance of a neoliberal value system in relation to social care education (Garrett 2010, Van Heugten 2011). These developments do not take into account the new era of registration and the as yet unknown thinking of the HSCPC and the SCWRB on social care education, which could have a profound impact on its future structure and content.

Social care education and social care work are interconnected. The HSE document on its role in education and training in the context of the legislation on health and social care professionals (2009) sets out its perspective and expectations of this relationship. The HSE document recommends this as one of its core principles 'in developing its strategic vision and policy framework for Health and Social Care Professions education and training':

> Education, development and training should be *service driven*, based on need which is identified through mechanisms such as service planning and workforce planning. It should be integrated with service requirements and fit in the context of overall strategic and business plans (HSE 2009: 18, emphasis in original).

The HSE is the major provider and funder of social care services in the state, and its views are therefore of great importance. One of the key themes that emerged from the HSE's consultation process with the various professional groups was a 'need for education, training and CPD [continuing professional development] to be service driven, based on need and evidence-based practice to ensure that both current and future health care needs are met' (HSE 2009: 12). The document reports that there was a 'need to ensure that graduating Health and Social Care Professionals are "fit for purpose" in terms of being able to work and deliver services in the context and manner required in the current and future health services' (HSE 2009: 12). The language of the HSE document is presented in the discourse of managerialism, one element of a neoliberal approach to public service management which has impacted on and transformed the welfare state (Dickens 2008, Wallace and Pease 2011). Dickens describes public service managerialism:

> The core assumptions of managerialism for the public services are that they can be managed more effectively, efficiently and economically through the introduction of private sector management techniques and market place principles; that the practice of front-line public sector workers needs to be closely regulated and scrutinized; that public spending must be tightly controlled and monitored; … These beliefs have resulted in the multiplication of procedural guidelines, performance indicators and performance

measurement technologies, such as audit and inspection. (Dickens 2008: 49)

A supposed tool in the effective and efficient management of health and welfare work is the notion of evidence-based practice (EBP), referred to in the HSE paper. The HSE (2009) does not say what it means by EBP. Gambrill defines EBP for social workers (the same definition is appropriate for social care workers): 'social workers seek out practice related external research findings related to problems clients confront, critically appraise what they find and share what they find with clients'. The social worker in consultation with the client then 'chooses courses of action on the basis of this systematic review of scientific evidence plus other factors' (Gambrill 1999: 348, cited in Cohen 2011: 337).

EBP is not without its challenges for the social professionals, one important stumbling block being the lack of interest in carrying out evidence-based research (McCrystal and Wilson 2009). Even more fundamentally Cohen (2011) questions the use of such an approach to address social problems, which by their very nature are complex and changing, and thus cannot be resolved by responses based on past findings. A further problem is the multidimensional nature of problems faced by users of social care services. Cohen (2011) says the complexity of such problems does not allow for an EBP response, which suggests problems are discrete and independent of each other. Apart from questions about the practical usefulness of EBP, its presentation in a scientific, politically neutral way does not stand up to scrutiny either. For instance, we might wonder how the identification of a lack of resources as the kernel of a social care service user's problems would go down with management who are attempting to reduce costs.

The issue of cost reduction and financial savings in public service provision leads us to a final point in our brief exploration of the relationship between neoliberalism and social care. Staff wages and associated costs are the biggest element of public service expenditure, and containing this cost is of primary concern for the state and its funding agencies. A feature of the employment model under neoliberalism is a shift towards insecurity in people's working lives (Garrett 2010). In the social professions this includes, according to Garrett, 'the growth of short-term contracts and insecure patterns of employment; perhaps especially in the growth of "agency" working where staff have few employment rights, "enjoy" low pay and, on occasions, even have difficulty in trying to determine who their actual, legal employer is' (2010: 346). In an earlier article Garrett (2009: 274) refers to what the National Social Work Qualification Board (2006) calls the phenomenon of a 'syndrome of permanent temporary posts' and 'casualisation' in social work employment in Ireland. While no equivalent assessment has been done on social care work in Ireland, there is certainly anecdotal evidence that Garrett's observation about job insecurity in social work is equally applicable to social care. This approach to employment policy in social care is detrimental not only to social care workers but also to service users and the integrity of services (see Carey 2007).

Where to for Irish Social Care?

Irish social care will enter a new phase of development when the SCWRB becomes operational. To date social care professionals have had limited input into the direction of the profession. Social care work has a relatively marginal status, although the workers make up a large professional group and there are improving educational standards. Van Heugten has observed that '[a]n occupation's status … is known to be closely associated with the status of the populations it services' (2011: 181). There is thus no guarantee that registration will greatly increase the profession's status, as social care workers serve populations that are 'the least powerful groups in society' (O'Doherty 2006: 25). The emergence of SCI could strengthen the profession's hand, but there are weaknesses to be overcome. SCI (and its constituent members) needs to broaden its representation through practical encouragement of others in social care to participate in existing professional associations or to promote the development of new ones. Many social care workers are not members of the IASCW. The RMA is an association only of managers of residential child care services, and IASCE represents its constituent colleges rather than academics who teach on social care programmes (see the various organisations' websites). As a result many of the voices of social care workers, managers and academics are missing from discussions on the future direction of social care. Social care students only have a minimum of representation, with the IASCW reserving a place for a student representative on its National Executive. Users of services do not feature at all.

A second challenge relates to the definition of social care. We have seen that there is a lack of clarity about definitions of social care work, and this puts social care at a disadvantage. This issue could be resolved by the SCWRB if it agrees on an inclusive definition. Social care as it is currently understood is diverse in nature and overlaps with youth and community work, so some people who regard themselves as social care workers could be excluded from the definition. There is no strong international dimension to social care, as there is no equivalent to the IFSW for social care workers. Five institutes of technology are members of a European association, the Formation d'Educateurs Sociaux Européens/European Social Educator Training (FESET) (FESET n.d.). FESET provides an international dimension to social care education for its Irish members, but it does not really impact more generally on social care education in Ireland. The European version of social care is based on the idea of social pedagogy, which is encompassed in the term 'social educator'. This could offer social care work a more solid theoretical and progressive practice base, and an international dimension which is acutely missing.

Social pedagogy, or social education, is the common term in Europe for the type of work social care workers in Ireland do with children and young people, particularly those in residential care, although its methods can also be applied to other user groups (Cameron 2004; Cameron, McQuail and Petrie 2007; Smith and Whyte 2008). 'It is a system of theory, practice and training that supports the overall development of the whole child. It can be defined as "education in the broadest sense of the word"' (Cameron et al. 2007: 25). Working with the whole child means that social pedagogues are 'aware that children think, feel, have a physical, spiritual, social and creative existence, and that all of these characteristics are in interaction in the person' (Cameron et al. 2011: 15). For social pedagogues, practical day-to-day direct engagement with the service user is one part of their practice. Presenting themselves as involved and emotional beings is a second element, and theoretical knowledge and self-reflection is the final necessary component of their professional competence – so it involves hands, heart and head (Cameron et al. 2011).

According to Smith and Whyte, '[t]he approach is based on the belief that you can influence social circumstances and social change through education' (2008: 20). Pedagogy tries to bring about social change 'by influencing the personal in society', and is grounded in opposition to individual approaches that deny the existence of 'the social dimensions of human existence' (Smith and Whyte 2008: 20). Social pedagogy, unlike the social care and social work traditions in Ireland, is not 'deficit-oriented' as it believes that all human beings are 'capable of always developing themselves further, provided the requisite resources are available' (Lorenz 2008: 636). However, Smith and Whyte (2008: 20) appear to distance social pedagogy from political action, which they say focuses on the 'external elements of society', such as 'structures, institutions and legislation'. The training curriculum of social pedagogy, as outlined by Cameron and colleagues (2007), also suggests that there is little room for political considerations in the work of social pedagogues. On the other hand Lorenz's historical analysis of the development of social pedagogy places it firmly in a socio-political space of importance. He says that rather than taking its influences from 'institutional objectives', social pedagogy should:

> network with and build upon the countless moments of 'expertise' with which people demonstrate their coping abilities in everyday informal and non-formal learning processes. Such interventions are not a flight from political action, but, on the contrary, identify political processes, issues of justice and equality, in life-world contexts in which they build social policy 'from the bottom up'. (Lorenz 2008: 639)

Conclusion

The purpose of this chapter was to argue for a political understanding of the nature and role of social care work. Social care is at something of a crossroads, facing registration which will shape its professional future. Even more importantly, it is part of a wider political process of neoliberalism which is about reconstructing 'social' relationships into economically dominated market relationships (Lorenz 2005, 2008). Social care students, and the profession, need to develop a critical understanding of broader political, economic and social processes, if social care is to be relevant and responsive to the needs of service users (Garrett 2010). Even the most progressive forms of individual-based work are not enough to alter the life chances of the many people who are struggling and facing a lifetime of poverty and disadvantage in a society where opportunities for economic independence are greatly restricted and unevenly divided. What is required will not come through individual work when fundamental policy changes are needed. Of course social care workers can find comfort in focusing on individual therapeutic relationships and avoiding the structural causes of service user problems (Lorenz 2005). Confronting structural problems is far more demanding, since they challenge us to move outside our comfort zone, and quite simply, it might seem beyond our capacity to effect change on that scale. Yet this is exactly what is required, with Lorenz calling for '[n]othing less than a head-on challenge of the basic presumptions of neo-liberalism and their manifold applications to social service provision delivery systems' (2005: 93).

To achieve what Lorenz is calling for will demand a rethinking of social care education. Suggestions of a possible way forward are provided by O'Connor, for instance, who argues that there is a need to 'fully appreciate the links between the different elements of social care education' (2009: 109). He continues, '[c]ontemporary examples from social policy and practice point to the need to incorporate structure, campaigning and advocacy into social care practice' (2009: 109). Another related approach comes from Hanlon (2009) and Mulkeen (2009a), who suggest a broadening of our understanding of social care to include the idea of equality, based on emancipatory practice. This should be the touchstone of social care practice, with its values of empowerment, authenticity, citizenship, partnership, social justice, and de-individualisation (Hanlon 2009: 8). To attain these values will necessitate challenging conservative social care educational programmes, neoliberal higher educational policy, and the organisational and philosophical values of the providing colleges, whose embedded hierarchical and patriarchal structures are less than empowering for academic staff, let alone students (see Collins 1998, Lynch 2005).

In the field of social care practice, we need to tap into a spirit of resistance, as service providers and users increasingly question the policy path 'of the troubling dimensions of neoliberal "modernization"' (Garrett 2010). The capacity for resistance is present in untold ways because providers and users of services 'do not merely "act like automatons envisaged in the governmental plans and strategies of the powerful"' (Clarke 2005: 159 cited in Garrett 2010: 343; see also Wallace and Pease 2011). An essential ingredient of resistance to 'the commoditization of social care' is joining forces with like-minded workers in associated professions, such as social, community and youth work, as well as forming alliances with service users (Van Heugten 2011: 176). Action on the 'political' in social care work is thus an imperative, and as will become evident in the following chapters, the 'political' is the essential ingredient of all social policy.

Further Reading

Unfortunately there is limited material on the politics of social care in Ireland. Much of the analysis and interpretation is through the lens of social work, and even that is mostly non-Irish based.

Essential Documents

Only one piece of legislation is directly relevant to social care work and has implications for social care education and practice: the Health and Social Care Professionals Act 2005. It is available at: www.irishstatutebook.ie/pdf/2005/en.act.2005.0027.pdf

Policy documents on social care are also scarce, but the text refers to three important ones in recent years.

The first is the HSE document *The Education and Development of Health and Social Care Professionals in the Health Services* (2009):

www.lenus.ie/hse/bitstream/10147/83537/1/EdandDvlp-mtofHealthSocialCareProfs09-2014.pdf

The second is *Awards Standards – Social Care Work* (HETAC 2010): www.hetac.ie/docs/B.2.9-5.5_Awards_Standards_Social_Care_Work_2010.pdf

CORU's *Framework for a Common Code of Professional Conduct and Ethics* (2010) is the third document which is essential reading for student social care workers: www.coru.ie/uploads/Framework%20Code%20of%20Professional%20Conduct%20and%20Ethics.pdf

General Reading

No one publication encompasses all the ideas addressed in this chapter. There are two pieces by Tom O'Connor from Cork Institute of Technology on structural issues and social care. One is the 2006 chapter 'Social-care practice: bringing structure and ideology in from the cold', in *Social Care in Ireland: Theory, Policy and Practice*, which he co-edited with Mike Murphy. The second is a 2009 chapter called 'Social care and social change: future direction or lost opportunity' in the second edition of *Applied Social Care: An Introduction for Students in Ireland*, edited by Perry Share and Kevin Lalor. Two chapters by Majella Mulkeen in the same volume, 'Equality: a challenge to social care' and 'Anti-discriminatory practice: a new direction for social care', offer a critical stance, as does the chapter by Jackie O'Toole, 'Gender and social care: mapping a structural analysis'. It is also worth reading Part 1 of Share and Lalor's book, which includes a number of chapters that cover some of the ground referred to in this chapter from an international perspective. Niall Hanlon's (2009) article 'Valuing equality in social care' provides an alternative to the dominant discourse on social care.

Celesta McCann James, Áine de Róiste and John McHugh's *Social Care Practice in Ireland: An Integrated Perspective* (2009), offers a political dimension to social care work by using critical sociological analysis as part of the framework for assessing social care practice scenarios. It makes an important contribution to broadening social care practice to include structural analysis. However, the practice applications they discuss do not lead to interventions that reflect the authors' critical analysis; they invariably revert to more traditional approaches and accommodations.

IASCE publishes the *Irish Journal of Applied Social Studies*, which as the name suggests contains a wide range of articles on social studies, some of which are relevant to the issues discussed in this chapter. The web address is in the useful websites section, and access to articles is free.

The bibliography includes material under the general umbrella of 'politics' which offers a chance to explore the issues covered in this chapter, but much of it is related to social work. Two authors deserve special mention because of their links to Ireland. Paul Michael Garrett is based at the National University of Ireland Galway, and writes prolifically on the 'politics' of social work. Walter Lorenz, formally of University College Cork, and now based in Italy, also writes extensively on the political nature of social work. The critical political analysis offered by both of these authors is very relevant to social care.

Useful Websites

CORU – www.coru.ie
FESET – www.feset.org
Irish Association of Social Care Educators – www.iasce.ie
Irish Association of Social Care Workers – www.iascw.ie
Irish Journal of Applied Social Studies – http://arrow.dit.ie/ijass/
Resident Managers Association – http://residentmanagersassociation.com/
Social Care Ireland – http://socialcareireland.ie/
Social Studies.ie – www.socialstudies.ie/

3

Poverty in Ireland:
'The Poor Will Always Be with Us'

Area of Social Care for which this Chapter Is Relevant

Many users of social care services experience poverty in its different guises on a daily basis, sometimes throughout their lives. For this reason it is essential that all social care graduates understand the concept of poverty, and the associated terms social exclusion, marginalisation and inequality, and their implications, and are familiar with policies for tackling the major problem they describe.

Key Words in this Chapter

Poverty, social exclusion, marginalisation, inequality, anti-poverty strategies

Key Themes in this Chapter

- Definitions and measurement of poverty
- Social exclusion – changing the understanding of the meaning of poverty
- The extent of poverty in Ireland
- Policies to combat poverty
- Poverty and inequality

Introduction

'The poor will always be with us' is a well-worn cliché, but regrettably it seems to be true. No society has eliminated poverty, although some do much better than others at reducing its destructive force. These differences exist because of the political beliefs pursued in different societies, their differing social and economic structures, and the shape of public policies that ameliorate or add to poverty levels (see Lister 2004). The issue of poverty is of such concern at a political level across the globe that it has become an area of policy-making through global institutions such as the United Nations, and closer to home at EU level. Yet poverty continues to impact on millions of people worldwide (World Bank 2012), the majority of whom live in developing countries in Africa, Asia, the Pacific and Latin America.

It is not just in the so-called 'poorer' countries that poverty has an impact. It also affects tens of millions of people in the wealthy advanced industrial countries (Lister 2004). For example, in 2010 in the United States, the most prosperous country in the world, 46.2 million people (15.1 per cent of the population) were living in poverty. The poverty rate varies from state to state, and is highest in Mississippi, at 23.2 per cent (Seefeldt et al. 2012). General poverty statistics hide a number of important aspects, as Seefeldt and colleagues point out (in discussing poverty in the United States): '[t]he increase in poverty since 2006 has been greater among Hispanics and African Americans than among Whites, greater among children than among the elderly, and greater among female-headed households than other households' (2012: 5). There are also high levels of poverty in many other countries in the developed world, including Ireland, the focus of this chapter, and many of the features are the same.

Because the terms 'the poor', 'poor people' and 'poverty' are so much part of our daily vocabulary, we can underestimate the complexity of their meaning. When we talk about 'poor people', what exactly do we mean? In everyday language these terms have a multiplicity of less than clear meanings. This chapter gives the officially accepted and widely used definitions of poverty in Ireland, along with an outline of poverty measurements. The chapter also explores the development of a more complex understanding of poverty by addressing the connected concept of 'social exclusion', which has become part of the language of poverty. Another important term which receives some attention in the chapter is 'inequality', which is of enormous significance in the politics of the poverty debate.

It is also necessary to examine the policies that the state has introduced to combat poverty. This chapter discusses the development of Irish policy with reference to the important international influences, particularly at EU level. The most significant national policy development was the introduction of the National Anti-Poverty Strategies (NAPS), first put in place in 1997. At the end of this discussion the most obvious question is, how successful has Ireland been in reducing poverty since it introduced its first anti-poverty strategy a decade and a half ago? The answer to that question is addressed in the final section of the chapter.

Definitions and Measurement of Poverty

As is outlined in Box 3.1, the modern understanding of poverty was given a legal basis in Ireland and Britain under the nineteenth-century Poor Law. This understanding was conceptualised primarily in economic terms, based on the notion of work, but it also had a strong moral aspect. Consequently, the earliest research in the United Kingdom into poverty by Charles Booth (1889) and Seebohm Rowntree (1901) defined poverty as a lack of income from not having work. It was not until the 1970s that the understanding of poverty began to change, through what was then the European Economic Community (which has now developed into the European Union) and through the classic pioneering work of Peter Townsend (1979) in *Poverty in the United Kingdom*. From this time it became accepted that poverty was not just about income, and as a result it was reconceptualised to include wider issues.

Box 3.1

Poverty and the Poor Law

Poverty and how to address it has been a concern for Western societies for hundreds of years. Politicians, social commentators and theologians viewed poverty as a political and moral concern from before the Middle Ages (Glennester et al. 2004). Legislation as far back as the Elizabethan Poor Law in 1601 was used to address the issue of poverty in Britain (Fraser 1984).

The classical liberal view of the relationship between poverty, work, the market, the individual, and the state came to dominate the understanding of poverty in the late eighteenth and early nineteenth centuries, and continues to hold sway in debates on poverty to this day (Lister 2004). This view regarded poverty as a matter for individuals, whose obligation it was to look after themselves and their families through work which they should find. It was not the responsibility of the state to provide for the poor. Intervention by the state was deemed to contribute to the conditions that gave rise to poverty in the first place – a growing population, idleness, and dependency (Kidd 1999). Work was the answer to poverty, and any relief should not interfere with that basic principle. This led to a model of poverty relief which was intended to be disciplinary and deter all but the most needy (Evans 1978). This response to poverty was incorporated into English law through the Poor Law Act 1834, which in turn heavily influenced the harsher Irish Poor Law Act 1838 (Crossman 2006). This legislation defined poverty in terms of 'less eligibility', where persons could only receive poor relief (through admission to a local workhouse) if they had less income than the poorest worker (Fraser 1984).

Townsend (1979) wrote of two forms of poverty, 'absolute' and 'relative' poverty. Absolute poverty is defined as not being able to meet the basic needs for food, shelter and clothing. Relative poverty is a broader concept. It includes meeting basic needs, but goes beyond this to understand poverty in relation to the social and economic standards of a particular society at a given time. In Ireland poverty is measured through two similar concepts, but with different names.

The Irish state and agencies that work with poor people have agreed a definition of poverty which was first used in the 1997 National Anti-Poverty Strategy:

People are living in poverty if their income and resources (material, cultural and social) are so inadequate as to preclude them from having a standard of living that is regarded as acceptable by Irish society generally. As a result of inadequate income and resources, people may be excluded and marginalised from participating in activities that are considered the norm for other people. (Government of Ireland 1997: 3)

As you can see, this definition expands poverty beyond income to include the inadequacy of other resources. These include material resources (possessing goods which are regarded as necessary in Ireland – for example a television or a mobile phone), cultural resources (being able to participate in your local Gaelic Athletic Association (GAA) club or go to see a show or movie), and social resources (being able to enjoy time out with family or friends). If individuals and families have so little of these resources that they cannot do the things people are expected to do in Irish society, then they are seen to be excluded and marginalised from society, and are thus in poverty.

The first government-approved poverty measure used in Ireland is 'consistent poverty', a concept developed by the Economic and Social Research Institute (ESRI) in 1987 and revised in 2006 (Social Inclusion Division n.d.). Consistent poverty has two elements. People are defined as being in consistent poverty if they have an income below 60 per cent of the median (see Box 3.3 for an explanation of median income) and also experience at least two elements of deprivation from the ESRI's list of deprivation indicators (see Box 3.2).

Box 3.2

Consistent Poverty

Consistent poverty is derived from two elements: income and deprivation. People are deemed to be in consistent poverty if their income is less than 60 per cent of median income, and if they are deprived of two or more goods or services considered essential for a basic standard of living. The following is the eleven-item index which determines deprivation:

1. Two pairs of strong shoes
2. A warm waterproof overcoat

3. Buy new not second-hand clothes
4. Eat meals with meat, chicken, fish (or vegetarian equivalent) every second day
5. Have a roast joint or its equivalent once a week
6. Had to go without heating during the last year through lack of money
7. Keep the home adequately warm
8. Buy presents for family or friends at least once a year
9. Replace any worn out furniture
10. Have family or friends for a drink or meal once a month
11. Have a morning, afternoon or evening out in the last fortnight, for entertainment

(Source: CSO 2012a: 94)

The second concept used to measure poverty levels is 'at risk of poverty'. This indicator identifies all those households that fall below a certain income level, which in the European Union (and in Ireland) is 60 per cent of the median income.

Box 3.3

Median Income

Many students have difficulty understanding what is meant by the term 'median income'. They often get it confused with average (or mean) income. The median income is the middle value of incomes in Ireland (half of incomes are below and half are above), and is different from the average income (where all incomes are added together then divided by the number of people who have incomes to give an average value). The median more accurately reflects the reality of income distribution in Ireland, while the average can give a skewed outcome (making it look as if individual incomes are higher than they actually are).

In Ireland the Social Inclusion Division of the Department for Social Protection is responsible for monitoring poverty levels and for promoting policies to combat poverty and social exclusion. On its website the Social Inclusion Division states that '[t]he official Government approved measure [of poverty] used in Ireland is consistent poverty' (n.d.), and draws attention to the limitations of the 'at risk of poverty' measure, particularly in making comparisons between different countries. Because this is a relative, not absolute, measure, Ireland tends to perform less well on it than some other Western countries whose overall wealth is lower (Bertelsmann Foundation 2011).

Table 3.1 shows the 'at risk of poverty' levels across the European Union (there are no figures available for consistent poverty). Ireland rated just below the EU average in 2008. Social Justice Ireland (2011: 65) points out that this was the first time that Ireland had fallen below the average, which it claimed was as a result of 'sustained increases in welfare payments in the years prior to 2008'. It is clear from the table that a significant number of people are at risk of poverty, not just in Ireland but throughout the European Union.

Table 3.1: At Risk of Poverty Levels in the European Union in 2008 as a Proportion of the Population of Each Country

Country	Poverty Risk	Country	Poverty Risk
EU average	16.5	Germany	15.2
Latvia	25.6	Belgium	14.7
Romania	23.4	Malta	14.6
Bulgaria	21.4	Finland	13.6
Greece	20.1	Luxembourg	13.4
Lithuania	20.0	France	13.3
Spain	19.6	Hungary	12.4
Estonia	19.5	Austria	12.4
United Kingdom	18.8	Slovenia	12.3
Italy	18.7	Sweden	12.2
Portugal	18.5	Denmark	11.8
Poland	16.9	Slovakia	10.9
Cyprus	16.2	Netherlands	10.5
Ireland	15.5	Czech Republic	9.0

Source: CSO (2010a: 97).

The Extent of Poverty in Ireland

Poverty levels in Ireland are measured by the Central Statistics Office, which since 2003 has carried out the *Survey on Income and Living Conditions (SILC)*, on an annual basis. From 1994 to 2003, poverty was measured by the ESRI through the *Living in Ireland Survey (LIS)*. The *SILC* is a comprehensive household survey on income and living conditions, and includes 'a number of key national poverty indicators' (CSO 2012a: 5). The 2010 *SILC* gives the levels of poverty and deprivation over a number of years in its summary of main results: see Table 3.2.

Table 3.2: Income, Poverty and Deprivation Rates

	2004	2005	2006	2007	2008	2009	2010
Income	€	€	€	€	€	€	€
At risk of poverty threshold (60% of median income)	9,680	10,057	10,566	11,890	12,455	12,064	10,831
Poverty and deprivation rates	%	%	%	%	%	%	%
At risk of poverty rate	19.4	18.5	17.0	16.5	14.4	14.1	15.8
Deprivation rate*	14.2	14.9	13.8	11.8	13.8	17.1	22.5
Consistent poverty rate	6.6	7.0	6.5	5.1	4.2	5.5	6.2

Source: CSO (2012a: 5).
*Experienced two or more types of enforced deprivation (see Box 3.2).

It is apparent from the CSO data that poverty, both at risk and consistent, was on a downward trend in the new century up to 2008. In contrast there has been a slow trend upwards since the beginning of the current economic crisis. For deprivation rates there was a sharp acceleration upwards during the economic crisis. The CSO explains that the increased deprivation rates relate to those 'NOT at risk of poverty' rather than those at risk of poverty (CSO 2012a: 7, emphasis in original). In other words people who are not defined as being at risk of poverty are reporting enforced deprivations. (See Box 3.2 for a list of deprivation indicators.) This would be the case if people had an income (at least over the short term) that kept them above the level that qualifies as 'at risk', but still found that it did not stretch to provide the goods and services people typically expect to enjoy.

This could happen, for instance, if people had planned their budgets based on a certain level of income, then found that perhaps because they became unemployed, their income level fell. They might have large commitments (for instance a big mortgage, or loan payments) which took up so much of their income that they had only a small 'disposable income' left. So they could not afford to buy other items, or enjoy social and cultural events. This obviously affects their overall standard of living, and on the definitions that are used, it leads them to experience deprivation. The *SILC* figures also show a decline in overall income for the population as a whole, and because being 'at risk of poverty' is measured relative to median incomes, this reduced the income threshold that applied.

What average figures do not show are differences between age groups and family types. Those most at risk of poverty are children, with 19.5 per cent of Irish children at risk of poverty in 2010, up from 18.6 per cent in 2009. The group least at risk of poverty are older people, those over 65 years. The percentage of this group at risk of poverty (9.6 per cent) did not change between 2009 and 2010. One in five children is at risk of poverty compared with one in ten older people. Lone parent families, defined as families with one adult and one or more children under eighteen, are more likely to be at risk of poverty than any other group. Of these families 20.5 per cent are at risk of poverty, down from 35.5 per cent in 2009 (CSO 2012a – the CSO warns that there is need for caution in interpreting this dramatic change, since technical reasons caused the figures to differ so greatly). It is noticeable that there was an increase in the at risk of poverty rate across all other categories of families in the survey with children under eighteen, between 2009 and 2010.

The overall level of consistent poverty in 2010 was 6.2 per cent. Children show the highest levels of consistent poverty, at 8.2 per cent in 2010, no significant difference from 2009 (8.7 per cent), although this follows an increase from 6.3 per cent in 2008. On the other hand the rate of consistent poverty for people over 65 is the lowest of all age groups, at 0.9 per cent in 2010.

There are some other important findings on poverty from the *SILC* reports. They have consistently shown that the lower an individual's level of education is, the more likely they are to be at risk of poverty, experience deprivation and be in consistent poverty. There is a similar correlation based on housing tenure. Those who own their own homes are least likely to experience poverty, while those who are in social housing are most likely to do so (CSO 2012a; Drudy and Punch 2005). The highest level of income is achieved by those in employment, followed by those over 65 years. Poverty and deprivation rates are much lower for these two categories than any other. People who are unemployed, those who perform home duties, individuals not in work because of disability or long-term illness, and students have a high risk of suffering poverty and deprivation (CSO 2012a).

The *SILC* report for 2010 shows significant difference in rates of poverty between urban and rural dwellers (CSO 2012a). People with medical cards are more likely to experience poverty and express higher levels of poor health than those with private health insurance (CSO 2012a; see also Farrell, McEvoy and Wilde 2008, Harvey 2007, and Wren 2006 for discussions on poverty and health). It is therefore evident that a number of crucial factors that impact on people's basic material well-being, such as income, education, housing and health, are interconnected and together have an effect on rates of poverty and deprivation. Without the support of the Irish state through what are known as social transfers (that is, all payments made by the state to individuals and families through the social welfare system), the levels of poverty and deprivation would be even greater.

> In 2010 if all social transfers were excluded from income the at risk of poverty rate would be 51%, indicating a steady increase from 39.8% in 2004. This increase over time demonstrates the increasing dependence of individuals on social transfers to remain above the at risk of poverty threshold. (CSO 2012: 26)

Social Exclusion – Changing the Understanding of the Meaning of Poverty

As part of the conceptual expansion of the meaning of poverty since the 1970s, a second and closely related concept emerged, that of social exclusion. A definition of social exclusion was included in Partnership 2000 (a national agreement between the government and its social partners: business representatives, trade unions, the farming community, and the community and voluntary sector): '[c]umulative marginalisation: from production (unemployment), from consumption (income poverty), from social networks (community, family and neighbours), from decision making and from an adequate quality of life' (Government of Ireland 1997: 3).

So social exclusion is a long-term multidimensional state which impacts on a number of key aspects of people's lives, and gradually drives them to the margins of society. From the 1970s there was a shift in public policy, from a dominant view of poverty based on lack of income, to seeing it as involving poor people's inability to enjoy social, political and economic rights (Geddes 2000). Supporting social inclusion and combating its opposite, social exclusion, have been long-standing objectives of EU social policy. As early as 1975 the Council of Ministers defined poverty as 'individuals or families whose resources are so small as to exclude them from the minimum acceptable way of life of the Member State in which they live', with 'resources' being defined as 'goods, cash income plus services from public and private sources' (Council of Ministers 1975, cited in Atkinson et al. 2005: 18). The European Union has gained increasing competence in the area of social exclusion, which has become 'central to the social policy agenda' (Levitas 2005: ix).

The concepts of social inclusion and social exclusion have come into common usage in the public policy debate around poverty, yet they are contested terms (Levitas 2005). Some believe that these concepts provide for a much deeper understanding of the multidimensional experience of poverty, rather than the traditional and narrower definition of poverty based on lack of income (Langford 1999). Others argue that these concepts have sanitised the idea of poverty (Coakley 2004). Some authors argue that these new concepts tend to remove from considera-tion inequality, a key element in the discussion of poverty. If inequality is not considered in addressing poverty, it means that the impact of broader social and economic structures on poverty is ignored (Levitas 2005, Lister 2004, Nolan and Whelan 1996; see also the section on inequality below).

Policies to Combat Poverty

The development of Irish anti-poverty policies coincided with Ireland's membership of the European Union. Langford (1999) traces the development of Europe's anti-poverty poli-cies, which had a profound impact on Irish government (and EU) thinking on the nature of and approach to poverty. For almost two decades three successive European-led anti-poverty programmes provided the foundations for reflection and action on poverty, leading to its greater prominence in national and European social policy.

The first anti-poverty programme, 1975–1980, is attrib-uted to pressure on the European Commission from the Irish government (Ó'Cinnéide 2010). This programme 'put poverty firmly on the European Community agenda for the first time', and it also succeeded in bringing about a re-examination of the prevailing ideas about poverty (Langford 1999: 91). The second anti-poverty programme, 1985–1989, emphasised prac-tical responses to poverty at local community level, and the 'joint themes of research and innovation' (Langford 1999: 92). This programme led to poverty being identified as a structural problem (a problem brought about primarily as a result of the organisation and structure of society, rather than by individual behaviour or characteristics). The third and final EU anti-poverty programme, 1989–1994, concentrated on the new concept of social exclusion, with its emphasis on the broader dimensions and the dynamic nature of poverty (Langford 1999, Ó'Cinnéide 2010). During this period of anti-poverty programmes there was a discernible shift in language, policy understanding and actions to deal with poverty, both in Ireland and at EU level. Although the groundwork had been completed for a fourth EU anti-poverty programme, objections by Germany and the

United Kingdom scuppered a further programme (Ó'Cinnéide 2010). However, this was not to prove a setback as public policy on poverty moved on in subsequent years.

Before we turn to these events, it is worth pointing to a number of developments in Ireland in the 1980s, since these provided a very important stimulus to the improvement in public policy on poverty. Ó'Cinnéide (2010: 25) suggests that in 1986 anti-poverty work in Ireland received 'a fresh impetus' with the publication of the *Report of the Commission on Social Welfare*, a major review of the welfare system in Ireland. He also draws attention to two other significant events which took place in that year: the beginning of the first extensive survey on poverty in Ireland by the ESRI, and the establishment of the Combat Poverty Agency as a statutory agency 'to spearhead research and promotional work on poverty in Ireland' (Ó'Cinnéide 2010: 25). Langford (1999) discusses experiments in partnership and participation at a local level as a part of initiatives on poverty and social inclusion. These she attributes to the development of local area-based partnership companies, which were established to combat long-term unemployment and social exclusion.

Ireland participated in the United Nations World Summit on Poverty in Copenhagen in 1995, and subsequently developed a ten-year *National Anti-Poverty Strategy: Sharing in Progress* (NAPS), published in 1997 (Government of Ireland 1997). In so doing Ireland was one of the earliest countries to give priority to tackling poverty in this manner, which was to become institutionalised as standard practice throughout the European Union within a few years (Stewart 2005). In preparation for the first NAPS three substantial issues emerged which had to be dealt with, if poverty was to be effectively eliminated:

- Addressing poverty needs to be based on an understanding of the multidimensional nature of poverty.
- Addressing poverty involves tackling the deep-seated underlying structural inequalities that create and perpetuate it.
- There is also a need to give particular attention to a number of key areas if any significant advance on poverty is to be achieved. These areas were identified as:

- Educational disadvantage
- Unemployment, particularly long-term unemployment
- Income adequacy
- Disadvantaged urban areas
- Rural poverty

(Government of Ireland 1997: 8–9)

The European Union made a formal commitment to combating poverty and social exclusion through what has become known as the 'Lisbon agenda' or 'Lisbon strategy', which was agreed in 2000 by the EU Council (Ó'Cinnéide 2010: 30). As a result of this commitment all EU member states agreed common poverty indicators, national plans were monitored, action plans to address poverty and social exclusion were required to be drawn up, and joint reports on progress were to be published (Ó'Cinnéide 2010). Later in the same year at a summit in Nice the EU Council agreed the *National Action Programme on Social Inclusion* (NAPincl), which came into operation from 2001. Ireland's 1997 NAPS was revised in 2001 to become the country's first *National Action Programme on Social Inclusion*, in order to meet its EU obligation. This revised action plan was more ambitious than the original plan (Considine and Dukelow 2009). The poverty reduction targets were revised. Where the original NAPS aimed to reduce consistent poverty from '9 to 15% to less than 5 to 10%' (Government of Ireland 1997: 9), the new plan aspired to 'reduce the numbers of those who are "consistently poor" [to] below 2% and, if possible, eliminate consistent poverty, under the current definition of consistent poverty' (Government of Ireland 2002a: 9).

The new Irish NAPincl maintained its original key objectives and added some new elements. Targets for health and housing were added for the first time, as were targets for 'vulnerable groups', which consisted of children and young people, women, older people, Travellers, people with disabilities, migrants and members of ethnic minority groups (Government of Ireland 2002a). On the expiry of the first ten-year anti-poverty strategy the government published its successor, the *National Action Plan for Social Inclusion 2007–2016* (NAPinclusion), which was to complement the social partnership agreement *Towards 2016* and the *National Development Plan 2007–2013*. The government set a new poverty target, '[T]o reduce the number of those experiencing consistent poverty to between 2% and 4% by 2012, with the aim of eliminating consistent poverty by 2016' (Government of Ireland 2007a: 13).

Of course this new strategy was published just as the Irish economy was about to implode, and policy commitments to poverty reduction have been reversed in subsequent budgetary measures taken by government. As we saw above, the consistent poverty rate remained at 6.2 per cent at the end of 2010. It was unlikely that the NAPinclusion target of 'between 2% and 4%' would be met by 2012, and with increasing challenges as a result of recession it is also difficult to see how the aim of poverty elimination by 2016 will be achieved (Russell, Maître and Nolan 2010).

Considine and Dukelow note a shift in emphasis in the methods of poverty reduction between the original NAPS and NAPinclusion. The original NAPS had a 'focus centred on reaching adequate levels of social welfare payment, whereas in the current plan activation policy takes precedence over further improvements to the adequacy of social security payments' (Considine and Dukelow 2009: 232). In other words in the new approach there is a shift in emphasis towards directing those who are unemployed into training, education and paid work. This is preferred to income support, which NAPinclusion suggests is a 'largely passive approach' (Government of Ireland 2007a: 44). The trend towards 'workfare' or 'welfare-to-work' has come to dominate welfare policies in OECD countries since the 1990s (Dostal 2007), so it is no surprise that it has reached the policy agenda in Ireland, particularly in light of the cost of social welfare to the state at a time when it is heavily indebted. The current Minister for Social Protection, in announcing changes in the 2012 Budget, demonstrated her views on the relationship between poverty and paid work, saying (about lone parent families) that '[t]he best route out of poverty is through paid employment' (Burton 2011). This pronouncement showed continuity in language and philosophy from the previous government's stance on the relationship between poverty and employment (Considine and Dukelow 2009), but seemed to signal a greater determination to implement activation policies.

Box 3.4

Paid Work and Poverty

The mantra 'the best route out of poverty is through paid employment' is not a new one. However, work does not necessarily lead to a poverty-free existence (Social Justice Ireland 2010). Poverty indicators suggest that a sizeable section of those in paid employment experience poverty. In the 2010 *SILC* survey 17.3 per cent of those in work in Ireland were identified as being at risk of poverty, and 9.9 per cent of the working population were in consistent poverty (CSO 2012a: 33, 66). It is argued that the welfare trap causes some people to remain unemployed, because the level of benefit is so high that it acts as a disincentive to the unemployed person to take up paid work (Gray 2004). These disincentives are tackled through 'in-work benefits'. In Ireland Family Income Supplement plays this role: it is a means tested, time-limited supplement to wages, available to employees with children. This system is in effect a subsidy to employers who pay wages so low that the employee cannot live on them. In addition, there is according to Gray, 'the growing tendency in European benefits systems to adopt ... a "workfarist" approach, obliging people to take any job however low paid, and often using compulsory "activation" measures to drive them to do so' (2004: 189).

These approaches to low-paid work appear to ignore the reality of the current jobs crisis (see Collins 2012 on the Irish jobs crisis and activation) and even more fundamentally the changing nature of work itself (Standing 2011). It can also be argued that the logic of the approaches suggests that governments support the needs of employers to make profit over the needs of workers (Gray 2004). Increasingly throughout Europe, young workers, women workers, migrant workers and unskilled male workers are being marginalised into 'atypical' or 'precarious' employment (see Gray 2004, Loftus 2012, Standing 2011). This form of employment casualisation is both insecure and poorly paid, but has become the norm for many workers in certain employment sectors. Loftus (2012) argues that Irish workers are particularly at risk because of the flexible nature of the Irish labour market, high levels of low pay, and poor labour protection. As a result many workers can expect to struggle with poverty. This risk of poverty, according to Tomlinson and Walker (2012: 67), emerges from structural factors in the labour market that are outside the control of workers, rather than from their 'personal attributes or circumstances'. They conclude that '[p]olicies that simply encourage people to find work, without paying attention to the kind of jobs that are available, cannot secure a marked reduction in recurrent poverty or a sustained decline in the poverty rate' (Tomlinson and Walker 2012: 67).

Poverty and Inequality

An increasing number of scholars believe that the relationship between poverty and inequality is of huge significance not just for dealing with the issue of poverty, but also for addressing social cohesion within societies (Kirby 2001; Kirby and Murphy 2008, 2011; Layte 2011; Wilkinson and Pickett 2010). Kirby sees this question as centrally important in addressing the issue of poverty:

> While using the vocabulary of social exclusion/inclusion, [Irish social policy] fails to realise that growing economic inequality is a central cause of social exclusion and that any commitment to social inclusion must include adopting policies to narrow the gap between rich and poor. (Kirby 2001: 28)

Kirby concludes that Irish social policy shows an understanding of the multidimensional nature of poverty, but has 'a relatively minimalist distributional objective, namely to reduce the numbers of those who are "consistently poor"' (2001: 28). Consistent poverty is the target for government anti-poverty strategies, despite the fact that poverty is defined by government and social partners in relative terms (at risk of poverty), as was outlined earlier in the chapter. Coakley is critical of this 'consistent poverty discourse', which she says was used to show government success in tackling poverty during the boom years. However, it ignores issues of growing inequality, and 'ideas of redistribution of wealth and resources and of social justice' (2004: 115).

In a powerful analysis of the impact of unequal societies in their much acclaimed book *The Spirit Level* (2010), Richard Wilkinson and Kate Pickett argue persuasively that inequality has a destructive effect on societies. They provide evidence that social problems are worse in the most unequal societies than in more equal societies. Layte (2011) also suggests that inequality has negative consequences which go beyond some people being poor, and impacts on an array of social problems. He says that for the individual, inequality brings about feelings of social inferiority and shame. Furthermore, inequality impacts on social cohesion as these feelings of social inferiority and shame lead to distrust between people (Layte 2011).

It is very difficult to fully establish the levels of inequality in Ireland because of the lack of available data – there is much available on the poor but little on the rich (Kirby 2001). Kirby and Murphy (2008: 12), pointing to a lack of research in this area, say that there is little information on the distribution of wealth in Irish society, which they claim 'is generally far more unequally distributed' than income. Both Kirby and Murphy (2008) and Social Justice Ireland (2011) show that income inequality increased over the period of the Irish boom. According to Allen (2012), inequality is continuing to increase in the post-boom period. Kirby and Murphy (2008) acknowledge that the incomes of the lowest decile (that is, the lowest tenth of the population) did increase during the boom period, but add that the greatest gain was in the top decile.

Social Justice Ireland (2011) uses Central Statistics Office (CSO) figures from the 2010 *SILC* to demonstrate the extent of the differences in disposable incomes between those on the lowest and highest levels of income. These show that the bottom tenth of the population had only 2.39 per cent of national income at their disposal, in comparison with 25.83 per cent for the top tenth of the population. Actual weekly disposable income was €210.45 for those on the lowest levels and €2,276.00 for those in the top decile. The top earners have just over ten times more weekly income at their disposal than those at the bottom (Social Justice Ireland 2011). It is also important to note that this is not just a one-off aberration of inequality. Social Justice Ireland demonstrates that over the period 1987–2009 income inequality in Ireland was persistent. The levels of disposable income for the bottom and top deciles remained quite consistent over this 22-year period, as can be seen in Table 3.3.

Table 3.3: The Distribution of Household Disposable Incomes 1987–2009, Bottom and Top Deciles

Year	1987	1994/95	1999/00	2004	2009
Bottom decile	2.28	2.23	1.93	2.10	2.39
Top decile	24.48	24.67	25.90	27.15	25.83

Source: Social Justice Ireland (2011: 70).

Income distribution is usefully understood in a comparative context; in other words it is useful to compare income distribution in Ireland with income distribution in other countries. Within the European Union Ireland is at mid-table for income distribution, as can be seen in Table 3.4 (CSO 2010a). The figures in this table refer to the top and bottom quintiles (top and bottom fifths of the income scale), and the higher the ratio, the more unequal the distribution of income in the member state.

Table 3.4: Income Distribution in the European Union, Top and Bottom Quintile Ratios 2008

Country	Ratio	Country	Ratio
Latvia	7.3	France	4.2
Romania	7.0	Belgium	4.1
Bulgaria	6.5	Cyprus	4.1
Portugal	6.1	Luxembourg	4.1
Greece	5.9	Malta	4.0
Lithuania	5.9	Netherlands	4.0
United Kingdom	5.6	Finland	3.8
Spain	5.4	Austria	3.7
Italy	5.1	Denmark	3.6
Poland	5.1	Hungary	3.6
EU-27 average	5.0	Sweden	3.5
Estonia	5.0	Czech Republic	3.4
Germany	4.8	Slovenia	3.4
Ireland	4.4	Slovakia	3.4

Source: CSO (2010a: 97).

Ireland does not have the most unequal distribution of income in the European Union. However, the ratio of 4.4 points to a level of inequality which reflects the neglect of a redistributive dimension to public policy-making. Redistribution of wealth is emphasised in Nordic societies, hence their position towards the front of the equality league. Furthermore, the 2010 *SILC* reported growth in inequality between 2009 and 2010, with the average income of those in the top quintile in 2010 being 5.5 times greater than for those in the bottom quintile (CSO 2012a: 10). The CSO said that this change had reversed 'the downward trend evident from 2005' (2012a: 10).

Conclusion

The targets set out by government for consistent poverty eradication since 1997 have not been achieved. These targets were not met during the boom period when resources were plentiful. As this chapter was being written after almost five years of recession and austerity (and more to come), it seemed very unlikely that the current target, poverty elimination by 2016, would be achieved either. If anything, the data suggests that the gains that had been made will be reversed. During this time of austerity there have been cutbacks in expenditure on different elements of welfare provision. Child benefit has been reduced, wages have decreased, and direct and indirect taxes have increased. Income tax (through the universal social charge) has been levied on many low earners who were previously exempt, and new charges have been introduced for formerly free services, such as for prescriptions for medical card holders. Non-monetary supports and services, including health and social services, education and housing, have all been limited or reduced, impacting most on those on low and marginal incomes. Even information and informed debate on poverty is much more difficult to access, as the flagship Combat Poverty Agency was one of the first agencies to be closed in 2009 when the government began to rein in its expenditure.

Much has been achieved in Ireland in developing an improved understanding of poverty since the early 1970s. Efforts at national and EU level, where Ireland has played a leading role, to agree definitions and measurement of poverty have given policy-makers the tools and the expertise to address poverty effectively. Yet the problem of poverty and social exclusion continues in spite of these advances. Tools and expertise can only work if there is a political will to eradicate poverty. But the evidence from Ireland is that this commitment has never been fully pursued, and that is less likely still in the current economic circumstances, which are dominated by a neoliberal response to welfare matters. According to the original NAPS in 1997, the elimination of poverty 'involves tackling the deep-seated underlying structural inequalities that create and perpetuate it' (Government of Ireland 1997: 8). What chance is there of such a policy direction? No chance, is the short answer. And the poor in Ireland will remain with us.

Further Reading

The Social Inclusion Unit website has key material on poverty and social exclusion, including the Irish government's anti-poverty strategies. The CSO provides up-to-date annual information through its *SILC* reports. Social Justice Ireland also provides a very useful and up-to-date analysis on poverty and equality matters, and as its name suggests, on a range of social justice issues. Although it is beginning to become dated, a great information source for materials on the different aspects of poverty remains the defunct (since 2009) Combat Poverty Agency. The Agency's website (www.cpa.ie) is still functioning, its materials are also available through the Social Inclusion Unit website of the Department of Social Protection.

Essential Documents

The *National Action Plan for Social Inclusion 2007–2016* is available from the Office for Social Inclusion Unit website, an important source of materials on poverty and social exclusion: www.social-inclusion.ie/documents/NAPinclusionReportPDF.pdf

The original *National Anti-Poverty Strategy* is an essential document for students, setting out the original thinking on how poverty in Ireland should be addressed: www.socialinclusion.

ie/NationalAnti-PovertyStrategy-SharinginProgress1997.pdf. pdf

The annual government budgets announced in the Dáil by the Minister for Finance and other government ministers in early December each year are important for public expenditure decisions which impact on poverty. The Minister's budget speech can be accessed through the Department of Finance website.

The annual *SILC* reports published by the CSO are a must-read for anyone interested in Irish poverty. They provide extensive statistical information on income and poverty in Ireland.

Social Justice Ireland publishes materials on poverty and other social justice topics. Of particular interest and value is the annual *Socio-Economic Review*.

The European Anti-Poverty Network, an umbrella organisation representing European non-governmental organisations that campaign on poverty issues, is a very useful source of information on poverty.

General Reading

Much of the reading about poverty may prove challenging for those who do not engage well with the technicalities of statistics. But not all reading materials are dominated by statistics, and the following are useful contributions to the understanding of poverty and related issues of social ex/inclusion and inequality.

On the evolution of poverty policy in Ireland and its relationship with the European Union, I suggest reading Séamus Ó'Cinnéide's 'From poverty to social inclusion: the EU and Ireland', in the European Anti-Poverty Network Ireland's edited book *Ireland and the European Social Inclusion Strategy: Lessons Learned and the Road Ahead* (2010). On a similar theme and equally worth reading is Sylda Langford's chapter, 'The Impact of the European Union on Irish social policy development in relation to social exclusion'.

I also recommend two British authors. Peter Townsend's classic *Poverty in the United Kingdom* (1979) and Ruth Lister's *Poverty* (2004) are excellent books. For an excellent theoretical discussion on social inclusion I recommend Ruth Levitas's *The Inclusive Society? Social Exclusion and New Labour* (2005).

On equality/inequality issues, material worth reading includes Peadar Kirby's chapter, 'Inequality and poverty in Ireland: clarifying objectives', in Sarah Cantillon et al.'s edited book *Rich and Poor: Perspectives on Tackling Inequality in Ireland* (2001). The acclaimed book by British authors Richard Wilkinson and Kate Pickett *The Spirit Level: Why Equality Is Better for Everyone* (2010) is a very important contribution to the debate on equality.

Useful Websites

Central Statistics Office – www.cso.ie
Department of Finance – www.finance.ie
European Anti-Poverty Network – www.eapn.ie
Office for Social Inclusion – www.socialinclusion.ie
Social Justice Ireland – www.socialjustice.ie

4

Shame of It: Child Protection in Ireland

Area of Social Care for which this Chapter Is Relevant

Everyone who works with children is expected to be familiar with child protection policies. This chapter provides students with a summary of the historical development and current state of these policies in Ireland.

Key Words in this Chapter

Child protection, legislation, guidelines, definitions of abuse, rights of children, familialisation, Catholic Church, crisis, failure

Key Themes in this Chapter

- Background to child protection in Ireland
- Important legislation
- Dealing with child abuse
- Rights of children
- The rights and wrongs of child protection in Ireland

Introduction

Issues of child protection and care still dominate many Irish social care courses, because work with children and young people remains central to social care practice. The majority of social care workers will at some time in their careers work directly with children and young people, or will need to consider them and their needs in working more widely with families and in the community. Child protection has become one of the most controversial aspects of social policy in Ireland. We have learned of the historical abuse of children in the care of religious orders, and tried to come to terms with it, but it is still a great challenge to Irish society and the Irish state to face up to the serious problem of child abuse.

It was correct to focus on the historic role of the Catholic Church in child abuse, but that is only part of the challenge. It must also be acknowledged that child abuse continues to be a problem, and that most child abuse occurs within the home, where children are abused by people who are related to, or at least known to, them. The Irish state has a poor record in confronting and responding to child abuse. It has been responsible for negligent policies and practices which have either led to the abuse of children or have not prevented abuse, and it has failed to protect children in need of protection. At the time of writing there are grounds for some optimism. The long-standing flaws in child protection structures and practice in Ireland might be addressed, as services for vulnerable children are receiving the greatest shake-up since the foundation of the Irish state.

Background to Child Protection in Ireland

The care of Catholic children in Ireland has for the best part of two centuries been in the hands of the Catholic Church (Powell 1992, Robins 1987). Catholic religious congregations' involvement in child welfare began in the early nineteenth century in Ireland, when the British administration lifted its penal restrictions on Catholics (Robins 1987). This role was supported by the British government as part of its efforts to control the Irish population. The British effectively handed over responsibility for governing the Irish people to the Catholic Church from the mid-nineteenth century (Inglis 1998). The Catholic Church's primary vehicle for executing its control was the education and care of children, in order to ensure their socialisation (Powell 1992). Throughout the nineteenth century and into the twentieth century the Catholic Church's care of children continued to grow. Irish independence in 1922 did not arrest this trend. In fact, as the British began to dismantle and overhaul their care system, the new Irish state allowed more and more children to be cared for by Catholic religious orders (Raftery and O'Sullivan 1999). This continued until the 1970s, when as a result of criticism of the care provided by the church-run institutions, the government began to change its approach to the care of children in need of protection (O'Sullivan 2009).

Child protection became an issue of public interest from the 1870s onwards (Ferguson 2004). The protection and care of children had effectively been privatised, as initially the country under British rule, and then the Irish state, gave over the care of children to the Catholic Church and the protection of children to the National Society for the Prevention of Cruelty to Children (NSPCC), which was founded in 1889. Its Irish successor, the Irish Society for the Prevention of Cruelty to Children (ISPCC), was formed when the Irish service separated from the NSPCC in 1956 (Ferguson 2004). The NSPCC/ISPCC operated along the same philosophical lines as the Catholic Church. It was concerned with controlling poor children, for not dissimilar reasons. The nineteenth-century bourgeoisie feared social disorder in British cities, and were happy to financially support new charitable organisations, including the NSPCC, which were established to bring about the moral reform of the poor working class (Ferguson 2004). Ferguson states that the emergence of organisations like the NSPCC, and the development of legislation to support legal intervention in the lives of families and the parent–child relationship, were unknown prior to this period (1996).

Ferguson identifies three key 'formative phases' for child protection in Ireland: 'the periods 1889–1914; 1970–1989; and 1990 to the present' (1996: 7). By the beginning of the twentieth century the conditions for the recognition of child abuse in Ireland were established, but it was not until the 1970s that the issue began to be acknowledged in Irish social policy. It was during this period that the state took over responsibility for the investigation of child abuse, as it restructured the health and social services following the passing of the 1970 Health Act. Community care teams were established throughout the state, and responsibility for child protection and welfare was given over to them (O'Sullivan 2009). This saw a greatly expanded professional service with responsibility for the protection of children. During this period important reports on child protection and care were published: the *Kennedy*

Report (Kennedy 1970) and the *Task Force on Child Care Services Final Report* (Department of Health 1980).

In the 1990s child protection entered the public conscious-ness as never before, when a number of high-profile child abuse inquiries reported (Ferguson 1996). Since then there has been no let-up in public disclosure of child abuse, particularly abuse involving the religious orders which had responsibility for the care of children deemed to be in need of protection, and the sexual abuse of children by Catholic priests. The role of the Cath-olic Church has been the focus of public discourse about abuse, but there is also a case for a broader investigation, as allegations of institutional abuse have also been made by former residents of Protestant-run establishments. Meehan (2010: 10) points to how the Irish state neglected these people, and says they 'feel they are the forgotten few'.

Important Legislation

Box 4.1

Ireland's Most Important Child Protection Legislation
• Cruelty to Children Act 1889
• Children Act 1908
• Child Care Act 1991

Considering the growing importance of child protection and care through the period from the 1870s, there is surprisingly little associated legislation on the Irish statute books. In all, there are three substantial pieces of legislation dealing with child protection and welfare, beginning with the Cruelty to Children Act 1889, which 'criminalised child cruelty and gave Inspectors new powers to remove cruelly treated children from parental custody' (Ferguson 1996: 7). The policy approach was to force parents to carry out their responsibilities to care for their chil-dren, and 'prosecution was a key strategy towards this objective' (Ferguson 1996: 9). Two other Cruelty to Children Acts were subsequently enacted in 1894 and 1904, and all of this legislation was incorporated into the Children Act 1908 (Ferguson 1996).

The Children Act 1908 was introduced during the period of what have been described as 'the Liberal Reforms' (Burke 1999: 20). The Act was a most enduring piece of legislation, as it became the framework for child protection in Ireland for 83 years. It provided for the removal of children who were neglected or abused by their parents to a 'place of safety', and for children to be placed in the care of a 'fit person'. This 'fit person' was normally either a foster parent or a residential institution (Richardson 2005). From 1908 there was a shift from an emphasis on punishing parents to a casework ideology and practice. This was based on supervision of the parent–child relationship within the home (Ferguson 1996). Both the 1889 and 1908 legislation was enacted under British rule, and while subsequent British governments updated the UK child protection legislation on a number of occasions before the end of the twentieth century, the same was not the case in Ireland under Irish rule. Burke observes that the 1908 Act 'was strong on aspiration but weak in implementation, particularly in Ireland where it long outlived its relevance for children at risk in the rapidly changing world of the second half of the twentieth century' (1999: 20).

It was not until the passing of the Child Care Act 1991 that an Irish government, for the first time in its history, introduced child protection and welfare legislation. For almost two decades prior to this legislation there had been calls for an overhaul of the law and policies on child protection in Ireland. The impetus for this began with the *Kennedy Report* (1970) and the establishment of CARE, a pressure group of professionals and academics which sought to bring about change in legislation along the lines recommended by the *Kennedy Report* (Richardson 2005). Under increasing pressure the government established a Task Force on Child Care Services in 1974.

In 1980 the *Task Force on Child Care Services Final Report* was published. This was a substantial document which highlighted the complexity of the care and protection of children. One of the terms of reference of the Task Force was 'to prepare a Bill up-dating the law in relation to children' who were deprived and at risk (Department of Health 1980: 1). It did not complete that particular task, and it took another ten years before legislation was passed.

The Child Care Act 1991 was greatly welcomed, and according to Ferguson and Kenny it 'represents one of the most important pieces of social legislation ever to reach the statute book in the Republic of Ireland' (1995: 1). The key feature of the legislation is summed up in Section 3 of the Act, where a statutory duty is placed on the health boards (now the HSE) 'to identify and promote the welfare of children who are not receiving adequate care and protection and to provide a range of family support services' (Barron 1995: 10). The legislation covers a range of other issues: it defines who is a child, allows for voluntary care, imposes a requirement on the HSE to address the accommoda-tion needs of homeless children, sets out a range of procedures for care proceedings, defines the role of the courts, outlines the responsibilities of the HSE in relation to children in its care, includes for the first time the regulation of pre-schools in the legislation, and also addresses the registration of residential services for children (Government of Ireland 1991).

The Child Care Act also included some key concepts, such as in Section 3, that the welfare of the child must be given paramount consideration, and that the child's view must be considered and taken into account in matters affecting him or her (Government of Ireland 1991). These concepts are central principles of the United Nations Convention on the Rights of the Child (UNCRC), which Ireland ratified in 1992. With this new watershed legislation in place at last, it might have been expected that child protection was to enter a new phase in Ireland. The new phase came, but not immediately and not with the success that was hoped for.

Two later pieces of legislation further improved the state's legislative commitment to child protection. While the Child Care Act 1991 is concerned with the welfare and care of chil-dren, the Children Act 2001 had as its primary objective matters related to children and criminal justice. Yet there are elements within this legislation that have the potential to assist the rele-vant agencies in their response to the welfare needs of children. These include family welfare conferences (in Part 2 of the Act) and the provision for the care and protection of children who are a risk to themselves or to others (in Part 4A) (Government of Ireland 2001a). The Health Act 2007 (Government of Ireland 2007b) provides for the establishment of the Health Information

and Quality Authority (HIQA), under which the Inspectorate of Social Services, originally set up in 1999, has been given
a statutory duty to inspect and ensure appropriate standards
in children's services, including residential units, special care
units, foster care, and, from 2012, children and family services
(HIQA 2012).

Dealing with Child Abuse

Box 4.2

Types of Child Abuse
• Neglect • Emotional abuse • Physical abuse • Sexual abuse (Source: *Children First*, DCYA 2011)

Although there has been state recognition of child abuse from
the latter part of the nineteenth century, with the Cruelty to
Children Act 1889 providing a legal basis to that recognition, it
was not until the 1970s that the first attempts were made to deal
formally with child abuse in Ireland. Awareness of the problem
of child abuse in Ireland developed from the late 1960s, with
the 'rediscovery' of child abuse in the United States and Britain
(Ferguson 1996). The first child abuse guidelines in Ireland,
the *Memorandum on Non-Accidental Injury to Children* (Buckley
1996), were issued in 1977. The title of the guidelines shows the
limited understanding of child abuse at the time, where abuse
was deemed primarily to be physical injury. Subsequently the
abuse guidelines were modified and the description of abuse
was extended 'to include neglect, emotional abuse and sexual
abuse' (Buckley 1996: 38). With each passing modification the
guidelines expanded and became more detailed. By 1987 the
child abuse guidelines had grown substantially in content, to
include the management, monitoring and coordination of child
abuse cases (Buckley 1996, Ferguson 1996). These guidelines
were supplemented in 1995 to enhance cooperation between
the health boards and the Gardaí (Office of the Children's

Ombudsman (OCO) 2010). But as Ferguson points out, 'remarkably, however, at no time did any Irish guidelines published in the 1970s and 1980s actually provide definitions of the phenomenon of NAI (non-accidental injury)/child abuse' (1996: 21).

This was to change with the publication of *Children First: National Guidelines for the Protection and Welfare of Children* (DHC 1999). These guidelines have been superseded by a more up-to-date version published in 2011, *Children First: National Guidance for the Protection and Welfare of Children* (Department of Children and Youth Affairs (DCYA) 2011). The original *Children First* guidelines offered a detailed approach to dealing with child abuse, addressing the many complex issues and relationships as well as the range of professional responsibilities. The aim of the guidelines was 'to assist people in identifying and reporting child abuse' (DHC 1999: 17). *Children First* was particularly concerned to help provide clarification about the contribution to child protection of various professionals in the statutory and voluntary organisations, and to encourage mutual understanding between them. The needs of children and families were regarded as the primary consideration of child protection activity, and an approach based on partnership was to inform the delivery of services. The guidelines aimed at ensuring consistency in application of child protection services across the country (DHC 1999).

In 2008 a review of *Children First* was published – *National Review of Compliance with Children First: National Guidelines for the Protection and Welfare of Children* (Office of the Minister for Children and Youth Affairs 2008). This document reported the views of staff in government agencies who deal with child protection and welfare issues as well as those of academics. The review was carried out for the Office of the Minister for Children and Youth Affairs in the wake of the *Ferns Report* (Government of Ireland 2005b) – an official government inquiry into complaints and allegations made against Catholic clergy in the Diocese of Ferns. According to the Minister in his foreword to the review of *Children First*, 'the main finding of this review is that the guidelines have stood up well to the passage of time and with minor amendments can serve us well in the future' (2008: v). The *Review* suggested that the problems with the guidelines derived from 'local variation and infrastructural issues, rather than from fundamental difficulties with the guidelines themselves' (2008: 3).

Even if the problems are explained in this way, there appear to be some significant shortcomings in the way the guidelines have been implemented. For example, survey respondents in the *Review* were asked about one of the key principles of *Children First*, participation by children and young people in matters that affect them. Fewer than half believed this principle was 'always' or 'usually' adhered to. One of the central elements of the guidelines is to promote information-sharing between key agencies involved in child protection and welfare work. However, the review suggested that information-sharing was not happening in the way it was envisaged. The review also highlighted that only 8 per cent of the respondents believed the *Children First* guidelines were working for vulnerable children – children with disabilities, children in foster care, children who are homeless and children in residential care. Other important issues highlighted as problematic were access to the HSE to raise child welfare concerns, and the lack of an out-of-hours crisis intervention service (Office of the Minister for Children and Youth Affairs 2008).

Research carried out by Buckley and colleagues (2008) on the views of service users also reported less than satisfactory interagency cooperation, and difficulties in accessing workers, even during office hours. The OCO (2010: 77–8), in an investigation into the implementation of the *Children First* guidelines by the HSE, found a number of instances 'of unsound administrative practice'. There was a lack of consistent definitions of abuse, lack of clarity and consistency in the basis for reporting child abuse, and a lack of local procedures in local health offices. For a number of years after its introduction the HSE failed to put in place adequate measures to implement *Children First* internally, as well as to drive forward interagency implementation. There was a failure to resolve the lack of implementation, and a failure to put in place quality assurance systems for the operation of *Children First*. The HSE was not transparent in the industrial relations problems that emerged around implementation. Finally, the investigation referred to 'the failure to implement the requirements of *Children First* on HSE/Garda cooperation' (OCO 2010: 78).

Children First: National Guidance for the Protection and Welfare of Children (DCYA 2011) is a shorter document than the original guidelines. Among the key changes are a much briefer contextual introduction, and the chapter on support services to children and families was dropped and replaced with a much shorter section called the 'provision of child welfare services' (DCYA 2011: 32–3). The OCO (2010: 94) called this decision 'surprising given the OMCYA review recommendation that early intervention and family support services be strengthened'. There was no explanation given for the changes to the contextual introduction and the dramatic change in emphasis on support services to children and families. A major change between the two documents was the scope for 'local procedures'. This issue was given a chapter (albeit a short one) in the 1999 guidelines, but was reduced to a few brief bullet points in the 2011 guidance, with little scope for any change to the national guidelines. Explicit references to regional child protection committees and local child protection committees were removed, since as the OCO (2010) as pointed out, they were not seen to be effective. They were not replaced by any other structures.

A very important feature in the context of the 2011 guidelines is the quite dramatic change in the political and policy background of child protection over the years since the publication of *Children First* in 1999. In 2011 a Minister for Children and Youth Affairs was appointed to the Cabinet for the first time, with responsibility for child protection as part of the brief , while a minister of state had held this responsibility in 1999. The relevant statutory and administrative changes introduced since the 1999 guidelines were included in the 2011 guidance, and the language and presentation were also updated, but the essential content remained very much the same as in the earlier guidelines, except that there was a much sharper edge and urgency to them. A hugely significant development in relation to the *Children First* 2011 guidance was the commitment by the Minister for Children and Youth Affairs to place the guidelines on a statutory basis (DCYA 2011, Fitzgerald 2012), which as we shall see below is a controversial step.

Rights of Children

Box 4.3

United Nations Convention on the Rights of the Child (UNCRC)

- Adopted by the UN Assembly in November 1989
- Ireland ratified the Convention without reservation in September 1992.
- General principles of the Convention on the Rights of the Child (United Nations 1989):
  - That all the rights guaranteed by the Convention must be available to all children without discrimination of any kind (article 2)
  - That the best interests of the child must be a primary consideration in all actions concerning children (article 3)
  - That every child has the right to life, survival and development (article 6)
  - That the child's view must be considered and taken into account in all matters affecting him or her (article 12)

Historically the Irish state has not distinguished itself in addressing children's issues (Martin 2000). From the 1970s, however, an awareness of the rights of children was developing as the problems of child abuse were gaining greater public recognition (Richardson 2005). The lack of children's rights derived primarily from the role of the family in Irish law. Irish child protection in the twentieth century was seen in the context of a 'family-centred ideology, focused firmly on parents' (Ferguson 1996: 9). Ferguson (1996) says that this policy direction was greatly influenced by Catholic social teaching (see Box 4.4), and consolidated in the Constitution of Ireland in 1937. Although the Irish family-centred ideology stems from specific historical and cultural influences, this is not solely a feature of Irish social policy, as the family–state relationship is a controversial one in other countries too (Daniel and Ivatts 1998).

Box 4.4

Catholic Social Teaching/Familialisation

Catholic social teaching

This is teaching on social issues from a Catholic Church perspective. One of its fundamental principles is that the state should not involve itself in the affairs of family life.

Familialisation

Ferguson (1996) is quoted above referring to 'family-centred ideology'. Another common term used to describe this is 'familialisation'. Familialisation refers to the fusion of childhood into the institution of the family, defining children only as an extension of their parents. Therefore, children only have rights within the rights of the family and do not possess individual rights (Daniel and Ivatts 1998).

Attempts have been made to improve the rights of children to protection and welfare, but the Constitution restricts the extent to which this can be done. However, since Ireland ratified the UNCRC there have been some notable achievements and an improving policy infrastructure, which has been to the benefit of children. Some key achievements are the establishment of the Department for Children and Youth Affairs, with a minister in the Cabinet since 2011; the setting-up of the Ombudsman for Children's Office; and the development and publication of an ambitious national strategy for children, *The National Children's Strategy: Our Children – Their Lives (NCS)* (DHC 2000), which has been partly implemented. The *NCS* places its aspirations in the context of the UNCRC principles. It has three national goals, based on the concept of the 'whole child': that 'children will have a voice in matters that affect them', 'children's lives will be better understood', and 'children will receive quality supports and services to promote all aspects of their development' (DHC 2000: 11).

Although progress has been made in the promotion of children's rights through the *NCS*, there have been criticisms. Kilkelly concludes that the *NCS* 'has not succeeded in unifying or addressing the fragmentation of policy and service provision or the ad hoc nature of many supports and services. There has also been a failure to take the necessary measures to translate into reality the commitment to hear children's voices' (2007: 94).

The UN Committee on the Rights of the Child acknowledged the progress made by the Irish state in its second report on Ireland in 2006. However, it too highlighted the need for Ireland to improve the right of children to express their views. It also made a number of recommendations regarding the NCS: it should incorporate all aspects of the UNCRC, it should be evaluated to ensure that its achievements are rights-based, and it should establish specific time frames and budgets for the implementation of the strategy (UN Committee on the Rights of the Child 2006: 3). The National Children's Advisory Council (Peyton and Wilson 2006) pointed to the failure to incorporate the strategy into relevant government departments. It was also critical of the lack of a strategic approach to a number of issues, including tackling child poverty, the protection of children from abuse, the provision of adequate health care for children and the provision of support for children with special needs; and finally, it was critical of the lack of political leadership to ensure the strategy was fully implemented.

It has been argued that the rights of children in Ireland would not be addressed properly until an amendment was made to the Irish Constitution. A Joint Committee on the Constitutional Amendment on Children (JCCAC) was established by resolutions of both the Dáil and Seanad in November 2007. It comprised members of both houses, from all political parties. Its *Final Report* (2010) recommended a constitutional amendment to enshrine and enhance the protection of the rights of children:

> This final report considers and makes recommendations in relation to the proposed constitutional amendment concerning the acknowledgement and protection of the rights of children, the best interests of the child, the power of the state to intervene in the family, and adoption. (JCCAC 2010: 1)

The Fine Gael/Labour government elected in 2011 made a commitment to holding a referendum on children's rights, echoing a pledge made by the previous administration as far back as 2006. The current Minister for Children and Youth Affairs confirmed that commitment in July 2012 when she said that a referendum 'which will strengthen children's rights in the Constitution' (Fitzgerald 2012) would be held. 'This is the bedrock of the Government's commitment to raising the needs of children up the political agenda. It is a critical milestone for 2012' (Fitzgerald 2012).

The government's commitment on a referendum was honoured when in November 2012 the 'Children Referendum' took place and was passed. The amendment to the Constitution was concerned with 'the rights of children' (Referendum Commission 2012: 3), and the changes included the recognition of these rights and a commitment to protect and vindicate them as far as possible. They give the state the power to act in the place of married and non-married parents who fail in their duty towards their children. The amendment provides for the adoption of the children of married and unmarried parents, and for the voluntary placement of children for adoption (Referendum Commission 2012). It also places in the Constitution the requirements that 'concerning the adoption, guardianship or custody of, or access to, any child, the best interests of the child shall be the paramount consideration', and that in all of these proceedings 'the views of the child shall be ascertained and given due weight having regard to the age and maturity of the child' (Referendum Commission 2012: 5).

The history books will note that the amendment was passed, but the victory was not as comprehensive as had been anticipated, nor were the final days of the campaign without controversy. Almost uniquely in Irish political contests there had been unanimous support for the amendment from all political parties and children's advocacy organisations. Such was the level of agreement that there was no public discussion on its merits until the last couple of weeks, when a small number of individuals began to argue for a 'no' vote. Only 33.5 per cent of the electorate voted, with 58 per cent in favour – a lower proportion than had been expected (RTE 2012) – and 42 per cent against.

The Rights and Wrongs of Child Protection in Ireland

Since the foundation of the Irish state in 1922, it can legitimately be said that child protection and welfare has not been a major concern of government or of Irish society. Despite the efforts at various times of a small number of individuals and groups to improve the protection and welfare of children, it was not until the 1990s that any significant public policy action was taken. The most important piece of child protection legislation introduced by the state, the Child Care Act 1991, was passed in that year but not fully implemented until 1996. This reflected the impact of the *Kilkenny Incest Investigation* (Richardson 2005). On the face of it Ireland appears to have the essential elements of a functioning child protection and welfare service in place. The Child Care Act 1991 was welcomed as a good piece of legislation, Ireland is a party to the UNCRC, there is a *National Children's Strategy*, there is an Ombudsman for Children's Office, Ireland has had an Office of a Minister for Children and Youth Affairs since 2005, and the state has developed child protection procedures. There is also an independent inspectorate – the Social Services Inspectorate – a part of the HIQA, which monitors children's residential provision and is to begin to enforce standards in child protection services. Why then does a sense of under-achievement and crisis continue within child protection and welfare policies in Ireland? The answer to this question appears to lie in the observation of the Office of the Minister for Children and Youth Affairs that 'a failure of modern child care practice is that national policy and legislation, in many instances, has not been fully implemented or has been unevenly applied' (2009: 62).

A range of individual and interconnecting issues impact on the government's child protection and welfare policies. There is little doubt that the historic role of the Catholic Church in the 'care and protection' of children had an enormous impact by undermining trust in the state's child protection policies. The Commission to Inquire into Child Abuse, more commonly known as the Ryan Commission, found that many children entrusted to the care of the religious orders over several decades had been systematically and brutally abused (Government of Ireland 2009a). Later in 2009 a second damning report on the role of the Catholic Church in the management of child abuse matters was published. This report from the Commission of Investigation into the Catholic Archdiocese of Dublin, also known as the Murphy Commission, examined the handling by church and state authorities of allegations and suspicions of child abuse against clerics of the Catholic Church in the Dublin Archdiocese (Government of Ireland 2009b). It found that a number of senior members of the Catholic hierarchy in Dublin had been aware of abuse by priests for many years. They had colluded in covering up these crimes, at times aided by senior members of An Garda Síochána.

These two reports along with the 2005 *Ferns Report* represented a crisis for the Catholic Church, but also for the child protection and welfare system which had been in place in Ireland for most of the twentieth century. The crisis is not just within the Catholic Church, and is certainly not solely a historical one. The state's approach to and handling of child protection matters, such as in the 'X' case in 1992, the Kilkenny incest case in 1993, and the Kelly Fitzgerald case in 1994, pointed to serious shortcomings in how state agencies collaborate with each other to deal with child abuse cases. A number of other issues of policy and practice were also identified. For example, the *Kilkenny Incest Investigation* (McGuinness 1993), which was the first inquiry of its type in Ireland, pointed to the difficulties professionals have in working on behalf of the state in a system which is based on principles of family autonomy and guaranteed by a constitution which supports parents' rights (the principle of familialisation). It highlighted a number of principles on which child protection policy should be based, and made recommendations to change some of what it regarded as the underlying deficiencies in the constitution and child protection practices (Richardson 2005). The *Kilkenny Incest Investigation* is very important as it set the standard for other investigations which were to follow. It also demonstrated the key failings of the child protection system, which have been repeated again and again in similar reports.

Box 4.5

Key Recommendations of the *Kilkenny Incest Investigation* (1993, cited in Richardson 2005)

The report outlined certain principles that should inform policy and practice:

- The rights of children
- Parental involvement
- Multidisciplinary involvement
- Inter-agency collaboration/cooperation
- The need for proper planning and evaluation of services
- The primacy of prevention
- The provision of treatment services
- The need to provide for a balance between child protection and the rights of parents

It also recommended:

- Changes in the constitution to take account of the rights of children
- Revision of the child abuse guidelines to include parameters for best practice
- A system of mandatory reporting
- The introduction of child abuse registers
- An emphasis on case conferences as a method of interdisciplinary contact and decision-making
- The extension of primary prevention programmes and family support services

Many of the recommendations from the *Kilkenny Incest Investigation* were subsequently adopted, a number of them in the *Children First* guidelines, although as noted above, there have been major difficulties with the implementation of *Children First*. Some other recommendations have been more problematic. For example, the recommendation on changing the Irish Constitution to take account of children's rights was very slow in being realised. Another recommendation on the introduction of mandatory reporting of child abuse (see Box 4.6) has also been problematic, as many child care professionals and academics point to difficulties with this approach to addressing child protection problems (Buckley 2009, 2012b; Shannon 2009). The central argument against mandatory reporting is that it inflates child protection referrals, as those working with children are fearful of not referring because of the possible legal consequences, and as a result already stretched child protection services come under even more strain (Buckley 2009). However, the passing into law of the proposed legislation to place certain aspects of *Children First* on a statutory footing, and the Criminal Justice (Withholding of Information on Offences Against Children and Vulnerable Persons) Act 2012, which 'creates a criminal offence of withholding information in relation to serious specified offences committed against a child or vulnerable person' (OCO 2012: 3), will in effect introduce mandatory reporting into Ireland. The OCO (2012: 3) regards these legal developments as of great significance 'in the legislative framework governing child protection in Ireland'.

Box 4.6

Mandatory Reporting of Child Abuse

This is a requirement in law for those who work with children to report suspicions of child abuse to the appropriate authorities. Failure to report would result in legal sanctions against the mandated individual (Buckley 2009).

The Irish state was slow to develop a properly resourced child protection and family welfare system. While there was an expansion of services from the 1990s, the resources have never been adequate to meet the needs of the child welfare and protection system. The system appears to limp along from crisis to crisis, with children and families often receiving a poor service, inadequate management systems and unsupported staff. However, the problems are not just about inadequate resources, and appear to be much more fundamental than that. A report for the HSE published in October 2009 (PA Consulting 2009) did not inspire confidence in the child protection system. It found that there was a lack of direction in the HSE child protection policies, pointing out that there 'is no shared view about what the "service model" should look like within the HSE' (2009: 4). As Box 4.7 outlines, the report's authors pointed to a number of fundamental problems with the provision of child protection services by the HSE. Nearly twenty years on from the publication of the *Kilkenny Incest Investigation Report* there remain significant problems with the child protection system in Ireland. Reports published more recently in 2010 and 2012 regarding other child protection failures once again show up systemic inadequacies (Buckley 2012a).

Box 4.7

> ### *Inspiring Confidence in Children and Family Services: Putting Children First and Meaning It*
>
> #### *Key findings of the report:*
>
> - There is an urgent requirement to set and communicate direction for the service.
> - There are significant and, in many cases, unnecessary variations across local health offices (LHOs) in how *Children First* is being managed and delivered.
> - More visible leadership is required across all levels of the service as well as tighter management.
> - Structures for delivering the service need to be simplified and clearer.
> - Connections with other services within the HSE and agencies need to be strengthened.
> - Supports to social workers and their managers are underdeveloped.
> - There is inconsistent application of practice in implementing child protection and supports.
> - The service is not managed based on current intelligence.
>
> (*Source:* PA Consulting 2009: 4–5)

Beginning with the *Kilkenny Incest Report*, there is a depressing repetition of failings in the findings of the many reports in recent years on the Irish state's child protection policies and practices. This was acknowledged by the Office of the Minister for Children and Youth Affairs (2009: 62) in its comment that the recommendations of the *Report of the Commission to Inquire into Child Abuse* (Government of Ireland 2009a) are 'also contained in previous reviews, inquiry and inspection reports'. The Roscommon Child Care Case (HSE 2010) and the most recent report, *The Report of the Independent Child Death Review Group* (DCYA 2012a), continue to highlight the many failings of the child protection and welfare system. This is despite all of the previous reports and the various commitments given by government and the relevant state agencies.

The report on the *Roscommon Child Care Case* (HSE 2010) makes evident a number of familiar failures in the child protection system, including poor knowledge of essential aspects of working with children, poor support of workers, poor management, and poor implementation of the *Children First* guidelines. The HSE and other services had years of contact with the family in question and yet six children in that family experienced horrendous abuse and neglect during that time. The *Report of the Independent Child Death Review Group* (DCYA 2012a) reviewed the files of 196 children who were in the care of the state, were in receipt of after-care services, or were known to the state's child protection services, and who died between 2000 and 2010. The Independent Review Group pointed to an inadequate response to children identified to be in need of assistance, poor record-keeping, poor case management, poor allocation of resources, inadequate care planning, and poor supervisory management of workers (DCYA 2012a).

In relation to aftercare the Independent Review Group found evidence of good practice in some cases, but its application was intermittent and not consistent. Of the total deaths reviewed, 128 were of children known to the HSE, but not in care or receiving after-care support at the time of their deaths. In these cases the Independent Review Group once again found good practice across a range of standards, but these were not adhered to at the level required to provide adequate support to these children and their families (DCYA 2012a). Among concerns expressed were the lack of proper risk assessment in families where drug and alcohol use was a feature of family life, and difficulties in working with children and/or parents with mental health problems. There was also concern about the lack of resources within the HSE to provide necessary support for children and their families, including the lack of an out-of-office-hours emergency social work service. Instead of allocating a social worker to families there was an over-reliance on duty social workers in a number of the cases (DCYA 2012a). The Independent Review Group referred to poor communications within the HSE and between the HSE and other agencies, including the Gardaí. There was also evidence of poor professional supervision and support for social workers, and of poor communications between the HSE and children and their families (DCYA 2012a):

> These reports thoroughly document that in spite of efforts of staff from varied agencies, the fragmentation and silos that exist in services are the systemic cause of the failure to meet children's needs. They have repeatedly pointed to a lack of accountability amongst agencies and professionals, and failure to meet the needs of the child, with devastating results (DCYA 2012b: iii).

Conclusion

The protection of children is part of a broader sweep of interconnected policies concerned with the needs and rights of children and their families. It is therefore not possible to examine child protection policies in isolation from the UNCRC, the National Children's Strategy, and the relationships between children, the family and the Irish Constitution. The Child Care Act 1991 recognises the essential place of family in protecting children. It reflects a view that it is better to protect children by ensuring that their families are sufficiently strong, resilient, and emotionally capable of providing for their children, rather than trying to pick up the pieces when things go wrong.

In child welfare and protection policies there is an emphasis on family supports as a priority, but in practice this appears not to be the case. To quote PA Consulting in its report for the HSE, 'there is an emerging sense that the focus needs to shift to providing supports and specialist services for children and their families to prevent the risk of harm' (2009: 4). This is a telling comment about the previous lack of actual support for children and families, although it has been an established policy priority for many years. In 2007 *The Agenda for Children's Services* was published by the Office of the Minister for Children (2007: 2). Its focus 'is on the key messages of existing policies in relation to children'. These promote 'a whole child/whole system approach to meeting the needs of children' and 'a focus on better outcomes for children and families' (Office of the Minister for Children 2007: 2). Yet, by the end of 2009 the HSE had 'still not agreed how it is going to implement' this national policy framework for children and families (PA Consulting 2009: 10).

The new Child and Family Support Agency, which will become operational from 2013 (Fitzgerald 2012), will take over the children and family services functions of the HSE. It aims to resolve the many problems in the system by providing an integrated service for children and families (DCYA 2012b). For the first time in the history of the Irish state the protection and welfare of children will have priority. However, to get to this point it was necessary to heed the views of the Ombudsman for Children:

> While we have had difficulty accepting the reality of child abuse in Ireland we must accept that children deserve the highest level of protection from our laws, policy and practice.
>
> Much needs to be done to improve protection and promote children's rights and welfare. This is not simply a matter of resources. Some of the problems identified – variable practice, a lack of internal scrutiny, a failure to get different agencies working together – indicate a need for a change of culture and attitude. (OCO 2010: i)

The 'need for a change of culture and attitude' must, however, go beyond the formal systems of child protection. The envisaged reorganisation and restructuring of children and family services is certainly to be welcomed. But it is not possible to conceive of addressing child protection and welfare needs through improved child protection systems as if they existed in isolation from the socio-economic concerns of families, such as poverty, lack of employment, poor housing and health, and lack of educational opportunity and achievement. This is not to advocate a continuation of family-oriented policies that ignore the needs and indispensable rights of children, but the problems encountered by children in Irish society cannot be met solely through a focus on the more individualised notion of children's rights and a narrow prescription of child protection.

A commitment to equality for children and equality for all family forms, irrespective of their social make-up and economic value, enhanced with a range of adequate supports, is a far greater challenge for Irish society. The recent amendment to the Constitution, in my opinion, reflects the narrow view of children's rights. The constitutional changes will be of benefit to some children (and the value of that cannot be underestimated), but the absence of a guarantee to socio-economic rights and equality will ensure that many children remain on the margins of Irish society. The state's unrelenting reductions in recent years to a range of welfare supports for poorer children and their families will leave a legacy of increased marginalisation of these children. The constitutional amendment will not have any impact on this policy direction, nor will it protect or improve the welfare of the children adversely affected by these policy decisions. That is to our shame.

Further Reading

There are many different possibilities for further reading depending on student requirements. The materials mentioned below have been grouped into essential documents, historical materials and general readings. All of the readings are in the bibliography at the end of the book, and in this section are only referred to by author, year and title.

Essential Documents

For anyone studying social care wishing to pursue a career with children and/or young people, knowledge of the following documents is essential:

- Constitution of Ireland (1937) as amended to include the new Article 42a passed in November 2012

- Child Care Act 1991: www.irishstatutebook.ie/1991/en/act/pub/0017/index.html
- *Children First: National Guidelines for the Protection and Welfare of Children* (1999): www.dohc.ie/publications/pdf/children_first.pdf?direct=1
- *National Children's Strategy: Our Children – Their Lives* (2000): www.dohc.ie/publications/pdf/childstrat_report.pdf?direct=1
- United Nations Convention on the Rights of the Child (1989): www2.ohchr.org/english/law/crc.htm

Historical Materials

A number of important readings provide information on the history and development of child protection and care in Ireland. In some, for example Fred Powell (1992), the information on child protection and care is only part of a wider account of the development of social policies in Ireland.

Harry Ferguson's *Protecting Children in Time* (2004) gives an excellent historical account of the development of child protection in the United Kingdom, with some references to Ireland, which for part of the period discussed was under British rule. His 'Protecting Irish children in time' (1996) is a shorter piece, and deals directly with the development of child protection policies in Ireland.

Fred Powell's *The Politics of Irish Social Policy 1600–1990* (1992) and in particular Joseph Robins's *Lost Children: History of the Charity Child in Ireland, 1700–1900* (1987), make important contributions to the historical development of children's welfare policies in Ireland.

Mary Raftery and Eoin O'Sullivan offer a more recent historical account of the role of religious orders in residential care provision for children in *Suffer the Little Children* (1999). Some of the material is shocking, only to be surpassed by the more recent *Ryan Report* (Government of Ireland 2009a), which runs into five volumes and to which Eoin O'Sullivan also contributes in Volume 4.

General Reading

Several readings should help with understanding child protection policies in Ireland.

Harry Ferguson and Pat Kenny's *On Behalf of the Child* (1995) gives a very good account of the significance of the Child Care Act 1991. While it is slightly dated, many of the issues discussed in the book are still relevant to child protection today. Paul Barron's chapter 'The Child Care Act 1991: an overview' is an excellent summary of the legislation. Of similar vintage is the edition of *Administration – Protecting Irish Children*, edited by Harry Ferguson and Tony McNamara (1996), which contains a number of very useful articles on child protection and associated issues. See Helen Buckley's work for discussions of different aspects of child protection, particularly mandatory reporting. Valerie Richardson's (2005) chapter 'Children and social policy' is a good general contribution on a range of issues affecting children in social policy. For a critical view on the state's record on promoting the rights of children, Ursula Kilkelly's (2007) report is excellently researched and presented.

Several reports are referred to in this chapter, and all but one is available on the internet. In relation to child protection and welfare matters I highly commend reports by the Special Rapporteur on Child Protection, Geoffrey Shannon, those from the Ombudsman for Children's Office, and HIQA. The report of the *Kilkenny Incest Investigation* is not available online.

After the completion of this chapter the *Irish Journal of Applied Social Studies* published a 'Special Issue on Child Abuse Reports' (2012) edited by Áine de Róiste and Fred Powell. It is available free online at http://arrow.dit.ie/ijass/

Useful Websites

Barnardos – www.barnardos.ie
Children's Rights Alliance – www.childrensrights.ie
Department of Children and Youth Affairs – www.dcya.gov.ie
Health Information and Quality Authority – www.hiqa.ie
Health Service Executive – www.hse.ie
Ombudsman for Children's Office – www.oco.ie

5

It Could Only Be Youth:
Hoodies and 'Folk Devils'

Area of Social Care for which this Chapter Is Relevant

Working with young people or 'youth' is one of the areas which greatly interests social care students. Based at community level it includes working with youth in disadvantaged areas, youth justice related programmes, and community drugs initiatives.

Key Words in this Chapter

Youth, theories of youth, youth justice, Garda Youth Diversion Projects, transitions, unemployment, policy ambivalence

Key Themes in this Chapter

- Understanding 'youth'
- Important legislation
- Policy developments and youth
- Youth justice, young people 'at risk' and the youth services
- Ambivalent policy perspectives on Irish youth

Introduction

Two images characterise the general public's view of children and young people. The first is a positive view that they are our future (Powell et al. 2010), and as such are deserving of protection and support from the adult population. The second scenario is a negative one, epitomised by the infamous call in 2005 by Limerick politician Michael Noonan (who is as I write Minister for Finance) to ban young people from wearing hoodies in shopping centres. This was described by the National Youth Federation at the time as 'negative stereotyping of young people' (*Irish Times* 2005). Although the stereotyping is apparent, this does seem to reflect a common adult perception of young people. In a 2008 Garda public attitudes survey, for example, 'juvenile/teenage crime', at 76 per cent, came third behind drugs and violent crime in the public's perception of major crime problems (Browne 2008: 58). Young people are thus a controversial group, as likely to be cheered as lambasted, and as likely to generate hope as fear.

Youth is a vague term. In Irish public policy it refers to a period that stretches from late childhood to adulthood, from ten to twenty-four years inclusive (Government of Ireland 2001b), and this chapter adopts that definition for both 'youth' and 'young people'. This wide span poses challenges for policy-makers in addressing the specific needs of young people. Children and young people can have very different needs and problems at different stages and at a number of levels during this prolonged period (see Lalor, de Róiste and Devlin 2007). They also differ for example in social and psychological development, maturity, levels of independence, legal status and entitlement to political rights. The term 'youth' is interchanged throughout the chapter with 'young people' (to refer to all those within the ten to twenty-four age group). For clarity or greater accuracy I shall also refer on occasion to 'children and young people' (those under eighteen years) and 'young adults' (those aged between eighteen and twenty-four). 'Adolescent' is used here only when other authors employ it, because it is closely aligned to a psychological/developmental perspective of young people and children, and is thus a more restrictive concept (Devlin 2009).

An enormous range of services are provided for young people in Ireland, through youth clubs, the GAA and other sporting organisations, as well as uniformed youth services such as scouts and guides (see Powell et al. 2010). This chapter does not address policy issues related to these groups, as its focus is on youth that social care students are most likely to work with in practice placements and in their future careers: young people who live in circumstances of poverty and disadvantage, and/

or have dealings with the youth justice services. This chapter begins by exploring what is understood by the term 'youth' through a number of theoretical approaches. The most important Irish legislation and policy developments relevant to youth are outlined before the chapter turns to the issue of youth justice, which has gained increasing significance in youth work in recent years. We then explore the idea of transition from young person to adulthood through the state's approach to youth unemployment and independence. Finally, the chapter assesses the policy approach in Ireland which, it will be argued, shows ambiguity towards the needs, role and contribution of young people, with a tendency to problematise them, a universal trend in Western societies (France 2007).

Understanding 'Youth'

Youth is not a new concept. Ariès's (1962) historical work on childhood suggests that prior to the seventeenth century, in the pre-modern age, children were not recognised as a separate category of people, but rather seen as miniature adults. However, this interpretation has been challenged (Archard 2004). France says that while there was not a vocabulary to distinguish differences in age categories, age groups were recognised in this period, but '[t]hese focused more on the distinctions between dependence (childhood), semi-dependence (youth) and independence (adulthood)' (2007: 6). The experience of semi-dependence was not uniform, as people's experience and situation varied socially and economically, and their gender also had an impact. Griffiths' (1996) work on the history of pre-modern youth in England points to a separateness of youth from the adult world, and also identifies anxieties about the role of youth in that period in English history, which echo similar fears in the twenty-first century.

With the move towards industrialisation and urbanisation, and the weakening of family control and regulation which accompanied these enormous changes, the greater independence of youth caused 'moral panic' as a perceived general immorality took hold. This was epitomised in the perception that youth crime was on the increase (France 2007). Two opposing views emerged on how to address the new challenges posed by children and young people in a changing society. One was to increase the state and newly developing agencies' control of the lives of young people and children, while a contrary view saw the need to offer them protection from what France calls 'the harsh realities of the day' (2007: 11), in which the moral and physical well-being of children and young people was under threat, especially among the poor. Thus began the dualism in thinking on young people and children, who are perceived as a threat to be controlled, and at the same time vulnerable and in need of protection. These perspectives continue to the present, but are now informed by psychological, sociological and, to a lesser extent, educational theories.

Box 5.1

'Moral Panic'

Stanley Cohen writes:

> Societies appear to be subject every now and then, to periods of moral panic. A condition, episode, person or group of persons emerges to become defined as a threat to societal values and interests; its nature is presented in a stylised and stereotypical fashion by the mass media ... [it can have] serious and long-lasting repercussions and might produce such changes as those in legal and social policy ... these groups have occupied a constant position as 'folk devils': visible reminders of what we should not be ... public concern about a particular condition is generated, a 'symbolic crusade' mounted.

(Cohen 1972: 9–11)

With the development of psychological and sociological theories in the nineteenth and twentieth centuries, our understanding of young people and children has improved. For a comprehensive review of the theories of youth, refer to Lalor and colleagues (2007) and Devlin (2009). Here I give a brief summary of the key theoretical approaches as outlined by these authors. Lalor and colleagues (2007) include a broader menu of theories than Devlin (2009), but their categories overlap, and the comment that Devlin (2009: 37) makes about his own categorisation of theories is applicable to the outlines provided by both sets of authors, that they 'are neither exhaustive nor mutually exclusive'.

Lalor and colleagues group the theoretical perspectives on youth as follows (2007: 23):

- The biological perspectives – concentrates on the physical development of adolescents
- Cognitive psychological perspectives – Piagetian theory (for adolescents there is a development in their thinking which becomes more flexible and creative) and Kohlberg's moral development theory (thinking on matters of morality develop during adolescence, which leads the adolescent to distinguish 'right' from 'wrong')
- Socio-emotional psychological perspectives – includes identity and psychodynamic theories and 'have focused in particular on self-awareness, emotional regulation and identity formation' (Lalor et al. 2007: 33)
- Sociological perspectives – generational, conflictual, transitional and constructivist (see Devlin's summaries below)
- Focal and ecological theories – which the authors believe 'provide a more holistic perspective on adolescence' (Lalor et al. 2007: 23). Focal theories, which are psychologically based, believe that young people make the necessary adjustments in their transition from childhood to adulthood, and deal with problematic issues as they emerge one at a time. Brofenbrenner's model is used as the theoretical framework for ecology theory, which 'places the young person's development within a multi-layered social context, seeing development as the culmination of many direct and indirect influences … which either facilitate or impede an individual's development' (Lalor et al. 2007: 53).

Devlin's categorisation (2009: 37–8) places a greater emphasis on sociological theories, and he tends to use the terms 'youth' and 'young people' rather than 'adolescent'. The following are the different theoretical perspectives as he describes them:

- Developmental – rooted in 'mainstream psychology', concerned with 'the processes of change which individual young people go through', such as physical, cognitive, intellectual and socio-emotional changes
- Generational – complements the developmental approach. Young people go through a shared developmental process, but can be identified as a distinctive group, singling them out as 'a separate generation'
- Structural conflict – rejects the idea of youth being one homogeneous group, and argues that this general categorisation of young people fails to reflect the broader inequalities in society based on 'class, gender, culture and ethnicity, sexuality dis/ability' differences
- Transitional – a post-modern perspective that emphasises the complexity of young people's lives as they move from one period of their personal and public lives to another, a period of increasing risk which they are obliged to manage and negotiate for themselves
- Constructionist – argues that youth is a social construction, a necessary categorisation in the industrialised world, but it can lead to contradictory views of youth, so that youth can be seen for example as either a social problem, as vulnerable or as idealistic

If, as Devlin (2009) suggests, theory 'critically examines the values and assumptions that underpin practice', the very significant Youth Work Act 2001 (see next section) implies a theoretical approach which is heavily informed by cognitive and socio-emotional psychological perspectives. The legislation places an emphasis on 'enhancing the personal and social development of young persons' (Government of Ireland 2001b: S.3), and this is done through informal and non-formal educational models (Devlin and Gunning 2009, Treacy 2009). As a result this educational approach, reflecting a developmental model, has a limiting effect on the form of youth work offered in Ireland (Jenkinson 2000).

Box 5.2

Theoretical Perspectives on Youth

Lalor, de Róiste and Devlin (2007):   Devlin (2009):

* Biological perspectives
* Cognitive psychological perspectives
* Socio-emotional psychological perspectives
* Sociological perspectives
* Focal and ecological theories

* Developmental
* Generational
* Structural conflict
* Transitional
* Constructivist

Important Legislation

Two pieces of legislation directly relevant to youth in Ireland were passed within a four-year period between 1997 and 2001. Kiely and Kennedy (2005) acknowledge that for the first time the Youth Work Act 1997 provided a basis for youth work in Ireland. This Act was short-lived, never fully implemented, and was replaced by the Youth Work Act 2001. The Fianna Fáil/ Progressive Democrat coalition government which took up office after the 1997 General Election believed that the recently passed legislation was not workable 'on the grounds that the proposed local education boards were an unnecessary bureaucracy and would only duplicate the work already being undertaken by the VECs [Vocational Educational Committees]' (Kiely and Kennedy 2005: 198).

The Youth Work Act 2001 gives legal effect to a number of important measures for youth work in Ireland. It defines youth work, it places responsibility for a number of statutory powers with the VECs, and it introduces both an Assessor of Youth Work and the National Youth Work Advisory Committee (Government of Ireland 2001b). Devlin (2010) highlights the positive benefit of having a definition of youth work in law (even if, as he says, the definition changes over time), and claims that this legislation places Irish youth work at an advantage over many other European countries and most of the social professions. The definition of youth work in the legislation underlines its historical role as an educational activity (Devlin 2010, Devlin and Gunning 2009), which is provided by the voluntary sector and defined as follows in Section 3 of the Youth Work Act 2001:

In this Act 'youth work' means a planned programme of education designed for the purpose of aiding and enhancing the personal and social developments of young persons through their voluntary participation, and which is –

(a) complementary to their formal, academic or vocational education and training; and
(b) provided primarily by voluntary youth work organisations.

(Government of Ireland 2001b: S.3)

Box 5.3

Youth Work Act 2001 – Key Features

- Definition of youth work
- Definition of the functions of the Minister for Education in relation to youth work
- Definition of the functions of the Vocational Educational Committees – coordination role, provide assistance including financial assistance to youth organisations, to ensure the provision of youth services
- To develop a Youth Work Development Plan
- To establish a number of offices and committees – Assessor of Youth Work, National Youth Work Advisory Committee, Vocational Education Youth Work Committees, Voluntary Youth Councils
- To authorise a representative youth organisation for the youth sector

(*Source:* Government of Ireland 2001b)

Devlin (2010) says that this legislation enshrines a number of key youth work principles: its educational basis, the voluntary nature of participation by young people (which the Act identifies as people between the ages of ten and twenty-five years of age), and the key role of voluntary organisations in the provision of youth services, with a limited role for the state. Devlin and Gunning (2009) make the point that the emphasis on 'personal and social development' is significant because it shows concern for young people both at the personal level and in their place in the wider world. In a later publication Devlin (2010) raises the issue of the definition of youth work in the Act, where he points out that there are those opposed to it as they see it as overly rigid. He holds a contrary view, as he interprets the wording as permitting a certain flexibility for youth work. Lalor and colleagues (2007) welcome the potential opportunity for greater cohesion of youth services which the proposed role of the VECs offers under the legislation.

Yet these authors also raise some questions which have yet to be clarified about the role of the VECs in the provision and financing of services, and their relationship with existing services (Lalor et al. 2007). At the time of writing of this chapter the sections of the legislation which refer to the VECs have yet to be 'commenced' (implemented) (DCYA n.d., Devlin 2012), and according to Devlin (2012) they are unlikely to be. Kiely and Kennedy (2005) draw attention to the bestowal by the Act of exclusive representation rights for young people and the youth sector on one organisation, the National Youth Council of Ireland (NYCI). Other criticisms of the Youth Work Act are more fundamental in nature. McMahon (2009: 121) observes that the Act is more about the youth services than young people, and is critical of the static nature of youth policy-making which includes the Youth Work Act 2001, stating that the Act 'makes virtually no reference to young people, their social context or their changing needs'. In the same volume Kiely (2009) questions the role of youth work as laid down in the Act, which she says is given a marginal and complementary status when placed alongside other agencies that also work with young people.

Policy Developments and Youth

Devlin (2010) traces the development of youth services in Ireland, which historically have been based on voluntarism, elements of religious sectarianism and nationalism, and segregated along gender lines. Voluntarism in youth work has reflected Catholic

109

ideas of subsidiarity, where services should be provided at family and community level, and only when these do not work, and as a last resort, should the state intervene. In the early 1930s the Irish state first made provision for youth policy when as part of the Vocational Education Act 1930 the VECs were given a formal role in 'the collection and communication of information with respect to employment of people under 18 years' (Kiely and Kennedy 2005: 192). But it was not until the 1940s that services for youth were provided by the state, when the *Annual Report of the Department of Education 1941–42* included an outline of a statutory service for young people (Kiely and Kennedy 2005). Devlin (2010) says that the trend of voluntary youth services was bucked in Dublin with the establishment of a statutory youth service scheme by the Dublin VEC through Comhairle le Leas Óige (Council for the Welfare of Youth, now called the City of Dublin Youth Services Board) in the early 1940s. This move was 'at least partly in response' to pressure from the Catholic Church, and the work of Comhairle le Leas Óige was to focus on addressing youth unemployment in Dublin, and to be carried out in youth training centres (Devlin 2010: 8).

The next significant policy development was the publication in 1951 of *The Youth Services After the War* by the Department of Industry and Commerce, which was responsible for youth affairs at that time. This report viewed the problem of youth unemployment in the context of unemployment more generally, and saw the two as being inextricably linked. Among its recommendations were the raising of the school leaving age, 'the introduction of special schemes designed to provide employment for young people and special measures to deal with "unoccupied youth"' (Kiely and Kennedy 2005: 193). The report also referred to other matters affecting young people, such as education, physical development, training and welfare, and juvenile delinquency. The thinking within the document was informed by a Catholic ethos, and the committee responsible for the report was chaired by the then Catholic Archbishop of Dublin (Kiely and Kennedy 2005).

In their outline of developments in youth policy, Kiely and Kennedy (2005) write that the 1960s saw an expansion in the provision of youth services, assisted by increased funding by the state. In 1967 the National Youth Council (NYC, now called the National Youth Council of Ireland, NYCI) was formed to represent the broader interests of Irish youth services. The NYC was to become the primary consultative link between youth services and the state, and as was mentioned in the previous section, this role was confirmed in the Youth Work Act 2001. In the 1970s a number of reports on youth affairs were commissioned by government ministers and the Department of Education. These included *The Development of Youth Services* (1974), *A Policy for Youth and Sport* (1977), *A Policy on Youth Work Services* (1978) by the NYC, and *The Development of Youth Work Services* (1979) (Kiely and Kennedy 2005).

Treacy (2009) describes the general movement in the 1970s and 1980s in the philosophy of youth services from a character-building model to a personal development model (see Box 5.4), and explains that the government reports of this period reflected the trend. He argues that both models 'seek to enable young people to slot smoothly into society and to negotiate and regulate their lives in ways that do not disrupt the status quo' (Treacy 2009: 182). However, it was in the 1980s that an important turn in official thinking on youth work took place, with the publication in 1984 of the *Final Report of the National Youth Policy Committee*, better known after its chairperson as the Costello Report (Jenkinson 2000, Kiely and Kennedy 2005, McMahon 2009, Treacy 2009). This report countered the 'static' conception of youth policy, according to McMahon (2009: 121), as it set out a different view of young people, their needs, and their role in society.

Jenkinson (2000: 108) summarises the philosophy of the Costello Report, which she says emphasises the empowerment of young people, supports their social and political education, and encourages their critical participation in society. In recognising the existence of inequalities in society, the report 'claims that greater equality can be achieved through greater degrees of participation in political, economic and social institutions'. A central element of the Costello Report was its proposal to establish a national youth service based on the needs of young people (Jenkinson 2000). However, as both Jenkinson (2000) and Treacy (2009) point out, this report did not bring about any real change in youth work practice. In the following ten years more reports and papers on youth policy were published both separately and as part of education policy documents, such as the White Paper *Charting Our Education Future* (Government of Ireland 1995). This White Paper provided the basis for the ill-fated Youth Work Act 1997, referred to earlier.

Box 5.4

Features of Character Building and Personal Development Models of Youth Work

Character building model:

- Needs of society are give priority over those of young people
- It is assumed that young people should learn to accept cultural norms and the dominant values of society
- It is also assumed that young people will contribute to maintaining the existing social order, its institutions and structures

Personal development model:

- Focuses on the individual
- Emphasises the personal needs of young people 'with little reference to the social situation or environment in which the young person lives'

(*Source:* Treacy 2009: 181–2)

Within two years of passing the Youth Work Act 2001, the first Irish youth work plan prepared by the National Youth Work Advisory Committee was published in 2003, the *National Youth Work Development Plan 2003–2007* (*NYWDP*). The *NYWDP* has four broad principles which are expanded into a number of actions:

1. To facilitate young people and adults to participate more fully in, and to gain optimum benefit from, youth work programmes and services
2. To enhance the contribution of youth work to social inclusion, social cohesion and active citizenship in a rapidly changing national and global context

3. To put in place an expanded and enhanced infrastructure for development, support and coordination at national and local level
4. To put in place mechanisms for enhancing professionalism and ensuring quality standards in youth work

(Department of Education and Science (DES) 2003: 17)

Devlin (2012: 41) informs us that a review of the *NYWDP* carried out in 2009 by a subcommittee of the National Youth Work Advisory Committee found that 'less than half of the proposed actions had been implemented'. But he sees constructive aspects to the plan apart from the specific actions, and says it 'was of significance in the very positive "vision of youth work" it contained: it strongly asserted youth work's educational ethos and purpose and its commitment to equality and social inclusiveness' (Devlin 2012: 41).

From the late 1990s the youth sector was represented in national social partnership agreements by the NYCI. This role placed the organisation at the heart of public policy-making, a position which was not without its critics and even caused some misgivings and jitters for the NYCI itself, as promised policy developments and reforms were not being implemented (McMahon 2009). The youth sector has entered a policy lull as it awaits a review of youth policy under the new Department of Children and Youth Affairs. State responsibility for youth fluctuated between the Department of Labour and the Department of Education from the 1930s until 2008, when it was relocated to the Office of the Minister for Children within the Department of Health and Children. This was done without any consultation with the youth sector; it caused shock and generated insecurity (McMahon 2009). This Office was in turn renamed the Office of the Minister for Children and Youth Affairs. Subsequently it became a separate government department after the general election in 2011, overseen by a full minister for the first time and called the Department of Children and Youth Affairs.

Youth Justice, Young People 'At Risk' and the Youth Services

Youth justice tends to be written about separately from youth work policy, but it is included in this chapter because of the apparent shifting sands of Irish youth work policy (Kiely 2009), and as an example of a trend towards the problematising of children and young people more generally (France 2007, Goldson 2001). While the vast majority of youth services in Ireland are not aimed at young people with specific problems or who are 'targeted' (Powell et al. 2010), a significant number of youth service providers are engaged, at least in part, with the provision of services linked to youth justice and other 'at risk' groups (Irish Vocational Education Association 2009, Irish Youth Justice Service 2008b, Powell et al. 2010). A full discussion on youth justice is beyond the scope of this section. The focus here is on the relationship of youth services to youth justice, and the possible implications of this connection for youth work. (For a more detailed description and evaluation of youth justice policy in Ireland, see Kilkelly 2006, 2011; Lalor et al. 2007; McCullagh 2006; Walsh 2005.)

Writers on youth justice describe this policy area as one that is less than coherent. For example, Muncie and Hughes write of British youth justice that the 'history of youth justice is a history of conflict, contradictions, ambiguity and compromise. Conflict is inevitable in a system that has traditionally pursued the twin goals of welfare and justice' (2002: 1). Kilkelly writes that 'Ireland has a relatively punitive approach to young offenders … and is thus closer than many states to the "justice" approach' (2006: xvii). McCullagh (2006) says of the Irish youth justice system that there has been an historical consensus on the broken nature of the Irish system. Furthermore, he highlights disagreement and contention between some of the main actors, and claims that deliberations on the youth justice system all ended in the same way, being ignored by successive governments (2006: 162). All of this was to change with the passing of the Children Act 2001, which was hailed as a huge breakthrough for youth justice in Ireland (McCullagh 2006). According to the Irish Youth Justice Service, the 'Act attempts to reconcile the need to hold young people to account for their offending behaviour, the need to protect the public from offending behaviour and builds upon the viable premise that most young people mature into adulthood and cease offending' (2008b: 1). The key connection of youth work services to the Children Act 2001 as amended in 2006 is through the Garda Diversion Programme.

Box 5.5

Garda Diversion Programme

The key features of the programme are that a child or young person must:

- Be between the ages of ten and eighteen years
- Accept responsibility for their criminal behaviour
- Consent to be cautioned and where appropriate agree to be supervised

(*Source:* Government of Ireland 2001a: Part 4 S.23(1)(a))

The Garda Juvenile Diversion Programme began in 1963 as the Juvenile Liaison Officer Scheme, and had as its aim 'to try and divert offending juveniles away from court and criminal activity' (Lalor et al. 2007: 254; see also Kilkelly 2011). This programme was placed on a statutory footing in Part 4 of the Children Act 2001. The young person must be admitted to the Garda Juvenile Diversion Programme, and if suitable is then given an informal or formal caution, depending on the seriousness of the crime. The victim of the young person's crime may also be invited to attend the cautioning (Government of Ireland 2001a). The period of supervision under this scheme is twelve months. In 2010 there were 17,986 individual children and young people referred to the scheme, and 12,899 (72 per cent) of those referred were cautioned formally or informally and admitted into the scheme (Committee to Monitor the Effectiveness of the Diversion Programme (CMEDP) 2010). Almost one-third (32 per cent) of all the referrals were for public order offences, followed by theft and related offences at 22 per cent. In the same year one-third of all admissions to the Garda Diversion Programmes were of seventeen-year-olds, a quarter were of sixteen-year-olds and one-fifth were of fifteen-year-olds, leading to a total of 76 per cent of all young people admitted to the programme belonging to this older age group. There were far more boys than girls referred, 78 per cent to 22 per cent (CMEDP 2010).

Box 5.6

Garda Youth Diversion Projects and the Garda Juvenile Diversion Programme

The reader may be confused when references are made to the Garda Youth Diversion Projects and the Garda Juvenile Diversion Programme. The two are different. Garda Youth Diversion Projects are community-based initiatives established to divert young people from crime, while the Garda Juvenile Diversion Programme (or as it is usually called the Garda Diversion Programme) is the actual programme set out in the Children Act 2001 as amended. One of the strategies used by the Gardaí for children and young people who are admitted to the Garda Juvenile Diversion Programme is to refer them to the local Garda Youth Diversion Project.

(*Source:* Irish Youth Justice Service 2008a – Appendix 2: 43 and 46)

In 2008 a *National Youth Justice Strategy* was published (Irish Youth Justice Service 2008a), in which the Garda Diversion Projects were deemed to be of central importance in reducing youth crime. In 2010 there were one hundred Garda Diversion Projects across Ireland, funded by the Irish Youth Justice Service. The following quote from the CMEDP *Annual Report* sets out the Gardaí's perspective on the nature and objectives of the Garda Youth Diversion Projects:

> The projects are community based, multi-agency youth crime prevention initiatives which primarily seek to divert young people who have been involved in anti-social and/ or criminal behaviour by providing suitable activities to facilitate personal development, promote civic responsibility and improve long-term employability prospects. The projects may also work with young people who are significantly at risk of becoming involved in anti-social and/or criminal behaviour. By doing so, the projects contribute

> to improving the quality of life within communities and enhancing Garda/community relations. (CMEDP 2010: 23)

One of the basic tenets of youth work, voluntary engagement by the young person (Kiely 2009), is challenged by the contractual nature of the relationship between the young person and the Gardaí implied in Diversion Programmes. This is further complicated by changes to some sections of the Children Act 2001 related to the Diversion Programme, which were amended by the Criminal Justice Act 2006. This amending legislation extended the criteria for admission to the Garda Youth Diversion Programme, adding anti-social behaviour to criminal behaviour. Furthermore, the 2006 Act changed the basis for the admissibility of certain evidence related to the child or young person's involvement with the Garda Diversion Programme. Under the original legislation a young person's involvement in the Programme, or their admission of criminal behaviour, could not be used in subsequent proceedings against them (Government of Ireland 2001b). Under the new legislation this position no longer applies. A court can take into account these matters (or admission of anti-social behaviour) if they are put before it when it is deciding on a sentence for a young person for an offence which occurred after admission into the Garda Diversion Programme. Both Campbell (2005), commenting before the anticipated legislative change, and Kilkelly (2011) subsequently, have criticised this move. According to Kilkelly, 'it is a substantial change to the terms on which young people enter the Diversion Programme. In particular, they can no longer be assured, as they would previously have been, that their participation in the Programme will not be taken into account in any subsequent criminal proceedings' (2011: 140).

It is not just the youth sector's involvement with the Gardaí that poses difficulties for the basic philosophy of youth work (Kiely 2009). The youth sector's cooperation with other statutory agencies and government departments, such as the HSE, VECs or the DCYA, also poses challenges for youth work. For example, funding under DCYA programmes such as 'Special Projects to Assist Disadvantage Youth' and 'Young People's Facilities and Services Fund' prioritises programmes that target children and young people deemed to be 'at risk'. This suggests there will be greater demands on youth organisations to meet funders' specified outcomes (Treacy 2009). Kiely (2009) says that to achieve them, youth providers might be pushed in a direction that does not sit well with their fundamental beliefs. This could alter relationships with their young service users.

Kiely also alerts us to another danger in 'interagency arrangements' where 'youth work agencies take referrals and are drawn in to perform "social youth work" without adequate resources, thus compensating for flagrant inadequacies in vital State supports for young people with difficulties' (2009: 22). Somers and Bradford (2006) place this issue in a broader context, the challenge of working in multi-agency partnership networks (which are very common in the Irish youth and community work model), where there is an imbalance of power between more powerful organisations (state agencies) and the less powerful (voluntary and community organisations).

Powell and colleagues (2010) found that the age profile of participants tends to be at the lower end of the youth spectrum, and youth service providers admit to a difficulty in engaging older teenagers. On the other hand the young people referred through the Garda Youth Diversion Programme tend to be at the mid-range of the youth spectrum, with one-third of all participants being seventeen, and two-thirds of participants aged between fifteen and seventeen (CMEDP 2010). This suggests that youth services struggle to provide for the mid-range of young people beyond the delivery of programmes which in effect pathologise them. This leads us to a wider discussion on the state's ambivalence towards young people, and more specifically young adults.

Ambivalent Policy Perspectives on Irish Youth

It is very difficult to locate specific data on young people, and more especially on young adults. Fahmy refers to this in the British context, saying that 'there is a tendency for youth to "fall between the gaps" in policy development where young people's needs are simultaneously considered alongside children . . . and adults of working age' (2006: 348), and the same can be said of youth needs in Ireland. There is no category for 'youth' in primary policy documents, such as the National Economic and Social Council's (2005) *The Developmental Welfare State*, which provides the framework for subsequent policy documents on the life cycle model of welfare. Official Irish social policy documents tend to consider children (those under eighteen years) and adults of working age separately (those aged eighteen and over, up to sixty-four, although in some documents the lower end can be fifteen years) without reference to 'youth' who overlap these age categories.

Census 2011 (CSO 2012b) shows that children and young people between the ages of thirteen and twenty-four make up 15.2 per cent of the population (699,244 persons). There was only a very small increase in the thirteen-to-eighteen age group from Census 2006, while the young adult group, 19- to 24-year-olds, was the only group to show a decline, with a 12 per cent drop (CSO 2012b). However at the lower end, in the pre-school group, the increase in population was greatest of all groups at 17.9 per cent. This reflects a growth in the birth rate since 2006. While there has been a decline in the youth population between the two most recent censuses, the growth figure for younger children suggests that the trend will not continue downwards, at least in the short term. Furthermore, the youth population at 15.2 per cent of the population is not insubstantial, and is greater than the population of older people (CSO 2012b).

Table 5.1: Population Breakdown by Age Group, Census 2012

Age Group (years)	Number	Percentage +/(-)
Pre-school (0–4)	356,329	17.9
Primary school age (5–12)	504,267	12.0
Secondary school age (13–18)	344,931	0.8
Young adults (19–24)	354,313	(12.0)
Adults (25–64)	2,493,019	9.6
Older people (65+)	535,393	14.4
Total	4,588,252	8.2

Source: CSO (2012a).

A significant finding from Census 2011 is that the majority of young adults still live at home with one or both of their parents. In the 2006 Census this was true of 59 per cent of young adults, and the proportion increased to 66 per cent in the 2011 Census. The number living in non-family households such as house or flat shares dropped from 22 to 18 per cent of this age group (CSO 2012b). This high level of dependence of young adults on parents draws us into the debate on 'transitions', a sociological term.

Coles (2003) draws a distinction between three forms of transitions that young people go through on the life course into adulthood. Completing education and entering the workforce is the first of these transitions, followed by 'attaining (relative) independence of families of origin . . . the domestic transition', while 'the third involves moving from the parental home, sometimes initially into "transitional accommodation", but eventually achieving a "home" independent of parents – the housing transition' (2003: 296). As is the case in other Western countries, the period of youth transition has extended (Coles 2003) in Ireland, partly because there has been a dramatic increase in the numbers of young adults continuing into tertiary education – see Table 5.2 (and see also Smyth 2008). If the first period of transition is extended, this has a knock-on effect on the remaining two phases, domestic transition and housing transition. For Lalor and colleagues (2007), the phases of these different transitions are not straightforward, with young adults moving in and out of the various transitions over many years.

Table 5.2: Past Enrolment of Full-Time Students in Third-Level Institutions Aided by the Department of Education and Skills

Academic Year	1970/1971	1980/1981	1990/1991	2000/2001	2010/2011
Number of students	24,680	40,613	68,165	119,991	161,647

Source: Department of Education and Skills (2012). [These figures can only be used as indicative of the dramatic increase in admissions to third-level education by young Irish people because the figures also include mature age and overseas students, which have also increased.]

It is evident from Census 2011 that there is an increase in young adults depending on their families to support them. A large proportion of them live with their families while completing third-level education. Young adults who do not continue into higher education and instead hope to enter the world of work after post-primary education are greatly dependent on their families too. The CSO (2011a) shows a large reduction in young people between the ages of fifteen and twenty-four in the work-force between 2008 and 2010. In 2008, 47 per cent of those in this age group were employed, 5 per cent were unemployed and 48 per cent were not in the labour force. By 2010 these figures had changed dramatically, with only 30 per cent in employment and 61 per cent of young people not in the labour force (CSO 2011a: 3). The Organisation for Economic Co-Operation and Development (OECD) reports that between December 2007 and January 2012, the rate of unemployment for fifteen to twenty-four-year-olds in Ireland jumped from 9.4 per cent to 30.3 per cent (Sedghi 2012). These high levels of unemployment are also borne out by Census 2011, where it is reported that there was a 74 per cent increase in youth unemployment between 2006 and 2011 (CSO 2012c: 14). Young males between fifteen and twenty-four are more likely to be unemployed than their female counterparts: the unemploy-ment rate is 45 per cent for males and 32 per cent for females (CSO 2012c: 14). The OECD also points out that its figures do not reflect the true extent of unemployment among young people, as there are many more who are not in education or training, and are not in the welfare system either (Sedghi 2012).

It is important to remember that, as Smyth (2008) suggests, not all young people experience the same difficulties in the labour market. Those who come from a higher social class and those who have achieved higher academic grades in upper-secondary education are less likely to experience unemployment. Smyth also says that '[w]hat is most noteworthy is the continuing labour market disadvantage among those young people who leave school without any qualifications' (2008: 327). The gap between the qualified and unqualified has been found to increase during periods of economic downturn (Smyth 2008). The implications of these outcomes are clear: the life chances of young adults who do not have family supports and a good education behind them are adversely affected.

There has been a policy shift in income and housing support for single young people in Ireland in recent years: the state now assumes that their parents and families can and should support young adults. The unemployed saw a reduction in jobseekers allowance to between €100 (for 18 to 21-year-olds) and €144 (for 22 to 24-year-olds) from January 2012, and if a young single person can show a housing need which allows them to move out from the family home and into private rented accommodation, they are required to make an increased contribution towards the rent of €30 per week. (Information on rates is available on the Department of Social Protection website.) This adds to the pressure on young adults to remain with their families, and impacts negatively on their transition to adulthood. This policy change helps to redefine the idea of 'youth' by making the transition to adulthood longer, at least for some young people (Fahmy 2006), and limits the opportunities for poor young people to grow into independent adults (Furlong and Cartmel 2007). France (2008) argues that rather than reducing income levels for young people in the transition process, a period that has increased costs associated with it, they should continue to be given financial and other support at least on a par with that received by adults.

O'Connor's qualitative study on youth unemployment in Ireland (2010) brought up a number of issues of concern. He found that the increased difficulty of getting a job means that unemployed youth can suffer from low morale, low self-esteem and hopelessness, leading in some cases to despair and depression. His research suggests 'that there has been no co-ordinated, coherent or focused policy approach developed in response to the pressing needs of young jobseekers in Ireland – particularly those who have yet to gain experience in the labour market' (2010: 8). Since 2010 the government has introduced initiatives to address the unemployment problem, such as the *Action Plan for Jobs 2012* (Government of Ireland 2012a) and its accompanying labour activation document *Pathways to Work* (Government of Ireland 2012b), but these do not specifically address youth unemployment. There is a commitment in the *Action Plan for Jobs 2012* to increase training places and provide more internships, and to 'review the structures and funding of youth work and support services to ensure that they support the development of the skills needed by enterprises', in the context of the new *Children and Young People's Strategy* (Government of Ireland 2012a). This approach by the Irish government suggests it is giving priority to the needs of business rather than those of young people, and it appears inadequate when the OECD Secretary-General Angel Gurría has called on member governments 'to address this economic and social problem [youth unemployment] with decisive and concrete action' (OECD 2012).

Conclusion

There are a number of pieces in the jigsaw of youth policy in Ireland – if we can go so far as to call it a policy, which is doubtful, since this suggests a coherence which I feel is lacking. The policy approach suggests an ambiguity towards young people, who do not fit neatly into policies on children or on 'working' age adults. Putting people aged from ten to twenty-five in one category might be convenient, but it is an artificial grouping, since people aged ten and twenty-five have little in common legally, economically, socially, psychologically or emotionally. Youth work and youth justice are currently the only two specific policy areas for which there are youth-related legislation and national plans, and this too suggests an ambiguity in youth policy. In their research on the youth sector, Powell and colleagues (2010) found that a close connection between the youth work and youth justice benefits youth organisations financially. There is effectively a two-tier system in place, as substantially more funding goes to special projects for youth, the targeted interventions for '"problem" groups of young people' which include the Garda Youth Diversion Project, than to general youth services (Powell et al. 2010: 70).

McMahon (2009: 106) questions the approach of youth services, which she says treat young people as consumers of services 'as opposed to youth work as a social movement for youth rights'. The approach to youth policy, dominated by youth work, is largely one-dimensional, and neglects the broader needs of young people, as well as their role in and contribution to society. That is not to negate the value of youth work itself, and its importance to young people who make use of youth services (Devlin and Gunning 2009). But it suggests that young people, especially those from working-class or poorer families, occupy an ambiguous space in society, in which they are problematised (France 2008), pathologised (Treacy 2009) and stereotyped (Devlin 2006).

In the socially constructed language of youth, with its primary policy emphasis on the younger to mid-range age groups, young adults are not only neglected but also face great uncertainty in the short to medium term in Ireland. The opportunity for transition from youth to adulthood is increasingly inhibited by a combination of poor economic circumstances and government policy choices. The policy intention is to discourage those who do not have the financial means to set up on their own from gaining independence from their family. This entrenches the inequality between young adults who have access to money and other resources and those who do not. For those who can take up the option, emigration could seem a rational and positive choice (O'Connor 2010), but many young adults cannot or will not choose this. As we have noted elsewhere in this volume, young people, and particularly young males, face numerous challenges which do not register on the policy agenda in any coherent fashion.

Further Reading

It is reasonably easy to obtain reading material on youth, which tends to fall within in a broad spectrum of youth work, youth justice, psychology and the sociology of youth. You should also look at youth-related legislation, and development and strategic plans, at least for certain aspects of youth policy.

Essential Documents

The two pieces of legislation, the Youth Work Act 2001 and the Children Act 2001 as amended, are essential documents for gaining knowledge of the state's relationship with youth work and youth justice.

Youth Work Act 2001: www.irishstatutebook.ie/pdf/2001/en.act.2001.0042.pdf

Children Act 2001: www.irishstatutebook.ie/pdf/2001/en.act.2001.0024.pdf

Criminal Justice Act 2006 (the amending legislation for the Children Act 2001 is found in Parts 12–13: Sections 120-166 of this Act): www.irishstatutebook.ie/pdf/2006/en.act.2006.0026.pdf

National Youth Work Development Plan 2003–2007: www.youth.ie/sites/youth.ie/files/nydp_03_07.pdf

National Youth Justice Strategy 2008–2010: www.dcya.gov.ie/documents/publications/IYJS_Strategy.pdf

General Reading

The most prolific Irish author on youth is Maurice Devlin from the National University of Ireland Maynooth. The reference section lists several of his works. I recommend his 2009 chapter on 'Theorising "youth"' to give an understanding of youth theories. His 2010 article 'Youth work in Ireland – some historical reflections' provides a good historical account of the development of youth work in Ireland. The book on Irish youth that provides the most comprehensive range of coverage is also co-authored by Devlin: *Young People in Contemporary Ireland* (2007) by Kevin Lalor, Áine de Róiste and Maurice Devlin. This is a must-read for anyone interested in Irish youth. There is a good overview of policy on youth in the chapter on 'Youth policy' by Elizabeth Kiely and Patricia Kennedy (2005) in *Contemporary Irish Social Policy*. I also recommend three chapters in *Youth and Community Work in Ireland: Critical Perspectives*, edited by Catherine Forde, Elizabeth Kiely and Rosie Meade (2009): Elizabeth Kiely's 'Irish youth work values: a critical appraisal', Sinead Mc Mahon's 'The voluntary youth work sector's engagement with the state: implications for policy and practice', and 'Irish youth work: exploring the potential for social change' by David Treacy. As the book title suggests, these chapters take a critical look at youth work in Ireland.

Specifically on youth justice I recommend Ursula Kilkelly's *Youth Justice in Ireland: Tough Lives, Rough Justice* (2006) and Dermot Walsh's *Juvenile Justice* (2005).

I also recommend two books on youth by British authors, both published in 2007: Alan France's *Understanding Youth in Late Modernity* and the second edition of Andy Furlong and Fred Cartmel's *Young People and Social Change: New Perspectives*.

Journals on youth studies include the international *Youth Studies*. *Youth Studies Ireland* was established in 2006 and publishes two volumes each year.

Useful Websites

Central Statistics Office – www.cso.ie
City of Dublin Youth Services Board – www.cdysb.ie
Department of Children and Youth Affairs – www.dcya.gov.ie
Foróige – www.foroige.ie
Infed: Youth Work – www.infed.org/youthwork (British website with useful articles on the theory and practice of youth work)
National Youth Council of Ireland – www.youth.ie
Youth Studies Ireland – http://www.iywc.ie/youth-studies-ireland-2/

6

Whither Disability Policy?

Area of Social Care for which this Chapter Is Relevant

The area of disability is one of great interest for students, and many social care workers are employed in this sector. This chapter is particularly relevant for students planning a placement or work in a disability service, but all social care workers should be broadly familiar with disability issues.

Key Words in this Chapter

Disability, models of disability, legislation, mainstreaming, rights, inclusive society, individualised model of support

Key Themes in this Chapter

- The meaning of 'disability'
- Important legislation and policy developments for disabled people
- Mainstreaming or rights-based policies?
- Disabled people and an inclusive society

Introduction

There has been an increased public awareness of disability over recent years in Ireland, highlighted at popular level through the Special Olympics movement and the extraordinary success of Irish athletes at the London Paralympics in 2012. Through the efforts of disabled people and their families, supported by advocates from both within and outside the disability sector, disability policy has also developed and changed in Ireland over recent decades. However, according to Quin and Redmond, 'those at the receiving end of services might have seen scant evidence of such changes in practice. Services for people with disabilities and their families have been characterised by the piecemeal approach of policy development in this field' (2003: 2). Disabled people still find it hard to participate fully in a world designed for the able-bodied, and have 'remained marginalised in many respects' despite service developments (Quin and Redmond 2003: 2). This suggests there is a lack of a commitment to true equality and human rights for disabled people.

Over the past fifteen years there has been a substantial increase in funding for services for disabled people in Ireland, and disability and equality legislation has been passed. However, much of the Irish legislation reveals limited expectations. It also has loopholes, and its implementation has been incomplete (Conroy 2010, De Wispelaere and Walsh 2007). Furthermore, the budgetary gains for disability policy and services have begun to be reversed as a result of economic recession. What has not changed is that disabled people of working age are more likely than other people to be without work, with all that implies for dependence, exclusion and poverty (Watson and Nolan 2011). Families remain the most important providers of care for disabled people, and the state has only a limited legal obligation to provide financial and other support for carers. Even more crucially, there is no statutory obligation to maintain disabled people who wish to live on their own, or do not want to (or cannot) depend on the support of their family. Despite all of the apparent progress, disabled people still cannot expect to live independently in Ireland at the standard that is the norm for others. And the simple but hugely important matter of human rights for disabled people has yet to be faced fully (Conroy 2010).

This chapter first explores the meaning of disability through opposing models of disability located in a historical context. This is followed by a summary of important Irish legislation and policy developments, then we turn to the important question of rights and the Irish policy approach of mainstreaming. The chapter next moves to the issue of social exclusion and its consequences for disabled people. Finally, there is a brief discussion on the future approach of Irish disability policy, as it shifts towards a model of individualised care.

The Meaning of Disability

As Charlton says, '[t]he dehumanization of people with disabilities through language ... has a profound influence on consciousness' (2006: 225). In other words how disabled people view themselves derives in no small part from the views of wider society, and this means it is very important to use appropriate language and establish a firm basis for understanding the meaning of disability. As in many other areas of social policy, there is a historical dimension to this, which we need to consider briefly.

Two important changes came about as a result of the rise of industrial capitalism. First, people who were impaired could not keep pace with the mechanised production in factories, and as a result they were increasingly seen as unproductive, and displaced from the world of waged work carried out by individuals (Barnes and Mercer 2003). Second, the system of waged work separated work from home, and 'the boundaries of family obligation towards disabled people were re-drawn' (Oliver 1990: 35). These two changes added to the segregation of disabled people from the workforce and from their families. The 'changing nature of ideas' during the period of industrialisation also altered irrevocably the relationship between disabled people and the world in which they live (Oliver 1990: 42). This tendency to exclude disabled people from work has yet to be reversed (Barnes and Mercer 2003).

The 1834 Poor Law (which applied in England and Wales) and the introduction of the Poor Law Act Ireland in 1838, saw the institutionalisation of disability. Stone points to the significance of the pauper categories of the Poor Law in England (1985, cited in Oliver 1990: 34). Five pauper categories were defined in the Poor Law, and four referred to disability – the sick, the insane, defectives and the 'aged and infirm' (the fifth was children). The implication was that people in these categories should be sent to workhouses and asylums if their families could no longer provide for them (Oliver 1990). The establishment of the workhouses and the incarceration of disabled people as paupers permitted the medicalisation of disability. As a consequence, Quin and Redmond (2005) inform us, the workhouse or insane asylum continued to be the preferred option in Ireland for caring for disabled people into the twentieth century. A movement away from large custodial institutions for disabled people did not begin until the late twentieth century. In Ireland significant numbers of disabled people remain in larger residential facilities, and even as late as 2010, there were 238 people with an intellectual disability in psychiatric hospitals (Kelly and Kelly 2011), down from 277 in 2009 (Kelly, Kelly and Craig 2010).

In exploring the meaning and language of disability we enter a controversial debate about models of disability. Historically the medical profession have dominated the thinking on disability (Oliver 1990). This led to the medicalisation of disability, which has in the past caused untold cruelties and experimentation (Doyle 1990, Toolan 2003). Barnes (2003) outlines three perspectives on disability: the traditional individualistic approach, the 'liberal' or inter-relational approach, and the radical socio-political approach. I shall briefly outline each one.

Box 6.1

Opposing Models of Disability

- Medical model – traditional model of addressing disability, dominated by the medical profession with a focus on disability as a medical problem, which gave disabled people little or no say over their lives.
- Social model – emerged in the 1970s, an overtly political approach, which believes that people with impairments are disabled by society and the way to address disability is to challenge the structures of society that prevent disabled people from full participation.

The Traditional Individualistic Approach

This approach, which is based on an individualistic medical model, has been historically the dominant approach to disability. Barnes (2003: 8) says that it has become associated with

the World Health Organization's (WHO's) International Classification of Impairments, Disabilities and Handicap (ICIDH)
published in 1980. 'Evidently, this typology is based on notions
of intellectual and physical "normality", and that disability and
handicap are caused by psychological or physiological "abnor-
mality" or impairment' (Barnes 2003: 9). A number of criticisms
of this approach are offered by Barnes (2003: 9). First, ideas
of normality and impairment 'are not easily defined, and are
subject to substantive temporal, cultural and situational variation'. His second criticism is that there is an assumption in the
ICIDH 'that the human body is flexible and adaptable whilst the
physical and/or social environments are not', and he argues that
this flies in the face of reality, as humans have always adapted
their environment rather than adapting to it (Barnes 2003: 9). His
third point is that the ICIDH suggests 'that impairment, disability and handicap are static states', which they are not (Barnes
2003: 9). In his final criticism Barnes argues that the classification
is culturally specific to Europeans ideas of normality. Impairments are seen as the primary cause of handicap and disability,
and thus 'disabled people become objects to be cured, treated,
trained and changed and made "normal" according to a particular set of cultural values' (Barnes 2003: 9–10).

The 'Liberal' or Inter-Relational Approach

This so-called middle-ground position on disability is not often
used in discussions on disability, as the debate normally focuses
on the opposed medical and social models. The liberal or inter-
relational model is based on an updated version of ICIDH by the
WHO in 2002, with some changes in language (Barnes 2003), and
renamed the International Classification of Functioning (ICF).
Barnes regards it as an improvement on the earlier version of
the ICIDH. However, it is 'unacceptable to many' (Barnes 2003:
10). This is because of issues of cultural specificity, the fact the
ICF emphasises the individual 'as the starting point for the
analysis of "bodily function and activity"', the tacit assumption
that programmes are to be professionally led and unaccount-
able to disabled people, and finally, that 'disability in the ICF is
presented as a "health" rather than a political issue', leading to

a continued dominance by the medical profession (Barnes 2003: 10–12).

The Radical Socio-Political Approach

This approach to understanding disability is also known as the 'social model' of disability, and has its roots in the 1970s radical opposition of disabled activists to the medical individual model of disability. The Union of the Physically Impaired Against Segregation (UPIAS), a group consisting exclusively of physically and sensorily impaired people, was the pioneer of this approach in Britain (Barnes 2003). In its manifesto the UPIAS declared that it 'is society that disables people with impairments' (cited in Barnes 2003: 12). It 'said that "[a]nalysis of the disabling society is built on a clear distinction between the biological (impairment) and the social (disability)"' (cited in Barnes 2003: 13):

> This approach centres on the various barriers: economic, political and cultural, encountered by people with accredited impairments. Thus 'disability' is not a product of individual failings but is socially created; explanations for its changing character are found in the organisation and structures of society. (Barnes 2003: 13–14)

Shakespeare (2003) has long been a critic of the social model. While he believes a social approach is necessary, and views the medicalisation of disability as 'inappropriate and an obstacle to effective analysis and policy', he claims there are a number of weaknesses with the social model offered by Barnes, Oliver and other disability activists (Shakespeare 2003: 203). First, the social model neglects 'impairment as an important part of disabled people's lives', and treats disability as if the individual impairment is not a problem that impacts on a disabled person's life (Shakespeare 2003: 200). The second weakness according to Shakespeare is that the social model 'defines disability as oppression' (2003: 201); it assumes disability is always oppression even if the disabled person is not oppressed. He claims that the third weakness in the model is the crude distinction between the related concepts of impairment and disability – the medical and social. How do you establish which is the root cause of a problem for the disabled person, the physical/intellectual/sensory/mental impairment or the social environment in which they live? Or to what extent is the problem caused by both? The final weakness is '[t]he concept of the barrier free-utopia' (Shakespeare 2003: 201). He suggests that the social model seeks a utopia in which there are no impediments, social or physical, but such a claim is unrealistic because this utopian world does not exist. Barnes of course rejects these criticisms of the social model, and says that:

> [the social model] is a concerted attempt to *politicize* disability in order to provide a clear and unambiguous focus on the very real and multiple deprivations that are imposed on people whose biological conditions are deemed socially unacceptable in order to bring about radical structural and cultural change. (Barnes 2003: 14, emphasis in original)

Important Legislation and Policy Developments for Disabled People

For much of the life of the Irish state, legislation and policy development for disabled people barely existed. Some policy papers were published in the 1960s and 1980s, but this all changed from the 1990s when policy development began apace (Conroy 2010). It is not possible to detail the significance of every policy development here. Box 6.2 lists the most important policy and legislative developments, while the discussion concentrates on the overall thrust of policy. Aspects of these developments are also covered in the next section on mainstreaming and rights-based policies.

Box 6.2

Most Important Legislative and Policy Developments for Disabled People
• *The Problem of the Mentally Handicapped*, White Paper (1960)
• *Report of the Commission of Inquiry on Mental Handicap* (1965)
• *Services for Disabled People, Towards a Full Life*, Green Paper (1984)
• *The Psychiatric Services: Planning for the Future* (1984)
• *Needs and Abilities: A Policy for the Intellectually Disabled* (1991)
• *Green Paper on Mental Health* (1992)
• *Report of the Commission on the Status of People with Disabilities* (1996)
• Employment Equality Acts 1998 and 2004
• Education Act 1998
• Equal Status Acts 2000 and 2004
• Mental Health Act 2001
• *Report of the Task Force on Autism* (2001)
• *Report of the Task Force on Dyslexia* (2001)
• Education for Persons with Special Educational Needs (EPSEN) Act 2004
• *National Disability Strategy* (2004)
• Disability Act 2005
• *A Vision for Change: Report of the Expert Group on Mental Health Policy* (2006)
• UN Convention on the Rights of Persons with Disabilities 2006 (signed by Ireland in 2007)
• Citizens Information Act 2007
• Health Act 2007 – establishment of the Health Information and Quality Authority
• *Time to Move on from Congregated Settings: A Strategy for Community Inclusion* (2011)
• *National Housing Strategy for People with a Disability 2011–2016*

The move from institutional to community care began to take hold in other Western countries as a result of the questioning of the benefits and cost of large custodial institutions. It also began to influence thinking on policies towards disabled people in Ireland (Quin and Redmond 2005). The earlier documents on 'mental handicap' published in the 1960s referred to the need for better services and the growing cost of institutional care. These documents and a later one, *Services for Disabled People: Towards a Full Life* published in 1984, favoured the provision of care for disabled people by religious orders and voluntary groups rather than state provision, 'a policy decision which still has a considerable impact on Irish service provision to the present day' (Quin and Redmond 2005: 143). However, community care has also found favour with government as it is regarded as 'a less expensive option' (Woods 2006: 177). Doyle (2003: 14) refers to the change of language in the 1984 Green Paper, *Services for Disabled People: Towards a Full Life*, which she says shows that 'a new mindset had emerged'. The 1984 Green Paper concluded that disability was an issue which went beyond the concerns of health and social services, an issue of 'employment, transport and public buildings as well as equality and fuller participation in social and cultural life' (Doyle 2003: 14). This was a significant shift in official thinking, but it still took another decade before that thinking was turned into substantial policy, with the publishing of the *Report of the Commission on the Status of People with Disabilities* in 1996.

The *Report of the Commission on the Status of People with Disabilities* came about as a result of the government's development of an 'equality agenda' (Doyle 2003: 15) and this was to become the catalyst for the changes which followed in disability policy (Considine and Dukelow 2009). Doyle claims the report was 'the most comprehensive examination of the needs of people with disabilities', and 'a fundamental review of the conditions necessary to allow people with a disability to participate, as fully as possible, in economic, social and cultural activities' (2003: 15). The Commission, with 60 per cent of disabled members, was hard-hitting in its comments about the treatment of disabled people in Ireland, and opened with the statement: 'People with disabilities are the neglected citizens of Ireland . . . many of them suffer intolerable conditions because of outdated social and economic policies and unthinking public attitudes' (Commission on the Status of People with Disabilities 1996: Para 1.1).

Subsequent legislation and policy development continued with the thinking set out in the Commission's report, which strongly advocated 'the need to move away from charitable and medical models to a rights-based model' (Toolan 2003: 177). Equality legislation followed, covering both employment and the supply of goods and services. New mental health legislation was introduced, as was legislation for special needs education. A key recommendation of the Commission's Report was to set up a National Disability Authority (NDA). The NDA, established in 2000, was mandated to take the lead role in policy development and coordination, to research disability, and to develop standards for disability programmes (Doyle 2003).

The *National Disability Strategy* (DJELR 2004) was to underpin the actions taken towards the participation of disabled people in society. It contained a number of elements: new legislation (the Disability Act 2005), a personal advocacy service, statutory sectoral plans for six government departments central to the lives of disabled people, and a multi-annual investment programme. These developments along with the newly passed Education for Persons with Special Educational Needs (EPSEN) legislation and the existing equality legislation were supported by a policy of mainstreaming (Department of Justice, Equality and Law Reform (DJELR) 2004), and were to provide the basis of a new era in disability policy. The Disability Act 2005's central provisions were for an independent assessment of need, a service statement (the services judged necessary by the disabled person, dependent on resources available to meet that need), the right to appeal an independent assessment decision through an independent appeals process, an obligation on the public sector to actively employ disabled people, access to buildings and services provided by the state, and six sectoral plans (Government of Ireland 2005c).

The Citizens Information Act 2007 gave statutory responsibility for advocacy services for disabled people to the Citizen's Information Board (Government of Ireland 2007c). A multi-annual investment plan was outlined in the *National Development*

Plan 2007–2013, where 'some €19.2 billion will be invested under the People with Disabilities Programme' (Government of Ireland 2007d: 258). Most of this money was to be spent through the health sector (€18.8 billion), with lesser amounts on education and on a disability-friendly environmental programme.

Box 6.3

Definition of Disability in the Disability Act 2005

'[D]isability', in relation to a person, means a substantial restriction in the capacity of the person to carry on a profession, business or occupation in the State or to participate in social or cultural life in the State by reason of an enduring physical, sensory, mental health or intellectual impairment. (Government of Ireland 2005c: S.2.1)

In the definition of 'disability' in section 2, 'substantial restriction' shall be construed for the purposes of this Part as meaning a restriction which:

(a) is permanent or likely to be permanent, results in a significant difficulty in communication, learning or mobility or in significantly disordered cognitive processes, and
(b) gives rise to the need for services to be provided continually to the person whether or not a child or, if the person is a child, to the need for services to be provided early in life to ameliorate the disability.

(*Source*: Government of Ireland 2005c: S.7.2)

The extent of the legislative and policy commitments by the Irish government to disabled people over the ten-year period from the mid-1990s was by any standard impressive. To quote Colgan, there was 'a sea change in disability policy' during this period (2006: 204). The final two sections of this chapter examine how far these commitments have actually progressed to improve the lives of disabled people and to bring them closer to achieving equality with non-disabled citizens.

Mainstreaming or Rights-Based Policies?

A feature of the policy developments that took place since the 1990s is the emphasis on the mainstreaming of disability policy. In 2006 the NDA published a *Mainstreaming Position Paper*, which defines mainstreaming. There are two elements to its definition. The first is to ensure 'that people with disabilities are enabled to participate fully in society alongside their non-disabled peers'. To achieve this objective a second definition, specifically aimed at public bodies, can also be used for mainstreaming: 'the integration of policy-making, planning and service provision for people with and without disabilities, while ensuring that services are tailored to the individual's needs' (NDA 2006). Mainstreaming is placed on a statutory basis in Section 26 of the Disability Act 2005: 'there will be a statutory requirement on public bodies to integrate, where practical and appropriate, their services for people with disabilities with those for other citizens' (Department of Justice Equality and Law Reform 2005: 8).

Fundamental political and civil rights normally taken for granted in society are much more difficult for disabled people to enjoy, as there are a range of barriers to them (Quin and Redmond 2005). Achieving social rights is even more challenging, as the fundamental existence of these rights is contested. Quin and Redmond explain that social rights 'encompasses what is required to be able to participate in social living in its broadest sense, including having a standard of living or lifestyle compatible with current social expectations as well as the use of social facilities similar to everyone else' (2005: 145). Doyle says that disability groups view social rights 'as a means of ensuring that state resources are available to fully meet each individual's disability-related needs with high quality public services or fully funded private services within a short time-frame' (2003: 22–3). The three guiding principles of the *Report of the Commission on the Status of People with Disabilities* (1996), equality, maximising participation, and enabling independence and choice, form the basis of that report's challenge to move towards a social model of disability which has social rights at its centre.

In an important analysis of the Disability Act 2005, which is the centrepiece of the *National Disability Strategy*, De Wispelaere and Walsh argue that the Act is not rights-based, stating that '[i]n essence, the Act confers a right on disabled Irish citizens to have their needs assessed, but no enforceable right to any of the services that may flow from such an assessment' (2007: 520). This approach by the Irish state counters the disability rights perspective which requires disabled people's rights to be enshrined in law, and in turn gives disabled people the right to claim these rights through legal remedies (De Wispelaere and Walsh 2007). There are two arguments which support the Irish government's reluctance to develop a legally based rights approach to disability, or any other marginalised groups. One is the economic feasibility argument and the second is about the nature of democracy (De Wispelaere and Walsh 2007, Doyle 2003). If government commits in law to funding the needs of disability, it may have implications for general budgetary policy and may limit the ability to provide funding to other groups in society. On the democracy issue, it is argued that legal commitment to a rights approach can limit policy choices by democratically elected parliaments (De Wispelaere and Walsh 2007, Doyle 2003).

De Wispelaere and Walsh (2007) outline a number of deficiencies in the Disability Act 2005, which they argue are not acceptable in a rights-based approach:

- The Act limits the areas of public provision for which the assessment of needs can be carried out to health and educational needs only.
- The definition of disability in Section 2 is a limited one (see Box 6.3). It does not allow for intermittent disability.
- The lack of ring-fencing of funds is apparent through the language used on the service statement and in other parts of the Act (language such as 'availability of resources').
- There is no minimum essentially guaranteed floor below which services will not be allowed to fall.
- The commitment to accessibility to public services, such as physical access to buildings, is also subject to cost considerations.
- The redress aspect of the legislation is too bureaucratic and is not independent of state service providers.
- There is no right to legal challenge.

Overall, the assessment of De Wispelaere and Walsh (2007) is that while the full implementation of the Disability Act 2005 would improve the status quo, the legislation was not the advance that government politicians were claiming it to be. 'The current legislation centres around a conception of disability rights as the right to a needs assessment, which is clearly too weak to adequately recognise the moral and political status of disabled people in Ireland' (De Wispelaere and Walsh 2007: 537).

Disabled People and an Inclusive Society

An important achievement in the provision of information on disability was the establishment of the National Intellectual Disability Database (NIDD) by the Health Research Board (HRB) in 1995. Another milestone was reached in 2002 when the HRB set up the National Physical and Sensory Disability Database (NPSDD). These databases provide baseline information on disabled people in Ireland, a point which was stressed as a major gap by the Commission on the Status of People with Disabilities (1996). The databases provide a profile of disabled people, the type of accommodation in which they live and the level of supports available to them, but neither addresses socio-economic conditions. The HRB reported that in 2009, 26,066 people with an intellectual disability were registered on the NIDD, which is a prevalence rate of 6.15 per 1,000 population (Kelly et al. 2010), and this number increased to 26,484 people in 2010, the highest number of people ever registered (Kelly and Kelly 2011). The majority of people with an intellectual disability, 17,112 or 65 per cent of those registered, lived at home with family members or with foster carers in 2010 (Kelly and Kelly 2011). The population of people with an intellectual disability continues to increase, as the lifespan of people with a moderate, severe or profound intellectual disability aged over 35 years is lengthened. The proportion of people over this age has 'increased from 29% in 1974 to 38% in 1996 and to 49% in 2010', and this has implications for service planning (Kelly and Kelly 2011: 12).

In 2010 the NPSDD reported 25,191 people registered with a physical or sensory disability (O'Donovan 2011). It is likely, however, that there are more people than this with physical and sensory disabilities in Ireland, as the register is voluntary. Only a very small number of people with physical and sensory disabilities, 803 people or just over 3 per cent, lived in residential care in 2010. The vast majority (85 per cent) lived with family members, and the remainder lived alone or in other arrangements (O'Donovan 2011). It is worth noting that the CSO (2008) in its analysis of Census 2006 found that just over 9 per cent of the population (393,800) reported a disability. Watson and Nolan (2011) state that a combination of the National Disability Survey and Census results give the best estimate of the number of people with a disability. Using these sources it is between one in five and one in six of the population. They also highlight that most disabilities are not present at birth but occur during the life course.

Although significant extra funding has been provided for disability services since the beginning of this century, Kelly and colleagues (2010) found that the Multi-Annual Investment Plan in the period 2005–2009 was insufficient to meet the demand for intellectual disability services, a demand which was expected to grow. Services across all aspects of provision, including accommodation, education and training, and therapeutic services, were insufficient to meet demand. Kelly and colleagues (2010: 88) conclude that:

> [d]espite increasing levels of service provision, there are still high levels of unmet need among a critical number of individuals …. Although the data in recent years highlight growth in services, demographic factors and historical under-funding of intellectual disability services are contributing to long waiting lists for these services, which are likely to continue into the future. (Kelly et al. 2010: 88)

Likewise O'Donovan (2011) points to a lack of adequate provision for people with physical and sensory disabilities. In other facets of life, beyond service provision, O'Donovan (2011) found that over half the people with physical and sensory disabilities reported barriers and restrictions to common activities such as sports and physical recreation (69 per cent), employment and job-seeking (66.9 per cent), socialising (59.5 per cent), shopping (59.3 per cent), and leisure/cultural activities (57.2 per cent).

All of these figures were an increase from the previous year (O'Donovan, Doyle and Craig 2010).

The Irish state recognises that poverty and social exclusion impact on disabled people, as they are one of the target groups named in successive national anti-poverty strategies. In *Towards 2016*, the national partnership agreement, the state and social partners' vision for disabled people is set out as follows:

> The parties to this agreement share a vision of an Ireland where people with disabilities have, to the greatest extent possible, the opportunity to live a full life with their families and as part of their local communities, free from discrimination. (Government of Ireland 2006b: 66)

This vision is to be achieved through a number of long-term goals such as an adequate income to sustain an acceptable standard of living; access to various social services and employment; access to public spaces, transport and information; support to lead full independent lives, to participate in society and live fulfilling lives; and, support for carers (Government of Ireland 2006b). The vision and long-term goals of *Towards 2016* and the *National Action Plan for Social Inclusion 2007–2016* (Government of Ireland 2007e) are to be met primarily through the *National Disability Strategy* set out in 2004. Prior to the publication of both *Towards 2016* and the *National Action Plan for Social Inclusion 2007–2016*, Gannon and Nolan, in their analysis of the dynamics of disability and social inclusion, found:

> that on almost all the measures studied, people with chronic illness or disability fared worse than others in their own age group ... [they] tend to have lower levels of educational attainment than others, and only a minority are in work. People with chronic illness or disability are more than twice as likely to be at risk of poverty, and more than twice as likely to be poor, using official measures of poverty. People with a chronic illness or disability are also less likely to be in a club or an association, to talk to their neighbours, friends or relatives most days, or to have a social afternoon or evening out. (Gannon and Nolan 2006: 11)

Since the re-statement of the Irish government's commitments to disability in *Towards 2016* and in the 2007 social inclusion strategy, what has changed in the policy outcomes for disabled people? We know from the most recent reports from the NIDD and NPSDD that despite improvements, there continues to be a deficit in support services for disabled people (see Kelly et al. 2010, O'Donovan 2011, O'Donovan et al. 2010). Government commitment to its own policy of mainstreaming is facing a severe challenge as a result of the budgetary constraints imposed because of economic recession (Carroll 2010, Inclusion Ireland 2010). In the face of these financial constraints we can only wonder how more recent policy proposals will progress. These policies include the HSE's Report of the Working Group on Congregated Settings, *Time to Move on from Congregated Settings: A Strategy for Community Inclusion*, (HSE 2011) and the *National Housing Strategy for People with a Disability 2011–2016* (Department of Environment, Community and Local Government (DECLG) 2011a). In keeping with the Irish government's stated commitment to mainstreaming, these interrelated documents are very important as they deal with a very basic right to housing and independent living. Ireland signed (but has yet to ratify) the UN Convention on the Rights of Persons with Disabilities in 2007, which in Article 19 clearly sets out the rights of disabled people to live independently and within the community:

> States Parties to this Convention recognize the equal right of all persons with disabilities to live in the community, with choices equal to others, and shall take effective and appropriate measures to facilitate full enjoyment by persons with disabilities of this right and their full inclusion and participation in the community. (United Nations 2006)

If the proposals outlined in *Time to Move on from Congregated Settings* and the *National Housing Strategy for People with a Disability 2011–2016* were to be fully realised, they could potentially further the rights of disabled people quite significantly, particularly those with an intellectual disability. The aim of the HSE's (2011) strategy on congregated housing is to close down traditional residential units (units that accommodate ten or more people) within seven years, and to replace these with ordinary housing and apartment accommodation dispersed throughout the community. The strategy states that in these large units, residents live isolated lives separate from communities and families. The intention is to move approximately 4,000 people into the community to live in small accommodation units of not more than four people for those who wish to home-share (HSE 2011). This proposal has been questioned by the Centre for Disability Law and Policy at National University of Ireland Galway, as it points to the possibility of institutional features being replicated in these smaller units: 'Institutions are defined not merely by their size but also by practices which regulate individual's routines in accordance with the needs of the group '(NUIG 2011: 3–4). It is expected that the HSE would continue to have responsibility for the personal and social needs of the residents and the Department of Environment, Community and Local Government would have responsibility for accommodation.

The disability housing strategy reflects the congregated housing strategy in much of its thinking. Both strategies place enormous emphasis on the importance of collaboration between the different actors involved if the housing needs of disabled people are to be met properly. How this process is to be financed is not fully addressed in the strategies. The congregated housing strategy expects that a transfer of existing funding to the new accommodation arrangements should suffice without incurring further costs (HSE 2011). The disability housing strategy does not go into any detail about funding, but expects that a funding agreement would be put in place to provide the necessary community supports, and that the cost would be borne by the HSE. The way the strategy refers to accommodation provision suggests that the existing routes into accessing housing would be used, but it does not tease out the financial implications of this approach (DECLG 2011a).

It is difficult to assess how these strategies will play out at this stage, but the *Value for Money and Policy Review of Disability Services in Ireland* published by the Department of Health in mid-2012, and informed by the Expert Reference Group on Disability Policy's (2011) *Report of Disability Policy Review*, proposes a fundamental change to how disability services are funded and provided in the future. This report is critical of how services are currently provided and funded, questioning value for money and quality of services for disabled people. It states that 'the current model of service delivery is not providing a sufficient quality and quantity of services at an affordable price' (Department of Health 2012: 22). Traditionally disability services have been carried out by a service provider, usually a voluntary, not-for-profit agency, funded by the state after application by the agency. A group-based, provider-led model of service provision dominated. The users of the service, the disabled people, had little say or choice in the type of services available to them, and were also restricted in their choice of provider (see Department of Health 2012). The approach recommended in this review is an individualised model of support provision, towards *funding people rather than places* (Department of Health 2012: 171, emphasis in original). The proposed new model is person-centred, and supports are individually chosen rather than provided on a group basis. The Disability Federation of Ireland (2012) has welcomed the review's commitment to the person-centred approach, but is critical of its narrow focus, and questions whether that the exercise might be more about reducing costs than liberating people with disabilities.

A substantial factor in the poverty and social exclusion of disabled people is the individual or private cost of disability (Cullinan, Gannon and Lyons 2008). In their paper on the estimated cost of disability, Cullinan and colleagues conclude that 'policies that aim to address the economic problems associated with disability ... do not go far enough in addressing the extra costs faced by the disabled community in Ireland' (2008: 18). In the current economic context it is unlikely that there will be the improvements implied in Cullinan and colleagues' comments. The reason for this is clear, as the *Value for Money and Policy Review of Disability Services in Ireland* states: '[i]n the short to medium term, the changed economic climate dictates that there will be little additional investment for disability services' (Department of Health 2012: 3). The advancement of the Disability Act 2005 has also faltered. Section 2 of the Act gives a right to individual assessment of need, but this important right has been deferred indefinitely for adults (Inclusion Ireland 2010). According to

Inclusion Ireland (2010), individual assessment for children has only been rolled out in part, for those under five years. Children above the age of five have also had their entitlement to an assessment of need deferred indefinitely. The full commencement of the ESPEN Act 2004 is still awaited, having been 'put on hold in 2008' (Inclusion Ireland 2010: 19). The Personal Advocacy Service set out in the Citizens Information Act 2007 has been 'placed on hold in 2008 due to lack of resources', although the less expensive Advocacy Programme for People with Disabilities in the Community and Voluntary Sector was established (Round Table Solutions/Pathfinder 2010: 41).

Social inclusion does not happen by chance for disabled people. Social inclusion demands a certain type of vision, as well as policy and operational commitment, and significant financial investment, if it is be achieved. Furthermore, it takes time and persistence at many levels. The changed landscape of Irish disability policy in recent years has shown that a new vision of social inclusion for disabled people was beginning to take shape. However, a transformed economic reality has stalled the progress of the policy path begun in the 1990s.

Conclusion

There is little doubt that much has changed in Irish disability policy and practice over the past decade and a half. Yet many challenges have still to be overcome. As far back as 1996, the Commission on the Status of People with Disabilities made the point that in their consultations with disabled people that '[a]nother theme to emerge ... was that of marginalisation.... Many people with disabilities felt that they were either being kept at, or pushed to, the margins of society' (1996: 1.4). The deficits in support services (see Kelly et al. 2010, O'Donovan 2011, O'Donovan et al. 2010) and the lack of funding to implement mainstreaming (Carroll 2010, Inclusion Ireland 2010) pose serious challenges for the vision of disability policy espoused in various recent policy commitments and legislation. The marginalisation and social exclusion of disabled people must be undone for disabled people to truly enjoy the same level of life opportunities as are expected by their able-bodied family members, neighbours and community.

Toolan's observation of a decade ago on the policy commitments to mainstreaming is still relevant today:

> [a]bsent from these statements, however, were the practicalities of incorporating existing separate provisions into the mainstream. The question remained as to whether specific supports, such as personal assistance, sign interpretation, accessible information, advocacy supports, needs assessments, would be incorporated into the mainstream framework. (Toolan 2003: 179)

Commitments to mainstreaming may no longer be absent from policy statements or legislation, but they remain as rhetoric until they are implemented. Ratification of the UN Convention on the Rights of Persons with Disabilities would put pressure on Ireland to improve its disability policies, with its obligation for regular progress reports and a public examination of these at not only national but international level. However, it is unlikely that even such pressure would change the disability policy landscape in Ireland from its current path of non-implementation of any policy commitments that will divert the state from its budgetary targets.

The existing producer-led (where service providers control services for disabled people) approach to Irish disability policy does not bring about individual freedom for disabled people. 'Disabled people have argued ... that choice is fundamental to achieving citizenship, social inclusion and human rights' (Glendinning 2008: 459). Clarke, Newman and Westmarland comment that '"[c]hoice" draws on a political imaginary of how life might be, often involving fantasies of exercising power and control' (2008: 246). This suggests choice is not the simple option it might first appear. It is still not clear what model of individualised service will emerge in Ireland.

The experience in Britain has shown that despite the positive welcome for this approach by disabled people, their families and disability activists, questions remain about the extent of the improvement in care services that follow (Wilberforce et al. 2011). Limitations with the individualised model which have arisen include:

- Lack of information to make informed choices (Glendinning 2008)
- Lack of resources (financial, knowledge of the system, personal skills, acquaintance with professional decision-makers) for people to access the services needed (Glendinning 2008)
- Added costs to providers (because of the extra administrative burden) which are passed on to service users (Glendinning 2008, Wilberforce et al. 2011)
- Restrictions on how resources are used (Pearson 2000)
- Differential services where less money available to an individual means poorer quality service (Glendinning 2008)
- Not all localities having an appropriate, diverse range and choice of services (Glendinning 2008)
- Choice is presented as a one-off action, which it is not; it is ongoing and complex amid changing needs of the individual over the life course (Glendinning 2008)
- As an individual purchaser of a service there is a lack of leverage to get better value for money (Glendinning 2008)
- As is the case in all market provision, inequalities emerge between 'consumers' (Glendinning 2008, Wilson, Riddle and Barron 2000)
- It may increase the burden on individuals and families/ carers as they take on the role of managing the care of the disabled person which was the responsibility of service providers (Glendinning 2008)
- There are difficulties in monitoring quality of individualised services (Wilson et al. 2000)
- Expectations of disabled people that cannot be met (Wilberforce et al. 2011)
- How to resolve potential difficulties in the power relationship between service users and professionals who provide the day-to-day services (Clarke et al. 2008, Glendinning 2008)

- Market discourse may become the main determinant of disability policy (Pearson 2000)

It is therefore open to challenge whether disabled people will be better served by introducing an individual model based on the values of the marketplace. The language used in the *Value for Money and Policy Review of Disability Services in Ireland* (Department of Health 2012) is that of the marketplace, and there is no doubt that whatever the aspirations for policy developments in disability and the wishes of disabled people, their families and advocates, market criteria, including so-called 'value for money', will dominate all disability policy decisions from now on.

Further Reading

There is no shortage of further reading on disability, both Irish and international. Disability is one of the areas in Irish social policy that has generated much academic work.

Essential Documents

There are a number of pieces of important legislation related to disability. The most significant is the Disability Act 2005, which provides the statutory basis for much government policy on disability. It is available at www.irishstatutebook.ie/pdf/2005/en.act.2005.0014.pdf

Other exclusively disability-related legislation includes the Mental Health Act 2001: www.irishstatutebook.ie/pdf/2001/en.act.2001.0025.pdf

the Education for Persons with Special Educational Needs Act 2004: www.irishstatutebook.ie/pdf/2004/en.act.2004.0030.pdf

and the Citizens Information Act 2007, which requires the Citizens Information Board to make provision for 'a personal advocacy service to certain persons with disabilities': www.irishstatutebook.ie/pdf/2007/en.act.2007.0002.pdf

Equality legislation is also of great importance and consists of two primary pieces of legislation, the Employment Equality Act 1998: www.irishstatutebook.ie/pdf/1998/en.act.1998.0021.pdf

and the Equal Status Act 2000: www.irishstatutebook.ie/pdf/2000/en.act.2000.0008.pdf

As can be seen in Box 6.2 (page 134), there have been many policy documents and reports on disability over the past 30 years. Of course all of them played their part in the development of disability policy, but the following are the most relevant to current policy developments.

Report of the Commission on the Status of People with Disabilities (1996): www.nda.ie/cntmgmtnew.nsf/0/9007E317368ADA638 025718D00372224/$File/strategy_for_equality_03.htm

UN Convention on the Rights of Persons with Disabilities (2006): www.un.org/disabilities/documents/convention/convention_accessible_pdf.pdf

Time to Move on from Congregated Settings: A Strategy for Community Inclusion (2011): www.hse.ie/eng/services/Publications/services/Disability/timetomoveonfromcongregatedsettings.pdf

National Housing Strategy for People with a Disability 2011–2016 (2011): www.environ.ie/en/DevelopmentHousing/Housing/PublicationsDocuments/FileDownLoad,28016,en.pdf

Report of Disability Policy Review (2011): www.dohc.ie/publications/pdf/ERG_Disability_Policy_Review_Final.pdf?direct=1

Value for Money and Policy Review of Disability Services in Ireland (2012): www.dohc.ie/publications/pdf/VFM_Disability_Services_Programme_2012.pdf?direct=1

General Reading

I can highly recommend two books published in the past decade on Irish disability policy. Suzanne Quin and Bairbre Redmond's edited collection *Disability and Social Policy in Ireland* (2003) has an excellent range of chapters on a variety of issues of importance in disability policy. However, as it was published a decade ago it is becoming dated. Patrick McDonnell's *Disability and Society: Ideological and Historical Dimensions* (2007) is an excellent book which explores disability and the evolving ideologies of Western societies and culture, and also includes Irish disability developments. A very good overview on disability is provided by Suzanne Quin and Bairbre Redmond in their chapter on

'Disability and social policy' in Quin et al.'s *Contemporary Irish Social Policy* (2005). Mairéad Considine and Fiona Dukelow (2009) also have a chapter on disability in their book *Irish Social Policy: A Critical Introduction*. I also highly recommend *The God Squad* by Paddy Doyle (1990), which is an autobiographical account of the disabled author's life in residential care. For up-to-date information on intellectual disability I recommend the National Intellectual Disability Database (NIDD) published by the Health Research Board (HRB). Particularly useful is the annual report of the NIDD. Likewise the HRB publishes the National Physical and Sensory database. It provides the most up-to-date annual information on people with physical and sensory disabilities.

An excellent general reader on disability matters is Lennard J. Davis's (2006) *The Disability Studies Reader*, which includes a wide range of writings on different aspects of disability. I also suggest that students interested in the politics of disability read any publications by Colin Barnes and Mike Oliver, whose works promote the perspectives and arguments of disability activists supportive of the social model. Tom Shakespeare, also a disability activist, wrote the book *Disability Rights and Wrongs* (2006) in which he rejects the social model.

Useful Websites

Citizens Information Board – www.citizensinformationboard.ie
Disability Federation of Ireland – www.disability-federation.ie
Inclusion Ireland – www.inclusionireland.ie
Health Research Board – www.hrb.ie
National Disability Authority – www.nda.ie
National Federation of Voluntary Bodies – http://www.fedvol.ie/

7

Travellers: The Most Excluded of All?

Area of Social Care for which this Chapter Is Relevant

Throughout Ireland there are Traveller projects which provide placement and employment opportunities for social care students and workers. Anyone working in a general social care service is likely to have contact with Travellers, and it is thus important for social care students to be familiar with the social circumstances of Travellers and the complexity of the policy issues surrounding them.

Key Words in this Chapter

Traveller, marginalisation, accommodation, health, education, ethnicity, racism, nomadism, anti-Traveller, exclusion

Key Themes in this Chapter

- A people apart
- The burden of disadvantage and marginalisation
- Important legislation
- Policy shift from the 1960s
- Ethnicity, 'racism' and exclusion

Introduction

I believe the best way to start a potentially vitriolic discussion in any social gathering in Ireland is to mention the word 'Traveller'. Travellers arouse fear, contempt, suspicion, derision, prejudice and racist reactions from the settled population in Ireland.

Historically these negative reactions by wider society have been reflected in the media, by politicians, and in the social policies of the state directed at Travellers (O'Connell 2002). At the same time the evidence shows that Travellers are at the bottom of all indicators of good health and well-being, educational achievement, political access and employment opportunity. Many also experience inadequate accommodation and extreme poverty (O'Connell 2002). The widely held negative views of Travellers and their poor socio-economic circumstances are not unrelated phenomena. The social, economic and cultural exclusion of Travellers is entrenched in the notion of 'othering', which according to Ni Shuinéar means the denial of 'equal legitimacy to individuals and cultures that do not conform to one's own arbitrary, ever-shifting criteria of normality' (2002: 177), and which she says has long historical roots in Ireland. The idea that Travellers are so different from the rest of the population is reflected in cultural, social and economic structures and relationships, which set Travellers apart.

In this chapter it is not possible to tease out in any depth the answers to the complex question of the relationship between Travellers and the wider community, although it is referred to. However, the chapter addresses a number of other matters, which may lead to a better understanding of the circumstances of Travellers in Ireland and the way in which the Irish state responds to them and their needs. This includes reviewing the existing literature to explain the position of Travellers in Irish society from historical and contemporary perspectives; examining census and other data to determine the population structure of Irish Travellers; showing the level of disadvantage experienced by Travellers in the key social policy fields of accommodation, health and education; determining government policy towards Travellers by highlighting relevant legislation and policy developments; and finally, placing the debate about the Traveller experience in the context of racism and anti-Travellerism (McVeigh 2008).

Box 7.1

Who Are Travellers?

Crowley says that 'Travellers are a minority ethnic group with a nomadic tradition. They identify themselves as a distinct community and are seen by others as such. They share common cultural characteristics, traditions and values which are evident in their organisation of family, social and economic life ... they have a distinct oral tradition and largely marry within their own community' (2005: 232).

The Equal Status Act (Government of Ireland 2000a: S.2.1) defines Travellers similarly: '"Traveller community" means the community of people who are commonly called Travellers and who are identified (both by themselves and others) as a people with a shared history, culture and traditions including, historically, a nomadic way of life on the island of Ireland.'

A People Apart

Nomadism and Traveller communities have a long historical presence in European society. Irish Travellers (unlike Gypsies and Romanies, who are not originally natives of the countries which they came to inhabit) are indigenous members of the native Irish population (Mac Laughlin 1995). At different points from the fifth century onwards (which Mac Laughlin says coincides with the first historical mention of Travellers as travelling artisans), nomadism peaked and troughed. Its popularity was subject to the ebb and flow of commerce, changing religious beliefs and the rise of science. Mac Laughlin links the 'demonization of nomadic people' in Europe to the emergence of capitalism, the collapse and disintegration of feudalism, and European modernisation (1995: 15). In times of social and economic upheaval the victimisation and scapegoating of nomadic people was particularly marked. In the case of Travellers, Mac Laughlin (1995) says that this victimisation took place in the late nineteenth century in Ireland, which was later than in the rest of Europe. The essential difference between what occurred in Europe and Ireland was that in the former the nomadic Gypsies were regarded as 'Outsiders', while 'in

Ireland discrimination was practised by the settled Irish on the indigenous travelling Irish' (Mac Laughlin 1995: 15). Ni Shuinéar (2002: 177) attributes this to the internalising of centuries of colonialism, which manifests itself in 'self-loathing and scapegoating'. She argues that what the settled Irish did was to play out and transfer their own form of 'othering' experienced by the population under English colonialism to the Traveller population.

Of course Travellers, like many other occupational groups, were also subject to colonial vagrancy legislation, which stigmatised anyone who came within its reach. Helleiner (2000: 31) places this in the context of the 'civilising of the Irish', which was equated, she says with 'a suppression of mobility'. Helleiner (2000: 33) also claims that even as late as the nineteenth century the British authorities did not make the distinction between Travellers and other wanderers, although the local Irish population did. As the nineteenth century progressed and Ireland moved towards national independence, the lifestyles of the wandering occupational groups in Ireland altered and became more sedentary, leaving Travellers to become a distinct social and cultural group with its own identity (Helleiner 2000, Mac Laughlin 1995). Mac Laughlin writes that the emerging effort of nation-building equated nationalism 'with progress and growth'. He continues, '[N]omadism on the other hand, and Travelling communities within Ireland, were looked on as social anomalies, relics from a "barbarous" past that was best forgotten because they represented all that was backward, unstable and evil about Irish society' (1995: 28). The essence of these sentiments of negativity towards Travellers did not change in the newly independent Ireland. The new state was unable and unwilling to accommodate Travellers ('tinkers') and what they supposedly represented, 'poverty, violence and hardship', within its institutions (Mac Laughlin 1995: 35). These citizens were a people apart and would remain so, with only one course of action open to them. In order to be accepted by Irish society they were expected to assimilate into the dominant sedentary culture and social norms, whatever the cost to them.

The Burden of Disadvantage and Marginalisation

It is not unusual for Travellers to be identified in the academic literature as one of the most marginalised groups in Irish society, or in similar language: 'Travellers are widely acknowledged as one of the most marginalised and disadvantaged groups in Irish society' (O'Connell 2002; 49); 'as one of the most marginalised groups in Irish society' (Silke 2005a: 268); '[t]here is little doubt that Travellers represent one of the most marginalised groups in Irish society' (Drudy and Punch 2005: 133); 'they are a particularly disadvantaged group in Irish society' (Watson et al. 2011: 54). In 1986 the ESRI observed that Travellers are 'a uniquely disadvantaged group: impoverished, under-educated, often despised and ostracised, they live on the margins of Irish society' (cited in O'Connell 2002: 49). This section details the levels of disadvantage and marginalisation experienced by Travellers, but first it gives a short demographic profile.

The CSO volume on *Religion, Ethnicity and Irish Travellers* (2012f), based on details from Census 2011, gives the most up-to-date information on the Traveller population. We know from Census 2011 that there has been a substantial recorded increase in the Traveller population since the last census in 2006. In 2006 the Census recorded 22,453 Travellers, which was 0.5 per cent of the population of the Irish state (CSO 2007). In 2011 the figure had risen to 29,573, which appears to be a dramatic increase of 7,120 people or 31 per cent. Nolan and Maître address this issue when they say that Census 2006 'may underestimate the number of Travellers in the country' (2008: 56). They point out that an annual count of Traveller families carried out by local authorities (see below) suggests a far greater number of Travellers than was recorded in Census 2006. The All Ireland Traveller Health Study Team estimates in its study that there are 36,224 Travellers in the Republic of Ireland (2010: 43). The national population now stands at 4,525,281, and the Traveller population remains a very low proportion at 0.6 per cent (CSO 2012d). Even if the Traveller population is still underestimated, it is very unlikely, on the basis of the available information, that it is higher than 1 per cent of the overall population. Travellers live predominantly in urban areas (81.7 per cent). They also make up a greater proportion of the population in Counties Galway, Longford and Offaly, in all of which over 1 per cent of the population are Travellers (CSO 2012f).

A significant feature in the make-up of the Traveller population in Census 2011 is its age profile, which is younger than for the settled population. Travellers are aged 22.4 years on average, in comparison with 36.1 years for the general population (CSO 2012f: 27). Over half (52.4 per cent) of Travellers are under twenty, with 29.1 per cent under nine years; this compares with 14.8 per cent of the general population. For those over 65 the difference is even starker: only 2.5 per cent of the Travellers are in this age group compared with 11.7 per cent of the general population (CSO 2011f). As a result of the population structure of Travellers, the number of middle-aged and older people is significantly smaller than the younger age groups. The Traveller population does not reflect the expectations of population structures in industrialised countries, and is referred to in one report as being 'more reminiscent of a pyramid of a developing country, characterised by high fertility and premature mortality' (All Ireland Traveller Health Study Team 2010: 11).

Table 7.1: General and Traveller Population Details, Censuses 2006 and 2011

Detail	2006	2011	% increase
Population of Ireland	4,239,848	4,525,281	+8.0
Traveller population	22,453	29,573	+31.0
Traveller % of total population	0.5	0.6	+0.1

Source: CSO (2007, 2012d).

Next we shall look at the three areas that receive most policy and research attention: accommodation, education and health. Of course employment, income adequacy and poverty (for example) are also crucially important to the well-being of Travellers, but they receive less attention in the policy literature – despite the fact that Travellers have been identified as a target group for social inclusion in all national anti-poverty strategies since 1997 and in social partnership agreements since 1991 (Silke 2005). For employment, Watson and colleagues, in their analysis of Census 2006, state that Travellers are 'markedly disadvantaged when compared with other white Irish people' (2011: 55), with very high levels of unemployment. This situation deteriorated between 2006 and 2011, with unemployment up from 74.9 per cent to 84.3 per cent (CSO 2012f: 33). It is noted that Traveller women are more likely (32.7 per cent) to look after the home and family instead of paid work than women in the general population (17.5 per cent) (CSO 2012f: 33). Nolan and Maître acknowledge that 'employment is crucial to a household's income' (2008: 64). They also make an important observation: '[t]he type of work traditionally common in the Traveller community, with an emphasis on self employment, trading and casual work, may mean that the Census and other statistical sources underestimate the percentage who are at work' (2008: 64).

Accommodation

Housing for Travellers has long been regarded as a social problem that has to be addressed (Coates, Kane and Cotter 2009). Travellers' housing needs were not given recognition by the Irish state until the 1960s (Drudy and Punch 2005), but have become a central plank of Traveller policy since then. In the first major report on Travellers, the *Report of the Commission on Itinerancy* (1963), housing was seen as key to solving the 'problem of itinerancy' (cited in Silke 2005: 272). Yet recommendations made in that report regarding the provision of halting sites by local authorities were not successful. The sites were never close enough to key services such as schools, and did not provide for 'maintaining family connections or traditional economic activities' (Drudy and Punch 2005: 134). Because of this lack of progress the Irish government set up a Review Body in 1981 to examine policies and services for Travellers.

In 1983 the *Report of the Travelling People Review Body* acknowledged that progress had been made over the previous twenty years; this included a substantial increase in housing from 56 families to 1,210 families (Silke 2005). The authors of the report were of the opinion that although serviced halting sites should be part of the housing strategy for Travellers, they should be kept to a minimum, reserved for 'those Travellers who are unable or unwilling to live in standard housing' (Coates et al. 2009: 93). The report also recommended that accommodation for Travellers should allow extended families to live together. Coates and colleagues (2009) suggest there were three broad trends between the publication of this second report and a third which followed in 1995, the *Report of the Task Force on the Travelling Community*: a further increase in the number of families living on halting sites, a large increase in the number of Traveller families living in group housing schemes, and that 'the numbers of families living on the roadside did not change significantly between the start and end of this period' (Coates et al. 2009: 94). In the period between the two reports the Traveller population had doubled (Silke 2005).

The *Report of the Task Force on the Travelling Community* (1995) highlighted the unevenness of the response by local authorities to Traveller accommodation, which still remained a major issue for Travellers. Among the report's recommendations was that 'standard housing and Traveller-specific accommodation be provided' and that a national Traveller Accommodation Agency be set up to oversee the implementation of a national programme for Traveller accommodation by the local authorities (Coates et al. 2009: 95). Silke says that the Task Force Report 'provides the framework for much of the current policy development in this [accommodation] area' (2005: 275). The subsequent policy approach was in keeping with the general thrust of the Task Force recommendations, but followed a different implementation path (Silke 2005). This included time-lined accommodation programmes, the establishment of a Traveller Accommodation Unit within the Department of Environment and Local Government, and a National Traveller Accommodation Consultative Group, set up by the Department, but granted advisory powers only.

The practical impact of these policies on accommodation can be observed in Table 7.2, which is a summary of the annual counts of Traveller families by local authorities. The most recent figures available are for 2011, which includes the counts from the previous two years. For comparative purposes annual counts from selected years are taken from Silke (2005). The figures tell us that since 1996 there has been an upward trend in Travellers availing themselves of standard housing. It is also notable that there has been a slow trend downwards in the use of official halting sites but a dramatic decrease in the use of unofficial halting sites (in other words living on the side of the road) since 2000. The explanation lies in the implementation of legislation on trespass from 2002, which is discussed in the next section. Yet there continued to be 327 families living on the roadside in 2011, despite efforts by the state and its agencies to curb this practice. Furthermore, many of those Travellers who live on local authority halting sites in caravans or mobile homes have poor living circumstances (Nolan and Maître 2008).

Table 7.2: Annual Counts of Traveller Families by Accommodation Type – Selected Years and 2009–2011

Accommodation type	1996	2000	2003	2009	2010	2011
*Social housing	2,135	2,653	3,554	4,618	4,643	4,675
Local authority halting sites	1,143	1,152	1,398	999	991	920
Unauthorised halting sites	1,040	1,093	788	422	444	327
Own resources (estimate)	—	—	443	511	561	563
Private rented (estimate)	—	—	293	2,003	2,380	2,558
Sharing housing	—	—	323	390	451	492
Total	4,138	4,898	5,740	8,943	9,470	9,535

Sources: years 1996, 2000 and 2003 from Department of Environment, Heritage and Local Government, cited in Silke (2005: 280); years 2009–2011 from Department of Environment, Community and Local Government (2012).
NOTE: * This term 'social housing' includes families in all local authority funded housing: standard local authority housing, local authority group housing, private houses assisted by local authorities, and housing provided by voluntary bodies with local authority assistance. Also note Silke's (2005: 280) point that 'when comparing figures from the different Annual Counts, it is important to keep in mind that the count format has been revised a number of times … it is only possible to focus on general trends'.

Education

Travellers suffer from severe educational disadvantage (Nolan and Maître 2008, Watson et al. 2011). In Census 2011 their level of educational attainment was shown to be very low. In the Traveller population 55 per cent had completed their education before the age of fifteen in comparison with 11 per cent of the general population (CSO 2012a: 32). Of Travellers aged fifteen years and over, 69 per cent had achieved only a primary education, while 21.8 per cent had completed Junior Cert level (up from 15.2 per cent in 2002) and 8.2 per cent had attained their Leaving Cert. This figure had more than doubled since 2002, when it was recorded that 3.6 per cent of Travellers completed their Leaving Cert (CSO 2012a: 32). One per cent of Travellers had achieved either a third-level degree or a comparable non-degree qualification; this compared with 30.7 per cent of the general population (CSO 2012a: 32).

The state has a long history of neglecting the educational needs of Travellers, and official concern was formally expressed for the first time in the *Report of the Commission on Itinerancy* in 1963, in which education policy 'focused on the reform of perceived Traveller deviancy and alleviation of destitution, and it promoted a segregated model of provision' (Kenny and Lodge 2004: 93). *The Report of the Travelling People Review Body* (1985) was of the view that education for Travellers should be 'compensatory' (Kenny and Lodge 2004: 93). Education is hugely significant for socio-economic well-being, achievement and participation in Irish society, and such was the concern about the poor quality of education access, participation, lack of cultural recognition, and outcomes for Traveller children that 167 recommendations for improvement were made in the *Report of the Task Force on the Travelling Community* (Task Force 1995).

In the same year, *Charting Our Educational Future: White Paper on Education* (Government of Ireland 1995) set out specific targets and timescales for Traveller children's participation in education. These included that all children of primary school age would be enrolled and fully participating in primary school education within five years, and 'that within ten years, all Traveller children of second level, school going age will complete junior cycle education and 50 per cent will complete the senior cycle' (Government of Ireland 1995: 57). However, as can be observed from the 2011 Census there are still high levels of early school leaving and poor achievement by Travellers in education (see also Crowley 2005, Irish Traveller Movement (ITM) 2011). There is a recognised problem of transition from primary to post-primary education, where Traveller children are at risk and more likely to drop out than settled children (Smyth, McCoy and Darmody 2004). One of the features of educational policy and practice in the past has been its segregationist approach, where Traveller children had either special schools or special classes in mainstream schooling. The separation of Traveller children from mainstream schooling has been almost completely eradicated, yet 'the issues of segregation and discrimination are very real' (Considine and Dukelow 2009: 436). They remain in the pre-school sector where there are still Traveller-only pre-schools in operation, although official policy is to phase these out (DES 2003b, 2006).

The Task Force report in 1995 recommended a Traveller education strategy, but this has yet to materialise. In 2006 *A Report and Recommendations for a Traveller Education Strategy* was published by the Department of Education and Science, but this strategy has not been implemented. The report provides a blueprint for the future development of Traveller education across all levels, pre-school to higher education, and contains a chapter on the inclusion of Traveller parents in the educational process (DES 2006). The report stresses that education provision for Travellers should be based on 'an inclusive, holistic approach' and delivered in an 'intercultural manner' (DES 2006: 90). There have been some policy developments around intercultural education over the past decade, with the publication of guidelines on intercultural education in primary and post-primary schools by the National Council for Curriculum and Assessment (NCCA 2005), and more recently the launch of an *Intercultural Education Strategy, 2010–2015* (Department of Education and Skills and Office of Minister for Integration 2010). The *Intercultural Education Strategy* is aimed primarily at the immigrant population, and while Travellers are referred to, it is only in passing. This seems to be at odds with the thrust of the policy approach in recent years of addressing education in an inclusive manner.

Supports for Traveller children and young people attending educational facilities have been seriously affected by cutbacks to services as a result of government financial retrenchment in recent years. Among the provisions of Budget 2011 was the withdrawal of Resource Teachers for Travellers, the withdrawal of the Visiting Teachers for Travellers Service, withdrawal of additional teaching hours for Travellers in post-primary schools, and the phasing out of Senior Traveller Training Centres (Hourigan and Campbell 2010, ITM 2011). Such changes could be seen to be beneficial if they were carried out in a planned way, with a spirit of improving education for Travellers at their heart. But this is not happening; these services are not being replaced with improved resources to ensure equal participation and improved outcomes in education for Traveller children and young people. It has been argued by the ITM that these cutbacks have been 'disproportionate' to other cutbacks in 'mainstream' education, and will 'undermine young Travellers' future life opportunities' (ITM 2011: 7). All of this is occurring when it has been observed that '[r]elative to the general population they are falling constantly further behind' (All Ireland Traveller Health Study Team 2010: 162).

Health

It has been noted that accommodation and education are key determinants in the level of health and well-being of Travellers (All Ireland Traveller Health Study Team 2010). Given the limitations in both accommodation and education policy, and especially in their implementation, it comes as no surprise that the levels of Traveller health and well-being are well below the standards enjoyed by the general population in Ireland. The starting point for an examination of health policy for Travellers is the *Report of the Task Force on the Travelling Community* (1995), which noted that there was a crisis in their health care provision. Among its many recommendations the Task Force suggested the establishment of a Traveller Health Advisory Committee, a national health strategy to improve the health of Travellers, better information-gathering on the health needs of Travellers, better communication between health service providers and Travellers, Traveller-specific services to complement the general health services, and the provision of appropriate training for health service personnel (Task Force on the Travelling Community 1995). Subsequently a Traveller Health Advisory Committee was established in 1998, which included representatives of Traveller organisations, and at regional level Traveller health units were set up (Considine and Dukelow 2009).

A potentially significant step in addressing the health care needs of Travellers was reached with the publication of *Traveller*

Health: A National Strategy 2002–2005 (Department of Health and Children 2002), in which the extent of Traveller health disadvantage was outlined. Many of the 122 recommendations of this strategy reflected those of the Task Force. Much of the emphasis was on attempts to improve Traveller access to health care and the use of health services, including the development of Traveller-specific interventions with Traveller participation, improved training of health staff to ensure awareness of Traveller health needs and cultural issues, and improved data collection.

This report was followed in 2007 by a HSE publication, the *National Intercultural Health Strategy 2007–2012*. This *Strategy* names a number of different groups including Travellers as its target for a more responsive health system, which would meet the diverse cultural needs of ethnic minority groups and immigrants in Irish society. The aims of the *Strategy* are to improve the design, access and delivery of services to these groups in a way which respects their cultural needs and differences (HSE 2007). The *Strategy* is formulated around three key themes. The first is access to services – being able to access services is seen as a 'prerequisite to attaining positive health outcomes'. The second theme is data, information and research, as there is 'little information' available on minority groups. The third theme concerns human resource aspects – this includes addressing the nature of the organisational culture; training, recruitment, support and retention of staff from diverse cultures; and training of staff from the majority culture (HSE 2007).

A major contribution to data collection on Travellers' health was carried out between 2007 and 2010 by the All Ireland Traveller Health Study Team, which published its findings in 2010 and was a direct outcome of the publication of the *National Traveller Health Strategy*. This cross-border study, the first large-scale study on Travellers in 22 years, includes a census of Traveller families, with an 80 per cent response rate, as well as quantitative and qualitative information on health and well-being. This report is accompanied by three technical reports and is hugely ambitious, covering a vast amount of information relevant to health and well-being. It makes for grim reading. Some of the key findings are outlined in Box 7.2.

Box 7.2

Some Key Findings from the *All Ireland Traveller Health Study* (2010)

- 'Travellers experience considerably higher mortality at all ages in both males and females. The problem stretches across the entire age spectrum' (p. 86).
- The infant mortality rate (the number of deaths under the age of one year of babies who were born alive per 1,000 births) of Travellers has only marginally improved between 1987 and 2008, declining from 18.1 to 14.1, while in the general population it declined by almost half from 7.4 to 3.9. The relative difference in the infant mortality rate between Travellers and the general population has 'deteriorated since 1987' (p. 87).
- The Traveller mortality rate is 3.5 times greater than the general population – described by the Study Team as a 'stark picture' (pp. 89/90).
- 'Traveller mortality has fallen over the past 20 years but at a slower rate than in the general population. The mortality gap between Travellers and the general population has widened' (p. 91).
- The highest cause of death for male Travellers, at 27 per cent, is external causes (accidents, poisonings, suicide and so on). This is 5.5 times higher than in the general population (p. 91).
- 'The suicide rate in male Travellers is a statistically significant 6.6 times higher than in the general population' (p. 94).
- There continues to be a considerable difference in life expectancy between Travellers and the general population. The life expectancy is 61.7 years for male Travellers and 70.1 years for males in the general population. For women the gap is less but there is still five years' difference, at 76.8 years for Traveller females and 81.6 years for the general population. The study notes that the life expectancy of Traveller men today is the same as that of the general population in the years 1945–1947, and for Traveller women it is the same as in 1960 (pp. 94–95).
- The study states that 'the gap between Traveller mortality and that in the general population has widened in the past 20 years' (p. 95).

Important Legislation

There is only one Traveller-specific piece of legislation, the Housing (Traveller Accommodation) Act 1998, although a number of laws refer to and impact on Travellers and their lives. Crowley (2005: 237) points out that the first piece of legislation 'to specifically name Travellers' was the Housing Act 1988. Section 13, under the heading 'Provision of sites for Travellers', refers to those who pursue a nomadic way of life, and says that local authorities 'may provide, improve, manage and control' halting sites (Government of Ireland 1988: S.13). The Housing (Traveller Accommodation) Act 1998 requires local authorities to respond to Traveller accommodation needs by assessing the need for halting sites in their areas, adopt a five-year accommodation plan for Travellers, and take reasonable steps to implement the plan. It provides for the local city or county manager to adopt a Traveller accommodation plan where the elected local councillors fail to do so. It also provides for the establishment of a National Traveller Accommodation Consultative Committee, and obliges local authorities to appoint local consultative committees (Government of Ireland 1998).

Box 7.3

Legislation of Importance to Travellers

- Prohibition of Incitement to Hatred Act 1989
- Unfair Dismissals (Amendment) Act 1993
- Housing (Traveller Accommodation) Act 1998
- Employment Equality Act 1998
- Equal Status Act 2000
- Housing (Miscellaneous Provisions) Act 2002

The introduction of anti-discrimination legislation is of great importance for Travellers and other minority groups and sections of the general population who are deemed to be at risk of unfair treatment. The Prohibition of Incitement to Hatred Act 1989 is described by Crowley as 'ineffective, owing to the difficulty of proving that actual hatred was incited' (2005: 243). The

Unfair Dismissals (Amendment) Act 1993 amended the Unfair Dismissals Act 1977 to include 'the employee's membership of the travelling community' as grounds for unfair dismissal from employment (Government of Ireland 1993: S.5). More substantive anti-discrimination legislation was introduced with the Employment Equality Act 1998 and the Equal Status Act 2000. Both name membership of the Traveller community as one of the nine grounds for recognising discrimination. The former prohibits discrimination in the workplace while the latter prohibits discrimination in the provision of goods and services, accommodation and education. The Equal Status Act also defined the 'Travelling community', as quoted in Box 7.1.

While these legislative developments were regarded as positive, the same cannot be said of the Housing (Miscellaneous Provisions) Act 2002. Section 24 made trespass illegal, and criminalised Traveller families who lived on unauthorised sites. The possible sanctions include confiscation of caravans and other personal belongings, imprisonment and/or fines (Government of Ireland 2002b).

Policy Shift from the 1960s

Irish state policy towards Travellers has progressed from the early 1960s. This shift is evident from the language and policy approach of the three key policy documents on Travellers: the *Report of the Commission on Itinerancy* (1963), the *Report of the Travelling People Review Body* (1983) and the *Report of the Task Force on the Travelling Community* (1995). These reports demonstrated a policy shift on Travellers which moved from the intention of eradicating them and their culture, through a process of assimilation, which is evident in the earliest reports (O'Connell 2002). By the time the Review Body reported in 1983, language such as 'absorption, settlement, assimilation and rehabilitation' was no longer thought acceptable and was discarded (O'Connell 2002: 50). The Review Body also brought an end to the use of the term 'itinerant' and replaced it with 'Traveller', which 'was a recognition of a distinct identity' (O'Connell 2002: 50). Yet, despite this progress in thinking by the Review Body, Crowley observes that the dominant view in the report was 'one of a community in need of reintegration whose difference was a product of disadvantage and poverty' (2005: 235), and it continued to neglect a central consideration of Traveller culture, nomadism.

The report of the Review Body did bring about a change in policy direction, albeit at a slow pace, and led to the beginnings of recognition for Travellers as a group within Irish society with distinct needs (for example on housing: see Norris and Winston 2005: 814). But it was not until after the publication in 1995 of what McVeigh (2008: 91) calls the 'groundbreaking' *Report of the Task Force on the Travelling Community* that more significant change began to take place in the policy approach. This report recognised Travellers as a community with a distinct culture and identity (Crowley 2005) and of 'equal value to that of the majority population' (Norris and Winston 2005: 803). Gradually a policy shift came about, as has been discussed above, with changes in legislation and policy on accommodation, education, health and equality. But the recognition of Travellers as a distinct ethnic group has yet to be achieved. For Travellers this is at the crux of state policy towards them (Crowley 2005).

Ethnicity, 'Racism' and Exclusion

There has been an incrementally positive shift in Irish state policy towards Travellers over nearly 50 years, and relevant policy documents now as a matter of course refer to Travellers as having a distinct identity and culture (McVeigh 2007). However, to date the state has resolutely refused to give recognition to Travellers as a minority ethnic group, although in 2011 there was the beginning of what appeared to be a softening of that stance, a point to which we shall return. Ethnicity is a contested concept (Considine and Dukelow 2009, McVeigh 2007), but at its core is the idea of claiming an identity and being conscious of that identity (Platt 2008: 380 cited in Considine and Dukelow 2009: 427). There is much at stake for Travellers in being recognised as a minority ethnic group. It would potentially alter their relationship with both the state and the rest of society. The lack of formal ethnicity recognition casts Travellers as a deviant group, or 'failed settled people in need of rehabilitation and assimilation', denied their history, language and cultural contribution, and defined as a 'sub-culture of poverty' (Crowley 2005: 232).

In an extensive analysis of Traveller ethnicity and the Irish state's approach to this centrally important issue for Travellers, McVeigh (2007) argues that the state's position on the matter is contradictory. On the one hand he argues that the state has consistently denied Traveller ethnicity (which he terms 'ethnicity denial'), demonstrated most clearly in its reports to the International Convention for the Elimination of All Forms of Racial Discrimination (CERD), where the government's view over the years has been that Travellers '*do not constitute a distinct group from the population as a whole in terms of race, colour, descent or national or ethnic origin*' (McVeigh 2007: 98, emphasis in original). On the other hand a number of political leaders, certain government departments, agencies and policy statements, all 'say that Travellers *are* an ethnic group' (McVeigh 2007: 100, emphasis in original). The official stance by the state in denying Traveller ethnicity has serious repercussions for Travellers. According to Considine and Dukelow, 'the denial of ethnic identity generates anti-Traveller racism which has material effects such as poverty and health inequality' (2009: 427). Kenny and McNeela demonstrate in their research that 'the racism of the dominant society' (2006: 59 and 61) also makes a more fundamental impact which results in negative and harmful internalised self and community images, where Travellers 'self-limit' their potential and their life expectations (see also All Ireland Traveller Health Study Team 2010: 118ff).

Almost twenty years ago Mac Laughlin wrote of Travellers being reduced 'to the position of social outcasts in contemporary Ireland' (1995: 80). Collins claimed that the situation of Travellers could best be described as 'one of exclusion and oppression' (1997). These observations still hold true; Travellers remain social outcasts. The original assimilationist policy aim of settling Travellers is well on its way to being achieved, as the vast majority of Travellers are now living in houses – see Table 7.2. This however, has not led to acceptance of Travellers by the settled population, and Travellers continue to be regarded as a problem (Kenny and McNeela 2006). Kenny and McNeela, suggesting that Travellers are 'damned if they do and damned if they don't', conclude from their research that 'it is not Travellers' nomadism, but their group identity, that triggers anti-Traveller racism. Whether they settle or travel, Travellers are not wanted. Racism prevents Travellers from continuing with their nomadic traditions and it prevents them from dropping them' (2006: 60). At a policy level Travellers have been failed, and continue to be excluded by the institutions of the state and by the general population. Policy efforts over the past 50 years have done very little to change that fact (Fanning 2002).

Conclusion

Contact with Travellers is not wanted by the majority population (Mac Gréil 2010), they are undermined by media coverage that promotes anti-Traveller racism (Kenny and McNeela 2006, O'Connell 2002), and they are failed by the state (McVeigh 2008). The incremental policy approach which has been in evidence over many decades has not succeeded (Crowley 2005). In fact, it is suggested by some that the policy turn in the Housing (Miscellaneous Provisions) Act 2002, where trespass was criminalised, highlighted a regressive policy attitude, or backlash, towards Travellers (Crowley 2005, Norris and Winston 2005, McVeigh 2008). For many years efforts made by Traveller representative groups, such as the ITM, the National Travellers Women's Forum and Pavee Point, supported by a relatively small number of activists and academics, helped to set the agenda on Traveller rights and recognition. Progress has been painstakingly slow, and rights and recognition for Travellers, whatever the policy language, have never been fully accepted by the state. Furthermore, the wider public have shifted their thinking on Travellers very little over the years. Mac Gréil's (2010) study, replicating his earlier studies on attitudes towards Travellers in the 1970s and 1980s, refers to a growing polarisation of attitudes in the general public towards Travellers. Studies referred to in this chapter highlight that oppositional, discriminatory and racist attitudes towards Travellers from the general public are a major stumbling point in progressing the basic conditions of Travellers (All Ireland Traveller Health Study Team 2010, Fanning 2002, Kenny and McNeela 2006).

It is of course very easy to lump all experiences of Travellers together into extreme disadvantage, and all responses from the general population into anti-Traveller attitudes, but this is too simplistic. Like all social phenomena and social relationships, the reality is much more complex. The All Ireland Traveller Health Study Team (2010) suggests that there are health and well-being differences between members of the Traveller population, and variations in personal and socio-economic circumstances. So, for instance, within the Traveller population there are very wealthy Travellers at one end of the spectrum and very poor Travellers at the other end. Similarly Mac Gréil's (2010) study found that not all members of the settled population are anti-Traveller. Yet these important differentiations do not get away from the funda-mental facts that on any basic understanding of well-being in the areas of employment, education, accommodation, health and poverty, Travellers as a section of Irish society do far worse than the majority population, and that there is considerable hostility towards Travellers by the settled population.

Absorption and assimilation of Travellers has been tried and failed. The alternative, which has yet to be attempted, is the recognition of Travellers as a minority ethnic group with equal rights. Taking such a course of action would not be without major challenges, but the present policy path has brought about only limited advancement for Travellers. There may be a chink of light, as the current government has indicated that it is '"seri-ously considering" conferring recognition of Travellers as an ethnic minority group' (Pavee Point 2011: 1). The Minister for Justice and Equality announced this during Ireland's hearing at the United Nations's Universal Periodic Review of Human Rights in October 2011. This has yet to become a reality.

Further Reading

There is a range of material for further reading on Travellers, addressing issues such as Traveller history, their socio-economic circumstances, and debates on ethnicity and racism. Among these are some older texts which are essential reading for gaining an understanding of the relationships between the state, Irish society and Travellers. These are as relevant now as when they were first published. There are a relatively small number of committed writers with expertise in this area.

Essential Documents

The three key documents which are a must for anyone interested in pursuing the changing policy approach of the state towards Travellers are the *Report of the Commission on Itinerancy* (1963), the *Report of the Travelling People Review Body* (1983) and the *Report of the Task Force on the Travelling Community* (1995). It is not easy to gain access to these documents now. Your college or even your local library might have copies. I have tried to locate them on the internet with only very limited success. An executive summary of the *Report of the Task Force on the Travelling Community* (1995) is available online at: www.lenus.ie/hse/bitstream/10147/45449/1/7868.pdf

Only one piece of legislation addresses the specific needs of Travellers, the Housing (Traveller Accommodation) Act 1998: www.irishstatutebook.ie/pdf/1998/en.act.1998.0033.pdf

Two very important pieces of anti-discrimination legislation which refer to Travellers along with other groups are Employment Equality Act 1998: www.irishstatutebook.ie/pdf/1998/en.act.1998.0021.pdf

and the Equal Status Act 2000: www.oireachtas.ie/documents/bills28/acts/2000/a800.pdf

There are a number of key policy documents, such as in education, *A Report and Recommendations for a Traveller Education Strategy* and an *Intercultural Education Strategy, 2010–2015*, both of which can be obtained through the Department of Education and Skills website.

For health there is *Traveller Health: A National Strategy 2002–2005*: www.dohc.ie/publications/pdf/Traveller_health.pdf?direct=1

The Department of Environment's *Annual Count of Traveller Families*, various years, can be found via the Department of Environment, Community and Local Government website.

The CSO's (2012) publication from Census 2011, *Profile 7: Religion, Ethnicity and Irish Travellers*, and *Census 2006: Volume 5 – Ethnic or Cultural Background (Including the Irish Traveller Community)* published in 2007, are very important sources of information.

General Reading

One of my favourite books is Jim Mac Laughlin's *Travellers and Ireland; Whose Country and Whose History?* published in 1995. It is a succinct and relatively short book but pulls no punches in its analysis, and regrettably its criticisms have not dated. Another very good book is *Irish Travellers: Culture and Ethnicity* (1994), edited by May McCann, Séamus O'Siocháin and Joseph Ruane, with chapters written primarily from anthropological and socio-logical perspectives. Jane Helleiner, a Canadian anthropologist who made an ethnographic study of Travellers in Galway while living on an unofficial halting site, gives what could be called an 'outsider's view' of the experience of Travellers in *Irish Travellers: Racism and the Politics of Culture* (2000). Other authors who have contributed considerably to our knowledge and understanding of the Traveller population's fight for human rights and recogni-tion, and who remind us of the central problem of anti-Traveller racism in Ireland, are Niall Crowley, Sinéad Ni Shuinéar and Robbie McVeigh. The readings in the references section are good examples of their work. John O'Connell's chapter (2002) is also an important contribution from an activist's perspective. Of recent studies completed on Travellers I highly recommend the *All Ireland Traveller Health Study* (2010). It is a comprehen-sive study covering not only health but a range of issues more broadly related to well-being.

Useful Websites

Central Statistics Office – www.cso.ie
Department of Education and Skills – www.education.ie
Department of Environment, Community and Local Govern-ment – www.environ.ie
Department of Health – www.dohc.ie
Irish Traveller Movement – www.itm.ie
National Traveller Women's Forum – www.ntwf.net
Pavee Point – www.paveepoint.ie
Social Inclusion Division of the Department of Social Protection – www.socialinclusion.ie

8

Will We Ever See the End of Homelessness?

Area of Social Care for which this Chapter Is Relevant

This chapter is most useful for students with an interest in homelessness, but it should be also of use for those who wish to work in the broader areas of social housing, housing advice or addiction services.

Key Words in this Chapter

Homelessness, contested, structural, individual, legislation, homeless strategies, housing need, young people, marketplace

Key Themes in this Chapter

- Understanding homelessness
- Important legislation
- The extent of homelessness
- Homeless policy developments
- Young people and homelessness
- Progress towards the end of homelessness

Introduction

Housing is a basic need in all societies (Silke 2005b). However, in Ireland there is no specific right to housing in either the Irish Constitution or legislation (O'Sullivan 2005). Housing in Irish public policy is regarded primarily as belonging to the marketplace rather than treated as a public good (Drudy 2005). There are three different types of tenure – home ownership, private rented and social rented. While Irish housing policy is officially committed to ensuring that everyone has access to accommodation which meets their needs in a tenure of their choice, the reality is that its main thrust is to support home ownership (Department of Environment 1991, Silke 2005b). This has been achieved primarily through a variety of initiatives including incentives for house-building and house purchase which favour home ownership (Fitzgerald and Winston 2005). These housing policies have operated in conjunction with policies on property development and land acquisition, as well as a myriad of tax incentives. They have been central to the recent history of boom and bust of the Irish housing market and the wider economy. The legacy of this period has been well catalogued: huge national debt, a surplus of housing, incomplete housing developments, a dramatic fall in house prices, negative equity, and great uncertainty for many thousands of householders who are unable to repay their mortgages because of loss of jobs and reduced income. But even before the bubble burst their housing circumstances were a problem for many people (Drudy 2005). Those confronted with the greatest difficulties during this period were people in private rented accommodation and those waiting to gain access to local authority housing (Drudy 2005, Fahey 2004).

Private rented accommodation has traditionally been regarded as a short-term form of tenure in Ireland, providing for a transitional population, such as students and young working people who have not settled down. Private rented accommodation has also filled a gap in the social rented sector. This is the sector for people on low incomes who expect to have their housing need met by local authorities or voluntary housing associations, which are not-for-profit organisations that provide housing for low-income groups. The state funds accommodation for many people in need of housing in the private rented sector because of a lack of social housing. This was done in the past through rent allowances, and also more recently through the Rental Accommodation Scheme (RAS), where a local authority has a direct contractual agreement with a landlord to provide accommodation for a low-income tenant (Department of Environment, Heritage and Local Government (DEHLG) n.d.; see Box 8.2).

There is a long history of policy neglect of the social housing and private rented sectors, primarily because of the dominant emphasis on home ownership at political level. This policy neglect has manifested itself in a number of ways: through the lack of long-term sustainable investment in these sectors; poor quality of local authority and privately rented housing; a lack of security of tenure and historically poor regulation in the private rented sector (see Silke 2005b). However, the quality of accommodation in both of these sectors has greatly improved over the past fifteen to twenty years. Legislation and regulation has also enhanced the rights of tenants in private rented accommodation, although there are still tenants living in poor accommodation and those who encounter difficulties with landlords. Census 2011 suggests that there is a shift in preferred housing tenure type, with 29 per cent of all households in the state renting their accommodation, up from 22 per cent in 2006. In contrast owner occupation has decreased to 69.7 per cent in 2011 from 74.7 per cent in 2006 (CSO 2012d). These figures suggest a return to the tenure types of the early 1970s (Silke 2005b). However, the increase in the use of rental accommodation may have more to do with economic circumstances than actual housing preference, as it has become difficult to access mortgages, unemployment remains high and economic uncertainty continues.

It is in this broader public policy context that homelessness is located. Therefore, addressing homelessness must be understood as part of a housing policy that is quite extensive but firmly placed in a framework of home ownership. As a result, people who are homeless and those working with them may find that the interests of homeless people are marginal to Ireland's broader housing policy. In this chapter a number of key aspects of homelessness are explored, including understanding homelessness, important legislation, homeless statistics, homeless policy developments, young people and homelessness, and progress towards the ending of homelessness.

Understanding Homelessness

There are essentially two elements to this debate. One is how homelessness is understood in a formal, policy and legal

framework, and the second is how homelessness is understood sociologically. This section explores the sociological
understanding of homelessness, and the following section on
important legislation discusses more formal understandings of
homelessness.

The understanding and definition of homelessness is
contested. In other words there is no agreement on the general
understanding of homelessness and its causes. Those involved
in the debate tend to take one of two opposing positions. One is
that homelessness occurs as a result of how society is organised
(the structural approach). The second is that it occurs as a result
of individual pathology. This approach blames individual weakness for a person's homelessness (Brandon et al. 1980, Drudy and
Punch 2005, Hutson and Liddiard 1994, O'Sullivan 2005, 2008).
In one of the earlier contributions to this debate, Brandon and
colleagues outlined these differences in their book *The Survivors*
(1980), about youth homelessness in London. They write of the
two approaches to homelessness, the structural (or political as
they describe it) and the individual. However, they go further in
explaining the individual approach by dividing it into a number
of models – the individual culpability model, the pathological
model, the child model and the spiritual/religious model.

The individual culpability model places responsibility on the
homeless individual, suggesting that becoming homeless is the
consequence of individual behaviour and choice. The pathological model does not hold the individual responsible, and instead
believes that homelessness is as a result of underlying issues
such as child abuse or mental health problems. Yet those who
become homeless as a result of these difficulties are still seen as
'socially inadequate' (Brandon et al. 1980: 68). The child model
applies only to young people. At the core of this model is imma-
turity and naivety, which leads young people into homelessness.
The final model, spiritual/religious, suggests that homelessness
occurs as a result of the young person falling from 'grace', but
within a wider societal malaise of the spirit (Brandon et al. 1980:
66). While this subdivision provides extra detail of the differences within the individual approach to homelessness, most
explanations of homelessness do not distinguish between people
in this way, and categorise them under the heading of individual

pathology. In other words, according to this perspective, the responsibility for homelessness rests with the individual homeless person.

How those who make, fund and implement homeless policies understand the nature of homelessness impacts on the approach they take to it. So for instance, as Drudy and Punch (2005) point out, if homelessness is seen as arising from individual culpability, then the problem is marginal and relevant only to a small number of possibly deviant people. This understanding of homelessness is supported by a neoliberal philosophy that places the emphasis on the individual's responsibility to cater for their own housing needs. In turn it plays down the role of possible state intervention in resolving the problem (Drudy and Punch 2005). If housing is seen as primarily a responsibility of the individual and not of government, then the state will only provide a minimum level of support to those in most need. Support services for the homeless are then left to charitable organisations. O'Sullivan (2005) says that the focus of homeless research in Ireland and internationally is on the individual pathology of homeless people. This research has shown that they suffer disproportionately from a range of afflictions such as mental illness, alcohol and drug addiction, and show high levels of institutionalisation. Homelessness then is described as a function of personal pathology, and 'explanations of homelessness that focus on structural factors such as housing market conditions' are dismissed (O'Sullivan 2005: 260).

The structural approach to explaining homelessness is premised on a more critical approach of how society is organised. It regards housing policies as part of a wider problem of disadvantage and exclusion encountered by vulnerable individuals and families. 'Homelessness is thus a stark reflection of this deeper problem of social inequality and disempowerment; in a sense, it exists in the shadow of privilege and affluence' (Drudy and Punch 2005: 123). From the structural perspective, the response to homelessness requires a more fundamental change in how society is organised, including how housing is provided and allocated.

The structural and individual explanations of homelessness are not polarised to this extent in the real world of homeless policy debate and implementation in Ireland. While the policy focus tends to be on individual explanations, there is also an acknowledgement of the structural issues around homelessness in the various policy initiatives (O'Sullivan 2005). It is also the case that the nature of homelessness, whatever its cause, may require responses at both the individual and structural levels. Those who are homeless may need more than accommodation. The experience of homelessness can bring a range of person-ally debilitating difficulties, and it may not always be possible to rectify them by taking a solely structural response. Conse-quently there may also be a requirement to provide a range of supports at an individual level. It is however important to emphasise, as O'Sullivan (2008) points out (see below), that such an approach is not relevant to all homeless people, and that the key to addressing homelessness is the provision of affordable and adequate accommodation.

Important Legislation

Without doubt the most important piece of legislation that is directly relevant to homelessness is the Housing Act 1988. Before it was passed there was no formal legal definition of homeless-ness in Ireland. According to Section 2 of the Act, a person is regarded by a housing authority as being homeless if:

(a) there is no accommodation available which, in the opinion of the authority, he, together with any other person who normally resides with him or who might reasonably be expected to reside with him, can reason-ably occupy or remain in occupation of, or

(b) he is living in a hospital, county home, night shelter or other such institution, and is so living because he has no accommodation of the kind referred to in paragraph (a), and he is, in the opinion of the authority, unable to provide accommodation from his own resources. (Government of Ireland 1988)

The Housing Act 1988 contains positive elements addressing the issue of homelessness. It provides a definition of homelessness, even if it is less than precise. Central to the legislation was that for the first time it 'specified the local authority as the statutory agency with responsibility for the homeless' (O'Sullivan 2005: 248), while before 1988 homeless people fell between the remit of the local authorities and health authorities (O'Sullivan 2005), causing confusion and ambiguity. Local authorities are required under Section 8 to carry out an assessment of homelessness in their administrative areas from time to time. In Section 10 the Act gives the local authorities power to assist homeless people, although it does not oblige them to do so. It also allows local authorities to support the activities of the voluntary housing sector as providers of housing to those in need of accommodation. Local authorities can give direct support to homeless people, either financially or by providing for rented housing or lodgings (Government of Ireland 1988).

The legislation can be criticised for limiting the role of local authorities: their role is an enabling one, and they are not obliged to address homelessness (Curry 2003, Kenna 2006). Yet as Phelan and Norris point out, the legislation has been praised for its 'implication that structural factors – i.e. lack of housing – are the cause of homelessness' (2008: 54). Phelan and Norris add that the legislation has been further praised for its broad definition of homelessness. While there was a positive view taken of the legislation, Curry points to problems in its implementation, and states that it soon 'became clear that some local authorities were either unwilling or unable because of the lack of finance' (2003: 66) to comply with guidelines issued by the Department of Environment and to facilitate the implementation of the legislation.

The most recent legislation with implications for homelessness in Ireland is the Housing (Miscellaneous Provisions) Act 2009. Under Chapter 6 (sections 36–42), all city and county councils are legally obliged to adopt a homeless action plan with the aim of preventing and reducing homelessness. There is a requirement for the response to homelessness to be coordinated through a local homeless consultative forum that includes all relevant statutory and voluntary bodies. The responsibility for the development of the plan and for overseeing its implementation rests with a statutory management group (Government of Ireland 2009c). The elements of the 2009 Act that relate to homelessness were welcomed (Finnerty 2010, MakeRoom 2009).

However, homeless organisations in the voluntary sector had lobbied unsuccessfully to have more far-reaching changes made to the existing legislation (MakeRoom 2009).

The Extent of Homelessness

Measuring the extent of homelessness is fraught with practical difficulties (Hutson and Liddiard 1994). Prior to the introduction of the 1988 Act the state did not keep official records of the number of homeless people in Ireland (Brownlee 2008). The 1988 Act required local authorities to measure the level of homelessness, and Table 8.1 gives the official figures from the DECLG's Housing Needs Assessments of the levels of homelessness recorded in each of the assessment periods. It shows that homelessness increased during the 1990s, doubling between the 1996 and 1999 assessments, and reached a peak in 2002, followed by a substantial decrease in the two subsequent assessments, in 2005 and 2008. This trend was again reversed in 2011.

Table 8.1: Housing Needs Assessments 1989–2011: Levels of Homelessness

Year	Number of Persons Categorised as Homeless
1989	1,491
1991	2,371
1993	2,172
1996	2,501
1999	5,235
2002	5,581
2005	3,031
2008	1,394
2011	2,348

Source: Department of Environment, Community and Local Government, Housing Needs Assessments, various years.

Some argue that flaws in the definition of homelessness and in the implementation of the 1988 Act have made it difficult to obtain a true picture of the number of homeless people, so these official figures should be treated with caution. Brownlee states quite categorically that 'we do not, nor have ever, been able to truly measure the extent and nature of homelessness in Ireland' (2008: 34). Phelan and Norris suggest that problems with the legislation include 'the ambiguity of the statutory definition of homelessness' (2008: 55), which allowed local authorities significant flexibility in defining the problem. *Cornerstone* (2009: 2) highlights the limitations of the mechanism for 'counting' the homeless, stating that the 2008 figure of 1,394 is not the total number of homeless households, because 'the assessment counts only those on housing waiting lists, and not all homeless people are registered on housing waiting lists'.

The CSO reported for the first time on the extent of homelessness on Census night 2011 (10 April) (CSO 2012b). It obtained agreement with the major stakeholders on the approach it took: people were counted as homeless if they were accommodated in homeless services or were sleeping rough. On Census night 3,744 people were in accommodation for the homeless and 64 were sleeping rough (CSO 2012g). The CSO found that homeless people are more likely to be unemployed, and had poorer health and lower levels of education, than the general population. They also showed significantly higher levels of separation and divorce.

O'Connor (2008), in a revealing discussion on the complexity and the politics of counting the homeless, points to two significant difficulties which he suggests are at the heart of the issue. First, there is no acceptable agreement on a definition of homelessness. Second, homelessness is an emotive issue, and this impacts on a valid discussion of measurement techniques, because they can be perceived as callous towards those who are homeless. O'Connor also outlines the motivation of the different approaches to measurement by the statutory and voluntary sectors. His conclusion states that the varying definitions of homelessness and the methods of measurement employed by different organisations have been used 'for different purposes' (O'Connor 2008: 63). Voluntary sector organisations that provide services tend to use a broad definition of homelessness on humanitarian grounds, while state funding agencies use a more limited definition to ensure best use of scarce resources (O'Connor 2008).

Homeless Policy Developments

In the first decade of this century there was a concerted effort to combat homelessness through a number of strategic and policy developments, led by government and supported by the voluntary sector. As well as the four strategic approaches, *Homelessness: An Integrated Strategy* (2000), *Youth Homeless Strategy* (2001), *Homelessness: A Preventative Strategy* (2002), and *The Way Home 2008–2013* (2008), there was a *Review of the Implementation of the Government's Integrated and Preventative Homeless Strategies* (2006). Over the decade separate homeless action plans were published for Dublin, where the greatest number of homeless people was located. Homelessness also became an issue on the agenda of the national social partnership agreements, culminating in *Towards 2016* where there was a commitment to 'the elimination of such homelessness by 2010' (Government of Ireland 2006b: 55).

Box 8.1

Strategies to Combat Homelessness in the First Decade of the Twenty-First Century

- *Homelessness: An Integrated Strategy* (2000)
- *Youth Homeless Strategy* (2001)
- *Homelessness: A Preventative Strategy* (2002)
- *The Way Home 2008–2013* (2008)

Curry (2011) explains that the first of the strategies, *Homelessness: An Integrated Strategy* (hereafter called the *Integrated Strategy*), was published by the government in 2000 as a result of increased homelessness. Three key aims can be highlighted in this first strategy:

- Statutory agencies (local authorities and the health boards, now the Health Service Executive (HSE)) are to work in full partnership with the voluntary sector to coordinate services for the homeless.

- In order to achieve the first aim, local homeless fora are to be established in every county, and these will formulate and oversee homeless action plans which should be drawn up every three years.
- Local authorities are the responsible agency for accommodation needs, while the HSE is responsible for the health and care needs of homeless people.

(DEHLG 2000)

While the *Integrated Strategy* focused on issues of coordination and cooperation among providers of services for the homeless, *Homelessness: A Preventative Strategy* (hereafter the *Preventative Strategy*) (2002), which was published two years later, concentrates on the prevention of homelessness in the first place, as its name suggests. This is to be done by targeting adults at risk of homelessness, such as individuals leaving prisons or mental health residential facilities. Although there has been a separate youth homeless strategy in place since 2001 (see next section for a summary of its key points), the *Preventative Strategy* includes young people leaving care and young offenders leaving detention centres. The strategy seeks cooperation between those responsible for discharging individuals at risk to ensure that there are appropriate discharge arrangements in place. These include follow-up support services, such as resettlement and step-down facilities, and the extension of education services for homeless adults across the country (Department of the Environment, Heritage and Local Government/DES/Department of Health and Children/Department of Justice, Equality and Law Reform 2002).

In 2006 Fitzpatrick Associates carried out a review of both the integrated and preventative strategies for the Department of Environment. This review concluded that much had been achieved in addressing homelessness but significant challenges remained. It stated that the majority of the proposed actions set out in the integrated strategy 'were considered to have been either fully or significantly progressed since the launch of the strategy' (Fitzpatrick Associates 2006: 3). It concluded that as a result, the integrated strategy had impacted substantially on how homelessness was perceived in Ireland, the level of resources to combat homelessness and the types of interventions used to address it. Most crucially of all, it pointed to the fall in the numbers of homeless people (Fitzpatrick Associates 2006). The review stated that problems still remained around funding for accommodation, over-concentration on homelessness in Dublin, and the need to develop more appropriate responses to meet the needs of homeless people with mental health problems. It high-lighted five priorities for future development:

- The provision of long-term accommodation
- Appropriate local treatment of homelessness
- Case management approach
- Improved coordination of funding
- Better data on homelessness

(Fitzpatrick Associates 2006)

Box 8.2

Rental Accommodation Scheme (RAS)

RAS is a scheme established by the government in 2004 to meet the accommodation needs of people normally in receipt of rent supplement for more than eighteen months. A central feature of the scheme is that local authorities source accommodation through the private and voluntary housing sectors, and enter into medium to long-term contracts to secure availability of the accom-modation. The local authority then leases it out to the tenants.

(Department of Environment, Heritage and Local Government 2010)

The Way Home 2008–2013 was published in 2008 (accompanied by the *Homeless Strategy National Implementation Plan*), and was intended to build on the earlier strategies and incorporate key recommendations made by Fitzpatrick Associates. This latest strategy sets out the ambitious vision that from 2010 long-term homelessness and rough sleeping will be eliminated. The strategy outlines six strategic aims:

- Prevent homelessness
- Eliminate the need to sleep rough

- Eliminate long-term homelessness
- Meet long-term housing needs
- Ensure effective services for homeless people
- Better coordinate funding arrangements

(DEHLG 2008: 7)

Loughnan (2008), on behalf of the MakeRoom campaign, welcomed a number of key elements of the strategy, including the commitment that no one will stay in emergency accommodation for more than six months, the placing of local homeless plans on a statutory footing, and the continued rolling out of the Rental Accommodation Scheme. But these positives were 'largely overshadowed by the general lack of clarity in the document' (2008: 10), which included the level of resources to be committed, the detail of actions that would be taken, responsibility for these actions, and the timeframe for delivery (Loughnan 2008). Other problems with the strategy included the omission of multi-annual funding for homeless services, and a failure to change the definition of homelessness in the Housing Act 1988.

Box 8.3

Vision of *The Way Home*

From 2010, long-term homelessness (i.e. the occupation of emergency accommodation for longer than six months) and the need for people to sleep rough will be eliminated throughout Ireland. The risk of a person becoming homeless will be minimised through effective preventative strategies and services. When it does occur homelessness will be short term and people who are homeless will be assisted into appropriate long term housing.

(Department of Environment, Heritage and Local Government 2008: 7)

Young People and Homelessness

It is essential for a number of reasons to highlight the challenge of youth homelessness. Homeless young people are extremely vulnerable, and at risk of exploitation, addiction, abuse and crime. Some develop a pattern of life which leads to long-term homelessness. The emphasis in explaining youth homelessness differs from that of adult homelessness, and there are separate legislation and policy responses to the needs of this group. Just as it is not easy to get an accurate count of the number of adult homeless in Ireland, it is challenging to establish the number of homeless young people. They may not show up in official data, because not all make contact with support services. Yet the problem of youth homelessness in Dublin was first identified during the early 1970s (Mayock and Vekić 2006).

Mayock and O'Sullivan studied homeless young people in Dublin (2007) and found the explanations for their homelessness to be similar to those for adults but quite differently balanced. They describe three main pathways into homelessness: a history of care, conflict and instability in family life, and 'problem' behaviour (Mayock and O'Sullivan 2007). Not all of those who participated in Mayock and O'Sullivan's study saw themselves as homeless. Some described themselves as 'out of home': in other words they had a home but could not make use of it. It was not until the Child Care Act 1991 came into force that the Irish state legally imposed responsibility (in Section 5 of the Act) for the accommodation needs of children and young people, on the health boards. The relevant body is now the HSE, which is obliged to provide accommodation for homeless children.

Box 8.4

> **Homeless Children and Section 5, Child Care Act 1991**
>
> Where it appears to a health board that a child in its area is homeless, the board shall enquire into the child's circumstances, and if the board is satisfied that there is no accommodation available to him which he can reasonably occupy, then, unless the child is received into the care of the board under the provisions of this Act, the board shall take such steps as are reasonable to make available suitable accommodation.
>
> (Government of Ireland 1991: S5)

Despite this legislation there continued to be many difficulties in meeting the accommodation needs of young homeless people. The first formal response to their needs was the Department of Health and Children's national strategy, the *Youth Homeless Strategy*, in 2001. It acknowledged that there were problems with the existing approach to youth homelessness and with services provided for young people who were out of home. It sets out twelve objectives under three headings: preventive measures, responsive services and planning/administrative supports. The strategy emphasised the importance of prevention in tackling youth homelessness, and sets out to achieve it through support to schools, families and communities (Department of Health and Children 2001b). When a young person is in an out of home situation, the strategy stresses the need for prompt and responsive action which is child-focused, with the aim of reintegrating the person into their local community as quickly as possible.

The strategy also emphasises the need for better inter-agency cooperation and coordination. An important element is the acknowledgement of a link between leaving care and homelessness. In response to this, the strategy sets out an aftercare protocol, to which the HSE, local authorities and other relevant statutory and voluntary agencies are required to subscribe (Department of Health and Children 2001b). The efforts to improve outcomes for young homeless people have shown some success, but there are many aspects of both the policy approach and the delivery strategies that need further improvement. There need to be more sympathetic and appropriate models of service provision, and more responsive services (Mayock, Corr and O'Sullivan 2008).

Progress Towards the End of Homelessness

A number of very important policy commitments have been made in the past decade. Most important of all was the commitment to end homelessness by 2010. The national partnership agreement, *Towards 2016*, states that 'the situation of homeless persons who are currently in long-term emergency accommodation is of particular concern. The revised strategies will have as an underlying objective the elimination of such homelessness by 2010' (Government of Ireland 2006b: 55). The most recent homeless strategy, *The Way Home* (2008), endorses that commitment (see Box 8.3).

The establishment of the Homeless Agency in 2001 in Dublin was a major milestone in the efforts to combat homelessness in the capital, where the vast majority of homeless people are located. The coordinating and policy role of the Agency played a central role in reducing homelessness in Dublin throughout the first decade of the twenty-first century. Any commitment to eliminating homelessness requires policies to be developed and implemented. I have already mentioned the main initiatives: *Homelessness: An Integrated Strategy* (2000), the *Youth Homeless Strategy* (2001), *Homelessness: A Preventative Strategy* (2002) and *The Way Home 2008–2013* (2008). Despite all of these commitments and the greater integration and coordination of homeless service delivery, there still remain people who are long-term homeless. A few months before the end of 2010 (the target date for eliminating long-term homelessness), the homeless charity Focus Ireland reached its 25th anniversary. Sister Stanislaus Kennedy, its founder, said she was 'very, very angry' that homelessness had not ended during the years of prosperity, and called it a:

Disgrace. There's no other word for it. They had the money, they had the resources, they had people like us reminding them all the time. They failed . . . . In 1991 there were 2,700 people homeless. Despite the increase in prosperity in the succeeding years, that figure has risen to almost 5,000. The Government had made a commitment to end long-term homelessness by the end of this year, but it was clear they would be reneging on that promise. (quoted in Kelly 2010)

It is not just at a policy and organisational level in Ireland that combating homelessness has been reimagined. In recent years there has also been a change in the theoretical understanding of how homelessness is overcome. Much of the literature focuses on the currently popular 'pathways' approach (Mayock et al. 2008, O'Sullivan 2008, Pillinger 2008). This acknowledges the complexity of homelessness, and is particularly interested in taking into account the views of homeless people. Previous accounts of homelessness tended to focus on its causes, but the pathways model gives important weight to the idea of leaving or exiting homelessness. According to Pillinger, 'the pathways approach provides useful insights into the complexity and diversity of people's routes into, through and out of homelessness by locating people's housing experiences, attitudes and perceptions to identify what works' (2008: 64).

As a consequence there has been a shift in approach, from a continuum of care to the provision of stable accommodation as the primary and most effective response to homelessness. O'Sullivan says that 'the growing body of evidence is that the provision of secure housing is more significant in achieving residential stability and ensuring that individuals do not return to homelessness than any other intervention and that enhanced service provision is only effective in specific contexts' (2008: 79). Therefore, the fundamental problem of the response to homelessness appears to rest with how the issue is conceptualised. O'Sullivan argues that there is 'a restricted understanding of the nature of homelessness in Ireland', which relates 'homelessness primarily to administrative defects and the absence of specialized programmes to reintegrate the homeless', with only a limited acknowledgement that 'structural factors may contribute to homelessness' (2003: 51).

Since the election of the current Fine Gael/Labour government in early 2011 there has been a change in emphasis in homeless policy. The new government continued with the commitment to eradicate homelessness, but underpinned its policy with a 'housing first' approach (DECLG 2011b). The Dublin Regional Homeless Executive (DRHE) sets out the context for this new approach:

> Initially outlined in *Government for National Recovery* (2011) as part of the outcome of the government's comprehensive spending review, the adoption of a 'housing first' approach means offering homeless people suitable, long-term housing in the first instance and thereby seeks to radically reduce the use of hostel accommodation and the associated costs for the Exchequer.
> (DRHE 2011: 1)

This policy approach 'was given further impetus and clarification' in late 2011 when the Minister for Environment, Community and Local Government, 'announced a new direction for the delivery of services for people experiencing homelessness that will see "the money follow the client", with the provision of funding linked directly to specific targets and outcomes' (DRHE 2011: 1). The housing first approach has been welcomed by the DRHE, which says is important in the implementation of the Dublin homelessness strategy *Pathway to Home* (DRHE 2013). However, as the Irish Council for Social Housing (2012) points out, there has been a significant reduction in the number of available social housing units.

Conclusion

In *Pathway to Home* (2009), the Homeless Agency refers to a number of barriers to exiting homelessness. The most important is 'the need for access to more appropriate and affordable housing options combined with supports in housing as required' (Homeless Agency 2009: 11). At the core of the homeless problem is the availability of affordable housing. Some analysts suggest that there is a need for Irish housing policy to develop a perspective that views 'housing as a home' (Drudy 2005, Drudy and Punch 2005).

For Drudy, housing should be seen as a 'central feature of development' (2005: 44), where the home is an element in the improvement of the quality of life of people and not something that is used simply for economic growth. He argues that using housing as a spur to economic advancement, a market-based approach, leads to segregation in housing (Drudy 2005). Those who become homeless are the most segregated or excluded from the housing market. Belatedly there is recognition of the problems associated with regarding housing as a means for wealth generation. In its *Housing Policy Statement* the DECLG says that '[w]e now know the consequences of encouraging people to choose their housing options on the basis of investment and yield rather than hearth and home' (2011b: 2).

The Irish model of home ownership has 'created significant inequalities' in Irish housing (Fitzgerald and Winston 2005: 243), inequalities which emerge from structural factors. The problem of homelessness has been redefined by policy developments in Ireland over the past ten years in what Phelan and Norris (2008: 67) describe as the 'reform agenda'. These developments have given some hope for the future of homeless policy. Ultimately though, according to Phelan and Norris (2008: 67), homelessness is regarded as the responsibility of individuals and 'external to the state's responsibilities'. If this depiction of homeless policy is true, there is little hope that we will ever see the end of homelessness.

Further Reading

Readings on homelessness in Ireland include materials from government departments and their agencies, organisations that work with homeless people, and a small number of academic and policy analysts who have a considerable track record on housing and homeless issues.

Essential Documents

Essential documents that give an understanding of homelessness include the Housing Act 1988 and the various strategies published by the DECLG and the Department of Health.

Housing Act 1988: www.irishstatutebook.ie/1988/en/act/pub/0028/print.html

Housing (Miscellaneous Provisions) Act 2009: www.irish statutebook.ie/pdf/2009/en.act.2009.0022.pdf

2000 – *Homelessness: An Integrated Strategy*: www.environ. ie/en/Publications/DevelopmentandHousing/Housing/FileDownLoad,1797,en.pdf

2001 – *Youth Homeless Strategy*: www.dohc.ie/publications/pdf/ythhmlss.pdf?direct=1

2002 – *Homelessness: A Preventative Strategy*: www.environ. ie/en/Publications/DevelopmentandHousing/Housing/FileDownLoad,1798,en.pdf

2006 – *Review of the Implementation of the Government's Integrated and Preventative Homeless Strategies*: www.environ.

ie/en/Publications/DevelopmentandHousing/Housing/
FileDownLoad,1800,en.pdf

2007 – *A Key to the Door: The Homeless Agency Partnership Action Plan on Homelessness in Dublin 2007-2010*: www.
homelessagency.ie/Research-and-Policy/Publications/
Action-Plans---Homeless-Agency/A-key-to-the-door-Action-
Plan-on-Homelessness-in-.aspx

2008 – *The Way Home 2008-2013*: www.environ.ie/
en/Publications/DevelopmentandHousing/Housing/
FileDownLoad,18192,en.pdf

General Reading

Some books specifically address the issues of homelessness, but much relevant literature deals with the general topic of housing. A good example is Eoin O'Sullivan's chapter on 'Homelessness' in Michelle Norris and Declan Redmond's (2005) edited book. Eoin O'Sullivan also contributed 'Marxism, the state and homelessness in Ireland' to Maura Adshead and Michelle Millar's (2003) edited collection. A Marxist context is rarely found in writing about homelessness, or most other issues in Irish social policy, so this provides an unusual and interesting perspective. A third chapter by O'Sullivan, 'Pathways through homelessness: theoretical constructions and policy implications' (2008), teases out various theoretical and methodological approaches to the favoured pathways model.

I also recommend *Perspectives on Irish Homelessness: Past, Present and Future* (2008) from the Homeless Agency, edited by Daithí Downey. It gives an excellent overview of the issues of importance, and its contributors include some of the most expert writers on homelessness in Ireland, including Eoin O'Sullivan, Brian Harvey and Paula Mayock. Mayock and O'Sullivan (2007) also collaborated on *Lives in Crisis: Homeless Young People in Dublin*, an important contribution on the experiences of young people who are out of home.

Some voluntary organisations that work with homeless people have also produced very high-quality research and publications by these and other writers. Check out the publications sections of their websites (see below).

Two earlier books on homelessness are worth looking at. David Brandon and colleagues's book (1980) about youth homelessness in London led the field. Susan Hutson and Mark Liddiard (1994) also cover youth homelessness. The challenges and debates these writers discuss are still pertinent over fifteen and thirty years later.

A very useful resource for anyone interested in homelessness is the magazine *Cornerstone,* which was published quarterly until the Homeless Agency was replaced in 2011 by the DRHE. It covered up-to-date debates and policy issues in relatively short and accessible articles. Archive copies are available through the DRHE website. Since early 2012 the DRHE has published a bimonthly newsletter, *Pathway,* available on its website.

Useful Websites

Department of Environment, Community and Local Government – www.environ.ie
Dublin Region Homeless Executive – www.homelessagency.ie
FEANTSA (European Federation of National Organisations Working with the Homeless) – www.feantsa.org
Focus Ireland – www.focusireland.ie
Simon Communities of Ireland – www.simon.ie

9

Lest We Forget the *Céad Míle Fáilte*: Immigrants, Refugees and Asylum Seekers

Area of Social Care for which this Chapter Is Relevant

Only a small number of specialised immigration organisations have the funding capacity to employ staff, but an increasing number of the users of most social care agencies are immigrants, so most social care workers will have contact with them, and need to know about the policies and initiatives that concern them.

Key Words in this Chapter

Migration, immigration, asylum seeker, refugee, social rights, integration, racism, social exclusion

Key Themes in this Chapter

- Gaining an understanding of migration
- Important legislation
- Immigration – facts and figures
- Policy developments in Ireland and the European Union
- Refugees and asylum seekers
- The *céad míle fáilte* (one hundred thousand welcomes)

Introduction

Immigration ranks amongst the most contentious and complex of policy issues. It prompts heated debate both at the political level and among the general population. Immigration raises the ire of many people, and is used by politicians and others to stir up hostility for their own purposes. In recent years an increasing number of anti-immigrant political parties have made electoral gains across Europe, and this has prompted the mainstream political parties to take increasingly harsh measures against immigrants. The anti-immigrant politicians claim that they are reflecting the views of a section of the population whose voice is not listened to. They tend to represent the fear and resentment of people who believe immigrants are taking jobs and welfare from locals. Much of this anti-immigrant feeling reveals both ignorance of facts and a genuine anxiety about a changing world over which people feel they have little control (Finney and Simpson 2009). Such attitudes are significant. While only a minority support overtly anti-immigrant political parties, they are sufficiently large in many countries to impact on national political systems and policy paths.

Immigration is not a new social phenomenon, and it is generally accepted that 'the greatest era for recorded voluntary migration was the century after 1815' (Hirst and Thompson 1999: 23). However, the recent stage of globalisation, starting in the final decades of the twentieth century, also led to mass movements of people, which has become a major global issue. People travel for all kinds of reasons: for holidays, to visit families, for education, for business and for adventure. These purposes are not the subject of this chapter, which centres around two specific migrant groups: those who migrate for economic reasons, in other words for work, and those who are forced to migrate. Forced migration is another term for people who are forced to flee their country of origin because of persecution. They are more commonly known as asylum seekers and refugees.

Ireland has been known for its long history of emigration, which has blighted the country for much of the past two hundred years. There were only two short periods in which the number of people entering the country outnumbered those who left, and the most recent of these, the ten-year period 1998–2008, was the most significant. Immigration outnumbered emigration then to such an extent that it added hundreds of thousands of people to the population (CSO 2011b). This unprecedented inward migration has posed many challenges to the policies of the Irish state and its people. In this chapter these challenges are explored.

Understanding Migration

Before we move to specific details about immigration into Ireland, let us examine some of the theories around migration. Why do people move from one part of the globe to another, often at great risk to themselves and their families, and often into circumstances which may be far from what they had hoped for? There are a range of complex reasons. Sales (2007) divides theories of migration into the individualist and the structural. She then adds a third lens, the gendering of migration. This section looks at each of these in turn.

The individualist model of migration is based on the idea that individuals attempt to improve their personal well-being by making rational choices which lead to the best outcomes for them personally. This includes moving from one part of the world to another if they believe this is in their best interest. This approach to understanding migration has a long history, and suggests that migration tends 'to take place from areas of scarce land and capital, low wages and poor employment opportunities towards areas where there was available land, economic opportunity and high demand for labour' (Sales 2007: 48). The costs and benefits are often described as the 'push' and 'pull' factors of migration, and any decision to migrate includes a weighing-up of these elements.

Sales (2007) accepts that the factors that influence individual decisions are important, but she argues that this is only part of the story. This particular model suggests that individuals have full knowledge of the choices that they make and that they are not impeded in any way by other factors. However, Sales says that 'migration is rarely a simple individual action' (2007: 48). In fact migration occurs as a result of a change in social and economic circumstances, when people find it too difficult to make a living in their home area or country. But there are structural restrictions in the process of migration, which go beyond the individual's decision-making capacity. These include access to information on the destination country, covering for example work opportunities, support networks and visa requirements. The individual model ignores these more complicated aspects of migration, and focuses on personal choice to improve well-being as if this potentially life-changing decision takes place in a vacuum.

Box 9.1

Some Important Definitions – Migrant, Immigrant and Emigrant

- **Migrant** is defined in this chapter as someone who crosses an international border for the purposes of work, education or business. This can be for a short or long period. (Refugees and asylum seekers are also migrants as they cross an international border, but the circumstances of their migration are different – see section on refugees and asylum seekers below.)
- **Immigrant** is the term used by the 'receiving' country for the migrant who has entered its territory.
- **Emigrant** is the term used by the country of origin to describe the migrant who leaves its territory.

The structuralist accounts of migration start from a very different theoretical perspective. These tend to see migration as an example of the exploitative relationship between the wealthier and the poorer regions of the world (Collinson 2009). Migrants move from poorer countries (often former colonies) to meet the labour needs of wealthier countries. In this account the receiving countries benefit from cheap labour, by young workers who do not claim benefits and have been educated by the poorer country of origin (Sales 2007). In this representation of migration the migrants are deemed to have little choice. They are obliged to move to support themselves and their families as a result of global structural inequalities. However, according to this perspective, migration is not just a simple act of moving, as rich countries put in place many barriers to control the movement of people, and are very selective about the types of worker they admit. Sales (2007) points to an important criticism of this explanation for migration, that the structuralist arguments tend to ignore the individual's wishes and actions. From the structuralist perspective migrants are regarded as passive actors in what is an extension of traditional class conflicts, but played out on a global stage (Collinson 2009).

Both individualist and structuralist theories tend to focus on male migration, but more recent analysis from a feminist viewpoint suggests that gender provides another dimension to migration. Sales says the development of an interest in gender and migration 'grew partly out of changing patterns of migration and the increased importance of flows in which women predominate' (2007: 51). In the individualist and structural accounts, women were seen as dependent and 'followers' of their men, rather than as initiators and leaders of migration. However, there is historical evidence that this is not always the case, as migrant women have travelled independently from Ireland for over a century (Delaney 2002). Considering women's role in migration does not only correct inaccurate accounts, but leads to a more diverse and richer understanding of the experiences and processes of migration. In more recent times women's migration is often associated with 'global care chains' (Yeates 2008) and the migration of women to work in the 'entertainment' industry and in prostitution (Sales 2007). Human trafficking for enforced labour, particularly for the purpose of prostitution, is another dimension of migration. Although it has at times had a high profile this is not new, as there is a long history of enslaving people and forcing them to migrate (Fredrickson 2002).

Box 9.2

Global Care Chains and Human Trafficking

Global care chains

'The term global care chain was coined by Hochschild (2000: 131) to refer to "a series of personal links between people across the globe based on the paid or unpaid work of caring"' (Yeates 2008: 238).

Human trafficking

Trafficking in persons shall mean the recruitment, transportation, transfer, harbouring or receipt of persons, by means of the threat or use of force or other forms of coercion, of abduction, of fraud, of deception, of the abuse of power or of a position of vulnerability or of the giving or receiving of payments or benefits to achieve the consent of a person having control over another person, for the purpose of exploitation. Exploitation shall include, at a minimum, the exploitation or the prostitution of others or other forms of sexual exploitation, forced labour or services, slavery or practices similar to slavery, servitude or the removal of organs.

(Article 3 of the UN Palermo Protocol to Prevent, Suppress and Punish Trafficking in Persons, Especially Women and Children, 2000)

More recent insights and theory development around migration stress the phenomenon of 'circular migration', where migrants move back and forth between their countries of origin and destination (Vertovec 2007). This approach 'emphasizes the importance of border-crossing social networks' (Vertovec 2007: 2). While these social networks have always existed for migrants, modern communication methods and cheaper transport allow for greater and more intense global connectivity. These transnational ties in turn give migrants a greater ease of movement, as they have people on the ground to facilitate their transition from one space to another. They also allow for increased opportunities to retain ties with communities of origin (Vertovec 2007).

Important Legislation

Before 1996 and the passing of the Refugee Act, only one set of legislation in Ireland dealt specifically with immigration, the Aliens Act 1935 and subsequent regulations made under it. The Aliens Act governed the entry and residence of non-Irish nationals, and gave the Minister for Justice extensive powers. From 1996 onwards the amount of immigration-related legislation changed dramatically: there were five substantial pieces of legislation between then and 2004. A number of other changes in law and related regulations also impacted on immigrants, covering for example work permits, social welfare entitlements, citizenship and nationality, movement of European Union citizens, and the European Convention on Human Rights (Quinn et al. 2008). In 2004 the Irish Constitution was changed after a referendum when a significant majority of the Irish electorate voted to alter how Irish citizenship was granted.

Box 9.3

Key Legislation on Immigration

- Aliens Act 1935
- Refugee Act 1996, as amended
- Immigration Act 1999, as amended
- Illegal Immigrants (Trafficking) Act 2000
- Immigration Act 2003
- Employment Permits Act 2006
- Immigration Act 2004
- Immigration, Residence and Protection Bill 2010
- Civil Law (Miscellaneous Provisions Act) 2011 – Parts 10 and 11

While the original Refugee Act 1996 gave rise to optimism over refugee policy in Ireland (Moran 2005), the subsequent amendments to it and other legislative developments between 1999 and 2004 were primarily about increasing the state's control over immigration. Many of the changes reflected what was occurring at EU level, to which we shall return later in this chapter. The Refugee Act 1996, as amended, incorporates into Irish law the 1951 Geneva Convention Relating to the Status of Refugees. It includes a definition of refugees, provides for the establishment of the key offices for determining asylum claims – the Office of the Refugee Applications Commissioner and the Refugee Appeals Tribunal – and sets out a structure for deciding on asylum claims (Government of Ireland 1996). The Immigration Act 1999 resolved a challenge to the constitutional powers of the state on deportation, as well as making substantial amendments to the original Refugee Act of 1996.

The Illegal Immigrants (Trafficking) Act 2000 introduced the offence of trafficking in illegal immigrants or people who intend to seek asylum. It also gave increased powers to the Gardaí on deportation orders, as well as widening detention for those awaiting deportation (Government of Ireland 2000b). The Immigration Act 2003 saw the completion of the amendments to the Refugee Act 1996, and particularly emphasised increased efficiency in the decisions on asylum applications (Fraser 2003). It also introduced carrier liability sanctions, where airlines or shipping companies could face sanction if they had not completed proper documentation checks of passengers destined for Ireland to ensure that they met Irish immigration requirements. The Immigration Act 2004 was introduced hastily because the state believed that High Court judgements which it faced undermined the Aliens Act 1935 and subsequent regulations, with adverse implications for the operation of immigration controls (Quinn et al. 2008).

From 2004 there was a long period of debate on immigration legislation, culminating in the Immigration, Residence and Protection Bill 2010, the third attempt at introducing a comprehensive piece of legislation which would repeal all existing immigration law. Its purpose was to set out 'a legislative framework for the management of inward migration to Ireland', and it addressed issues such as family reunification, long-term residence, trafficking, the process of applying for a visa, deportation and independent appeals (Government of Ireland 2010c: 231). The Bill is not without its critics, and Charlton (2010), on behalf of the Immigrant Council of Ireland (ICI), said that it would have to be revisited if it was to be a 'fair and comprehensive immigration policy'. She stated that the proposed legislation was not comprehensive, that there were problems in relation to family reunification, and that it lacked an independent and transparent appeals process (Charlton 2010). The new government elected in 2011 agreed to proceed with this Bill, but at the time of going to press little progress had been made. While the re-emergence of this Bill is awaited, the current immigration legislation is characterised by Charlton as 'restrictive and out-dated' (ICI 2011: 4). She also says that immigration policies and procedures lack clarity, and 'while some improvements have been made, on the whole, Ireland's immigration system remains chaotic, bureau-cratic, cumbersome and lacking in transparency. The complexity of current policy has led to a system that is disjointed, difficult to understand and even more difficult to navigate' (ICI 2011: 4).

Immigration – Facts and Figures

It is difficult or even impossible to get an accurate measurement of movement in and out of Ireland. Because of the lack of control at Irish borders the figures can only be estimated (Quinn et al. 2008). The primary data sources used include the aggregate inward and outward flows provided by the CSO on an annual basis in its *Population and Migration Estimates*; the number of work permits granted by the Department of Enterprise, Trade and Innovation; the number of Personal Public Service Numbers (PPSNs) generated by the Department of Social Protection; and data on asylum seekers from the Office of the Refugee Applications and the Reception (ORAC) and Integration Agency (RIA) (see O'Connell, Joyce and Finn 2012). Every five years the most important data on the population are made known when the CSO carries out the National Census, which includes questions on ethnicity status and nationality.

In the four-year period up to Census 2006, net immigra-tion into Ireland was 192,000, and in the next census period it increased by a further 125,000, which according to the CSO (2012d: 10) is significant 'given the recent economic situation in Ireland'. Between Census 2002 (the first time a question on nationality was included in the Census) and Census 2006 the number of non-Irish nationals living in Ireland almost doubled from 224,300 to 419,733. This number increased by a further 29.7 per cent to 544,357 non-Irish nationals or 11.9 per cent of the total population, in Census 2011 (CSO 2012d: 33). A feature of migration is the dominance of those of working age, particularly young working adults, who are most likely to move in search of employment opportunities. Census 2011 confirmed this pattern, as the highest numbers of immigrants fell within the 25–40 age group (CSO 2012d). The period between the 2006 and 2011 Censuses showed a new development, with a significant increase in the number of non-Irish women. 'This rise is reflected in an increase of 28,569 women at work among this group' (CSO 2012c: 26). In the same period the number of non-Irish-born children aged fourteen years and under went up 49.7 per cent, and the number of older non-Irish-born people also increased significantly, by 26.9 per cent (CSO 2012d: 34).

The number of non-Irish nationals in the workforce continued to rise between 2006 and 2011, by 9.7 per cent (CSO 2012c), giving a total of 74.2 per cent participation rate in the workforce in April 2011. 'While the number of non-Irish at work has increased, so too has the number who were unemployed, more than doubling between 2006 and 2011 from 33,587 to 77,460. This gave an unemployment rate of 22.4 per cent compared with 18.5 per cent for Irish nationals in April 2011' (CSO 2012e: 25). The CSO (2012e) recorded that of the different non-Irish national groups, Nigerians were the nationality with the highest number of unemployed at 39 per cent (down from 45 per cent in 2006), followed by Romanians, Russians, Ukrainians and Latvians. This adds weight to Fanning's observation that 'Africans generally experience the greatest difficulties in accessing employment' (2011: 143). At the other end of the scale, migrants from three Scandinavian countries, Denmark, Sweden and Finland (CSO 2012e), had the lowest levels of unemployment, at under 10 per cent.

By far the highest proportion of non-Irish nationals worked in the hotels and restaurants sector (38.1 per cent), followed by business activities (19.6 per cent), manufacturing (18.4 per cent) and the wholesale and retail sector (17.8 per cent) (CSO 2012e: 27). Nolan and Maître (2008: 47) make the point that this concentration of immigrant workers in these 'relatively low-skill occupations suggests that weak English language skills may be a contributory factor'. This point was highlighted in Census 2011, which found a correlation between poor competence in English and higher levels of unemployment. Immigrants who spoke English 'well or very well' were more likely to be employed, while almost one-third of those who did not speak English 'well or at all' were unemployed (CSO 2012c: 20). Barrett, McGuinness and O'Brien (2012) drew attention to the earnings differences between Irish nationals and non-Irish nationals in Ireland. They found a negative earnings gap between immigrants from the ten East European and Mediterranean island states that joined the

European Union in 2004, and Irish nationals in similar work. The earnings gap was less in employment sectors with lower pay and lower educational requirements, and greater as people moved up the pay and qualifications ladders.

This suggests that other issues are at play because, according to Barrett and colleagues, 'immigrants in Ireland are also unusual in having levels of educational attainment that are higher than the native population' (2012: 14). Nolan and Maître found 'some evidence' that East European immigrants 'are working in unskilled jobs that only pay around the minimum wage' (2008: 47). Barrett and colleagues suggest this is as a result of the lack of 'a full-return on human capital' (2012: 478). In other words these immigrant workers do not benefit from the education and skills they acquired in their country of origin. These are not the only group of immigrant workers who face workplace difficulties. Nolan and Maître stated that workers from outside the European Union who are in Ireland on work permits 'may be particularly vulnerable to exploitation' (2008: 47), given the restrictive nature of work visas. They claimed that greater protection is offered since the introduction of the Employment Permits Act 2006. Fanning (2011) laid the blame for a lack of equal participation in employment on racism in Irish society and institutional failure by the Irish state to assist with the development of English language skills and other supports necessary for immigrants to participate in the labour market. He also referred to the deliberate policy path pursued by the state to 'source low-skilled workers from within' the European Union (2011: 26).

Box 9.4

'Racism'
There is no scientific foundation for 'racial' difference. 'Race' is therefore a social construct and not based on any scientific truth. Penketh (2006) says that as people believe that 'race' exists, there is need for a definition.
'Racism' occurs '[w]here a group of people is discriminated against on the basis of characteristics which are held to be inherent in them as a group' (Penketh 2006: 89).

> Central to an understanding of 'racism' are prejudice (attitudes and opinions leading to the belief that certain individuals/groups are inferior based on perceived 'racial' differences) and discriminatory behaviour (actions that result from these attitudes and opinions). 'Racism' is not only the actions of prejudiced individuals; it may also be reflected in the institutions and structures of society (Penketh 2006; see also Fanning 2002, 2011).

Fears about the amount of state money spent on social protection for immigrants give rise to much public debate and controversy (Barrett et al. 2012). Yet there is evidence that immigrants tend to receive less welfare than Irish nationals (Barrett et al 2012, O'Connell et al. 2011). According to Fanning this is because of the nature of the welfare system that has developed over the past decade: '[i]n May 2004, to coincide with the enlargement of the European Union, the Irish government decided to remove many benefit entitlements from new immigrants and their families for an initial two-year period' (2011: 134). This refers to the habitual residency condition that was introduced as part of the Social Welfare (Miscellaneous Provisions) Act 2004. As well as needing two years of residency in Ireland, applicants for benefits must demonstrate that Ireland is their 'centre of interest' (the place to which they are normally connected). Gaining social protection under this legislation can be an arduous task. Many immigrant workers are in low-paid work and vulnerable to losing their jobs, so they and their families can easily find themselves in dire circumstances (see Migrants Rights Centre Ireland (MRCI) 2005).

Policy Developments in the European Union and Ireland

The European Union and its member states are ostensibly concerned about migration for work purposes, illegal immigration, asylum and integration. However, as Huysmans (2000) argues, migration is also part of the European Union's policy on security, as migration is regarded as having a destabilising effect on the integration of European society and public order. (See Fanning 2011 for a discussion on migration and security in Ireland.) Ireland's migration policies are inextricably bound up with those of the European Union, although under EU legislation member states make their own decisions on its migration policies. Brady (2008: 2) describes the nature of EU migration reform as 'elusive', in spite of years of debate and discussion. He says that the problem centres on the lack of 'clear political objectives for such a policy' (Brady 2008: 2). Yet the European Union has attempted to bring about greater coordination in immigration policy, beginning with the Tampere Agenda (at which EU leaders began the process of agreeing policies on justice matters, including immigration), which was agreed by the European Council in 1999. In subsequent years a number of EU legal instruments addressed issues of immigration and asylum. However, immigration and asylum are contentious issues for EU member states, and Ireland, along with the United Kingdom, has secured opt-outs from regulations on many migration-related issues on a case-by-case basis, while Denmark has opted out entirely from this area of policy making (Brady 2008, Quinn et al. 2008).

Two of the more significant policies concern the free movement of people and integration. The European Union has a principle of free movement of people: citizens of EU states can move from one member state to another without the need for visas or residence permits. However, some restrictions apply, particularly to the two newest member states, Bulgaria and Romania, whose citizens will not have free movement to work in other EU states until 2014 (Brady 2008). After three months 'they must be working, studying or financially independent if they wish to stay' (Brady 2008: 12).

The integration of immigrants into EU countries is a policy area of vital importance for social care students. Fanning says migrant and minority ethnic groups in the European Union 'are disproportionately represented in forms of poor and insecure work and are disproportionately unemployed' (2006: 82). The marginalisation of immigrants and ethnic minority groups suggests that despite generations of inward migration to EU countries, there remains an economic and social challenge of major significance. EU member states need to improve how they integrate immigrants if they are to cope with an increasing number of them (Brady 2008). As part of its efforts to develop a more coherent policy on immigration, the European Union has given consideration to the integration of immigrants through the

Hague Programme in 2004 and *Common Basic Principles for Immigrant Integration Policy in the EU* in 2005 (European Union 2007). This developing framework was followed by the introduction of the European Integration Fund in 2007 to support integration of third-country nationals (people originally from countries outside the European Union and now living within it) in member states (European Commission 2007).

Even with this commitment at EU level to the idea of integration, the policies face critics and opposition. At a conceptual level, some people believe integration is part of a racist policy of assimilation, where difference is not accepted and immigrants and minority ethnic groups are forced to give up their identities to be accepted as part of the communities in which they reside (Penketh 2006). At a political level some oppose the integration of immigrants, believing not only that it does not work, but that immigration is a burden, causes many problems for the host society and should be reversed (Finney and Simpson 2009). There has been an increase in anti-immigrant sentiment across many European countries, and its expression includes increased support for anti-immigrant political parties. In response, legislation on immigration at EU level and in different member countries has become increasingly restrictive and controlling (Sales 2007).

Irish policy on immigration issues has shifted considerably over the past fifteen years, but it is still far from being cohesive and well thought-out. Quinn and colleagues say that 'it has been argued that the updating of Irish immigration and asylum policy to the present time has been piecemeal, reacting to specific problems as they arise' (2008: 21). The lack of a coherent policy impacts greatly on immigrants, and reinforces uncertainty and insecurity. In 2010 the ICI reported on its information and referral service, and highlighted some of the problems. Issues mentioned most frequently included renewal of status, family reunification and citizenship (ICI 2010). The ICI pointed to a lack of clear guidelines available on the renewal of status and an absence of family reunification legislation for immigrant workers. It also claimed that an 'exclusionary' approach is taken to citizenship (ICI 2010). This information and referral service report revealed the extent of immigrants' needs and the inadequacy of immigration policy to meet them.

Refugees and Asylum Seekers

Asylum seekers and refugees face many of the same problems as other immigrant groups, but their reasons for migration and the legislation and administrative practices covering them are different. Furthermore, their personal, social and economic circumstances can be quite different from those of other immigrants. Refugees and asylum seekers are known as 'forced migrants', as they are forced to leave their home countries because they fear persecution there. The Irish Refugee Act 1996, as amended, uses the definition of a refugee outlined in the 1951 Geneva Convention Relating to the Status of Refugees, and specifies the conditions under which refugees are granted recognition. The individual must apply for refugee status from outside of their country of origin, and demonstrate a well-founded fear of persecution based on one or more of the following grounds: race, religion, nationality, membership of a particular group, or political opinion.

A number of categories of people are given different forms of protection by the Irish state – see Box 9.5. There are some differences between those with refugee status, programme or quota refugees, and those granted leave to remain, but these groups for the most part are treated like Irish citizens for the purposes of receiving services and benefits, and are allowed to work or start up a business. Asylum seekers (that is, those who have applied for but not yet been granted refugee status) are much more restricted in access to services and benefits, and in their general access to what might be described as the normal expectations of living in Ireland (see Free Legal Advice Centres (FLAC) 2009).

Box 9.5

Different Statuses of 'Refugee' Protection in Ireland

- A **refugee** is someone who is recognised as a refugee under Irish law in accordance with the 1951 Geneva Convention Relating to the Status of Refugees.
- An **asylum seeker** is a person who has applied for recognition as a refugee under the 1951 Geneva Convention and is

granted temporary residence in the state until their application is determined.

- A **programme/quota refugee** is a person who has been invited to reside in the state (either long-term or short-term) by the Irish government under a particular humanitarian programme, normally at the request of the United Nations High Commissioner for Refugees (UNHCR).
- A **person given leave to remain on humanitarian grounds** is someone who has been through the asylum process and has failed to be granted refugee status but is granted permission to remain in the state on humanitarian grounds at the discretion of the Minister for Justice and Equality.

Since 1999 asylum seekers have been required to live in accommodation centres set up throughout the country under a programme of dispersal. This programme was broadened to include what is known as direct provision (that is, the provision by the state of accommodation, food and other necessities) in April 2000. Taken together, dispersal, accommodation centres and direct provision for asylum seekers have been described as a 'parallel' system of welfare (Moran 2005) or as a form of 'racialised containment' (Moran 2009). Asylum seekers cannot obtain support for accommodation outside these centres, because the state deems that the centres meet their housing needs. The centres provide full board. Adults receive an allowance of €19.10 and children receive €9.60 per week. These payment levels have not changed since the system was introduced in 2000. Child benefit is not paid to asylum seekers, but they are entitled to exceptional needs payments from the local community welfare officer. Asylum seekers are entitled to medical cards. Children are obliged to attend school up to the age of sixteen, and may remain in schooling till the end of their secondary education. Those attending third-level college must pay full fees as non-EU nationals, and adults are not allowed to attend state-funded education or training courses, although there are some limited exceptions (FLAC 2009). Asylum seekers are not allowed to work or start up a business. In short enormous restrictions are placed on the lives of those pursuing claims for recognition as refugees.

Twenty years ago in 1992, 39 people applied for asylum in Ireland, but from the mid-1990s the numbers increased dramatically, peaking in 2002. Since then they have fallen back steadily in each subsequent year. Table 9.1 shows the trend of asylum applications for selected years from 1992 to 2011. The downward trend continued in 2012, with 388 applications by the end of May, down from 572 for the same period in 2011 (RIA 2012: 2).

Table 9.1: Applications for Asylum in Ireland – Selected Years

Year	1992	1996	2000	2002	2003	2006	2008	2009	2010	2011
Number of applications for asylum in Ireland	39	1,179	10,938	11,634	7,900	4,314	3,866	2,689	1,939	1,290

Source: Office of the Refugee Applications Commissioner (2012: 59).

The Irish pattern reflects a more general downward trend across European states and other industrialised countries (United Nations High Commissioner for Refugees (UNHCR) 2011). There are a number of possible and interrelated reasons for trends in asylum applications, and the choice by asylum seekers of a country in which to make their claim (Kate 2005, Neumayer 2005, UNHCR 2011). According to the UNHCR:

The number of people requesting international protection has fluctuated significantly between countries and years, largely depending on political developments in countries of origin or changes in asylum polices in receiving countries. However, other factors may also be of relevance, such as the existence of social networks of certain communities in destination countries, improved capacity to register asylum-seekers, and the fact that some countries are perceived as being more likely to grant refugee status than others. (UNHCR 2011: 8)

Countries vary in the proportion of claims for asylum (or recognition of refugee status) that they accept (Kate 2005, Neumayer 2005). Ireland's recognition rates are low in comparison with other EU member states. Eurostat's (the European Union's statistical office) most recent full-year statistics for asylum recognition are for 2010. In that year Ireland gave judgement on 1,600 applications for asylum, and granted 1.6 per cent of them (in other words, it conferred refugee status or gave humanitarian leave to stay in 25 cases). In Belgium the rate was 21.6 per cent, in Denmark 41 per cent and Finland 37 per cent (Eurostat 2011: 10). In the first quarter of 2012 Ireland's rate of positive decisions was 5.8 per cent, while the rates for Belgium, Denmark and Finland were 16.7 per cent, 42.5 per cent and 40.5 per cent respectively (Eurostat 2012: 12).

Although the number of asylum applicants has decreased substantially over the past decade in Ireland, the number of persons living in direct provision has declined much more slowly, because applicants tend to spend a long time in the system. The RIA, a functional unit within the Department of Justice and Equality, reports that the average length of stay in direct provision is just over three and a half years, and 2,997 (60 per cent) of the current residents have lived in direct provision accommodation for over three years (RIA 2012: 20). At the end of May 2012 there were 4,949 people living in direct provision (RIA 2012). Most of these were adults between the ages of eighteen and forty-five, but 35 per cent of all residents were children, with 1,733 under eighteen and 1,581 under twelve (32 per cent of the direct provision population) (RIA 2012). For anyone, but particularly for children, spending long periods of time in an institutional environment is difficult. Arnold (2012) has researched children in direct provision accommodation. She questions the negative impact on their well-being and the risks they face, in the context of both the UNCRC and *Children First: National Guidance for the Protection and Welfare of Children*. She concludes that 'Direct Provision is an example of a government policy which has not only bred discrimination, social exclusion, enforced poverty and neglect, but has placed children at a real risk' (Arnold 2012: 7).

Direct provision accommodation is provided in thirty-seven centres across seventeen counties in the state. Seven of the centres are state-owned and the remainder are contracted from private property owners, They include buildings which were originally 'hotels, guesthouses (bed & breakfast), hostels, former convents/nursing homes, a holiday camp and a mobile home site' (RIA 2012: 14). The centres are run by private firms on behalf of the Department of Justice and Equality. There are no statutory regulations or inspections to ensure appropriate standards of service. The RIA has responsibility for the system of direct provision and has published a code of practice for persons working in accommodation centres, but it does not appear to take a role in monitoring the implementation of the guidelines. In fact the RIA guidelines state that '[w]here these guidelines are not being observed by persons working in accommodation centres this should be addressed by contacting the management of the centre' (RIA 2005: 6). Those who live in direct provision are vulnerable people, and without independent monitoring they are exposed to an undue risk of poor treatment. Arnold points to 'the long list of complaints, grievances and child protection concerns reported by the residents, children, non-governmental organisations and support agencies' (2012: 7).

Ireland's management of asylum seekers through direct provision is not unique, as other member states of the European Union pursue similar policies. The Amsterdam Treaty was a move towards the harmonisation of refugee and asylum policies. Under this treaty Ireland has opted out of the minimum standards for the reception of asylum seekers (because they allow asylum seekers to work after twelve months, a policy the Irish government does not support), but it follows the overall thrust of EU policies, which is one of control and exclusion (Fanning 2006, Moran 2005). The term 'Fortress Europe' has been applied for many years by refugee analysts and even the office of the UNHCR. The measures used are intended to keep the borders of Europe secure, to combat illegal immigration and deter abuse of the asylum system. They include non-arrival policies, diversion policies, restrictive applications of the Geneva Convention, and deterrent policies (UNHCR 2000) – see Box 9.6. Such measures are deemed to be justified because such a low proportion of asylum seekers are granted refugee status. The UNHCR has suggested EU governments believe most of those who claim asylum are really economic migrants attempting to get into European Union via the asylum process (UNHCR 2000). The problem with this approach is its heavy-handedness. Even those who have a genuine right to refugee status have to surmount huge obstacles to prove their case. Often the primary obstacle is to get into a European country in order to make an asylum claim.

Box 9.6

Policies to Control Illegal Immigration and Abuse of Asylum Systems by the European Union

- Non-arrival policies – prevention of 'aliens' from entering Europe by using visa restrictions and carrier sanctions
- Diversion policies – shifting responsibilities for assessing asylum seekers to countries surrounding Europe
- Restrictive applications of the 1951 Geneva Convention – to exclude certain categories of claimants from the scope of the refugee definition
- Deterrent measures – increased use of detention, denial of social assistance, and restriction of access to employment

(*Source:* UNHCR 2000)

The *Céad Míle Fáilte* (One Hundred Thousand Welcomes)

The context in which Irish immigration and asylum policy operates goes beyond national policy-making, for as we have seen, it is rooted within a broader EU policy framework. EU immigration and asylum policy has been described by its critics primarily as one of exclusion, through the use of terms like 'Fortress Europe'. What does this mean for those immigrants and asylum seekers who have successfully gained access to member states like Ireland? In Ireland we have long believed and taken pride in the notion that we extend a *céad míle fáilte* (one hundred thousand welcomes) to strangers. Yet any examination of Ireland's history and approach to those who seek protection or who enter the state as economic migrants suggests that the welcome is not always as fulsome as we would like to believe.

For instance, it is argued that Ireland was far from generous in its response to those escaping Hitler's Germany and Franco's Spain (Fanning 2012, Ward 1996). After Ireland joined the

United Nations in 1956, one of its earliest international actions was to accept a group of Hungarian refugees. This turned out to be an unmitigated disaster, and the refugees received such poor treatment that they went on hunger strike. Eventually the group were relocated to Canada (Ward 1996). This was not an isolated incident (Moran 2005). Ireland's policy approach to immigrants, refugees and asylum seekers has consistently emphasised control and restriction, and as a result has limited their opportunities to participate fully in Irish society.

Box 9.7

Refugee Resettlement Programme

One of the positive aspects of Irish refugee policy has been its resettlement programme. Ireland joined the UNHCR-led reset-tlement programme in 1998, when the Irish government agreed to admit ten applicants and their immediate families (approxi-mately 40 people) each year for resettlement in Ireland. This increased to 200 people per year in 2005. The UNHCR reset-tlement programme, carried out in partnership with a number of countries around the world, provides a settlement solution for people who are deemed to be in 'protracted refugee situations'. In other words there is little hope of return to their country of origin or settlement in the country in which they find themselves as refugees. Long-term resettlement is offered by 26 countries, including Ireland.

Since the Irish resettlement programme began, 1,043 people have been resettled in different parts of Ireland from 30 different countries. The biggest groups (over 100) have been Democratic Republic Congolese, Iranian Kurds, Burma-Karen and Suda-nese. The Office for the Promotion of Migrant Integration has a resettlement team that works to support the integration of the refugees. Resettlement work is carried out at local level through the county and city development boards.

(*Source*: Information from the website of the Office for the Promotion of Migrant Integration – see useful websites at the end of this chapter)

Yet a number of policy decisions and programmes suggest that the Irish state recognises the vulnerability of immigrants, refugees and asylum seekers. Specific policies for these groups are set out in key economic and social programmes such as the National Development Plans and social partnership agreements from 2002. They are also listed among the 'vulnerable groups' in the government's national anti-poverty strategies (Government of Ireland 2002a), but none of these initiatives can be regarded as convincing (see Fanning 2011). The National Action Plan Against Racism might have been significant, but it was relatively short-lived (2005–2008), and although teachers were appointed to schools to support the English language development of immigrant children, their number has been reduced. Quinn (2008) writes that integration support was available only to refugees prior to 2006. From 2006 funding was made available to support policies aimed at the integration of the broader immigrant community. In 2007 a Minister of State for Integration was appointed, with the subsequent establishment of the Office of the Minister for Integration. One of this office's achievements was the publication in 2008 of *Migration Nation*, a policy statement on the direction of integration policy in Ireland – see Box 9.8.

Box 9.8

Migration Nation – Statement on Integration and Diversity Management

Five key principles underpin the integration policy outlined in *Migration Nation*:

- A partnership approach between government and non-governmental organisations as well as civil society
- A link between social inclusion policies and strategies
- A public focus to avoid parallel communities and ghettoes in urban areas – this requires a mainstream approach to providing services for immigrants
- A commitment to effective local delivery of services aligning the needs of immigrants and local host communities

> • A funding plan for integration is aimed at local authorities, sporting organisations, faith-based groups and political parties
> (*Source*: Office of the Minister for Integration 2008)

The Fine Gael/Labour government, elected in March 2011, did not renew the position of a minister with specific responsibility for integration. Responsibility for integration matters was transferred to the Office for the Promotion of Migrant Integration, an office within the Department of Justice and Equality (Joyce 2012). The Programme for Government made a commitment to reform immigration, residency and asylum procedures and to bring greater transparency to the appeals system. There was also a commitment to promote social inclusion and greater participation of ethnic minorities in all aspects of life in Ireland (Joyce 2012). There is as a sense of *déjà vu* with these policy commitments. Since immigration policy became an issue of concern with the rise of asylum applications in late 1990s the efforts have been ad hoc, short-term and lack an overall policy direction of real benefit to immigrants, refugees and asylum seekers.

An analysis of policy developments in the first decade of this century, including the National Development Plans, social partnership agreements and anti-poverty strategies, shows there was a lack of consistency and implementation (SONAS DP 2005). There are questions about the extent to which government was ever committed to addressing immigration, and particularly asylum issues, through the partnership process which underpinned the policy decision-making approach during this time (Fanning 2011, Hardiman 2006). As a result many from these new communities remain marginalised within Irish society and vulnerable to poverty and racism. Fanning accurately observes that 'many of the barriers of integration that immigrants must reckon with are those either imposed deliberately or permitted by the host society' (2011: 185).

Box 9.9

Separated Children Seeking Asylum (Also Called Unaccompanied Minors)

A group of asylum seekers not referred to in the body of the chapter are separated children seeking asylum. 'Separated children are children under 18 years of age who are outside their country of origin and separated from both parents or their previous legal/customary caregiver' (Separated Children in Europe Programme 2004:2). Approximately 3,000 separated children came to Ireland over the past decade to seek asylum and were placed in the care of the HSE (Barnardos 2011). At the peak in 2001, 1,085 children sought asylum, but the number was as low as 105 in 2011 (Fitzgerald 2012a). 'There is no dedicated instrument dealing with unaccompanied minors in Ireland' (Joyce and Quinn 2009: 20). However, under Section 8(5)(a) of the Refugee Act 1996 an immigration officer must inform the HSE if a child presents as unaccompanied. Then the provisions of the Child Care Act 1991 are invoked to provide for the welfare of the child. Children under twelve were routinely placed with foster parents but those over twelve were mostly placed in privately run hostel-type accommodation, which was outside of the normal children's residential inspection system.

This practice has been roundly criticised for treating separated children at lesser standards than Irish children in need of state protection (Fanning 2011, Joyce and Quinn 2009, Mullally 2011). Joyce and Quinn (2009: 20) refer to Ireland's obligation under the UN Convention on the Rights of the Child to give unaccompanied minors the same protection as Irish minors deprived of a family environment. Ireland's record of caring for separated children has been a cause for concern over many years, highlighted by the fact that '[a]n estimated 503 separated children have gone missing from state care since 2000 and 441 of those remain missing'. The presumption is that many of these children have fallen prey to human traffickers, 'primarily for the purposes of sexual exploitation' (Mullally 2011: 635). Problems with the lack of after-care for young asylum seekers who have 'aged out' (turned eighteen years) also persist (Crosscare 2010, Mullally 2011). A commitment to improve the service for separated children began with the implementation of the HSE's Equity of Care

Policy in late 2009, to give separated children equal treatment in care with Irish children. This resulted in a commitment to close all hostel-type accommodation, increase the number of foster carers for those over twelve years, and have services come under the state's statutory inspection system (Mullally 2011). Joyce (2012) reports that all separated children have been cared for in foster homes or residential services since the closure of hostel accommodation.

Conclusion

The nature of migration has changed in a globalised world, where the flows of people take a variety of forms – for purposes of education, trade, economic migration, asylum, trafficking and leisure. Yet the movement from poorer countries to wealthier ones tends to dominate the policy debate in the West. The theoretical understanding of migration has tended to focus on individualist and structural explanations (Sales 2007), although there has been a move in recent years to other explanations, such as 'circular migration' (Vertovec 2007).

Irish immigration and asylum policy, a relatively new departure for the Irish state, is firmly locked within a broader EU policy context, although Ireland does maintain a certain independence and distance by excluding itself from some policy commitments. Even where Ireland has not officially entered into policy agreements it has tended to follow the EU line in practice. There appears to be an underlying contradiction in the EU and Irish policy approach to immigration. The attempt to control migrants and asylum seekers contrasts with attempts at the social inclusion of these groups and the establishment of a resettlement programme. This contradictory stance leads to a number of potential problems. A contradictory message is given about migrants, refugees and asylum seekers to the citizens of the European Union, including Ireland. On the one hand they are not welcome, and on the other they are often popularly portrayed as enjoying favourable advantages over locals. A second problem with this approach is that it allows governments to act harshly in defending the integrity of their borders, and at the same time deny immigrants and asylum seekers basic human rights (see FLAC 2009).

Some authors believe this approach is based on ideas of exclusion which are embedded in racism (Bloch and Schuster 2002, Duvell and Jordan 2002, Fanning 2006). This is a controversial position, which governments deny. Yet there is much evidence that immigrants and ethnic minorities (mostly descendants of immigrants) in European countries do worse than their ethnic majority counterparts in comparative studies of social and economic inclusion (Fanning 2006). The social and economic exclusion of immigrants and ethnic minorities is a feature of society not just over a short period, but over decades and through generations. We do not as yet know the long-term significance of Ireland's immigration and asylum policies, but a glance over our shoulders at our European neighbours might give some indication of the likely outcomes.

Further Reading

A small but growing number of people write on immigration and asylum in Ireland. Many are academics, but the small number of non-governmental organisations that work in the areas of immigration and asylum has contributed enormously to the available materials. Statistical information is available from various governmental agencies and departments.

Essential Documents

Unlike other policy areas, government policy documents in the field of migration and asylum are very limited, essentially to legislation and a small number of reports and strategy documents.

Refugee Act 1996 – the URL is for the original Act which has been amended in subsequent legislation: www.irishstatutebook.ie/1996/en/act/pub/0017/index.html

Immigration Act 1999: www.irishstatutebook.ie/1999/en/act/pub/0022/index.html

Illegal Immigrants (Trafficking) Act 2000: www.irishstatutebook.ie/2000/en/act/pub/0029/print.html

Immigration Act 2003: www.irishstatutebook.ie/2003/en/act/pub/0026/index.html

Immigration Act 2004: /www.irishstatutebook.ie/2004/en/act/pub/0001/print.html

Immigration, Residence and Protection Bill 2010: www.oireachtas.ie/documents/bills28/bills/2010/3810/b3810d.pdf

Integration: A Two Way Process (2000) is a report on the integration of refugees by an Interdepartmental Working Group established by the DJELR: www.integration.ie/website/omi/omiwebv6.nsf/page/AXBN-7WMK3Z1533318-en/$File/INTEGRATION%20-%20A%20Two%20Way%20Process.pdf

Migration Nation (2008) Statement on integration strategy and diversity management: www.integration.ie/website/omi/omiwebv6.nsf/page/AXBN-7SQDF91044205-en/$File/Migration%20Nation.pdf

General Reading

The most prolific Irish author and academic in the area of immigration, asylum and racism is Professor Bryan Fanning of University College Dublin (UCD). His three best known books are published by Manchester University Press: *Immigration and Social Cohesion in the Republic of Ireland* (2011), *Immigration and Social Change in the Republic of Ireland* (2007) which he edited, and *Racism and Social Change in the Republic of Ireland*, second edition (2012).

A very good book which discusses Britain and its immigration and refugee policies, but is of use to Irish students, is Rosemary Sales's *Understanding Immigration and Refugee Policy: Contradictions and Continuities*(2007).

The European Migration Network (EMN), whose Irish partner is the Economic and Social Research Institute, publishes research and information on an ongoing basis. Its *Annual Policy Report on Migration and Asylum* is an excellent review of developments in both Ireland and the European Union. The most recent report for 2011 was written by Corona Joyce (see bibliography for details). The Office of the Refugee Applications Commissioner (ORAC) and the Reception and Integration Agency (RIA) are Irish government sources of information on asylum and refugees and give the most up-to-date information on the number of asylum applications and direct provision.

Translocations: Migration and Social Change is an Irish online journal that addresses migration issues, supported by a number of Irish universities and migration agencies: www.translocations.ie/

FLAC, ICI, Integration Centre, the Irish Refugee Council, MRCI and NASC are non-governmental organisations that have contributed greatly to the research literature on immigration in Ireland, refugees and asylum seekers. It is worth visiting the publication section of their websites.

Useful Websites

European Migration Network (Ireland – ESRI) – www.emn.ie/
Galway Refugee Support Group – www.grsg.ie/
Immigrant Council of Ireland – www.immigrantcouncil.ie/
International Organization for Migration (Ireland) – www.iomdublin.org/
Irish Refugee Council – www.irishrefugeecouncil.ie/
Migrants Rights Centre Ireland – www.mrci.ie/
NASC – the Irish Immigrant Support Centre (Cork) – www.nascireland.org/
Office for the Promotion of Migrant Integration – www.integration.ie/
Office of the Refugee Applications Commissioner – www.orac.ie/
Reception and Integration Agency – www.ria.gov.ie/
The Integration Centre – www.integrationcentre.ie/Home.aspx
United Nations High Commissioner for Refugees (Ireland) – www.unhcr.ie/

10

Ambiguity: Ireland's Alcohol and Drugs Policies

Area of Social Care for which this Chapter Is Relevant

Alcohol and drugs play a substantial role in many of Ireland's social problems. Substance use cannot be ignored by social care workers whatever their field of employment. Social care students may obtain placements in drug and alcohol treatment and community prevention projects, and for some, work opportunities are available in this area after qualification.

Key Words in this Chapter

Alcohol, drugs, public health approach, disease model, prohibition, harm reduction, politics, ambiguity, socio-cultural approach

Key Themes in this Chapter

- Understanding the issues
- The extent of alcohol and drug use in Ireland
- The development of alcohol policy in Ireland
- The development of drugs policy in Ireland
- The ambiguity and politics of Irish alcohol and drugs policy

Introduction

We have become accustomed to headlines which characterise the people of Ireland as having an unhealthy relationship with alcohol, something seen as a long-standing feature of Irish life. More recently the increased prominence of illicit drug use in Irish society has also gained headline notoriety. However, there is an ambivalence towards the use of alcohol in Ireland, which is not so obviously the case with illicit drugs (O'Mahony 2008). Associated with alcohol and drug use are problems that have an enormous impact on Irish society, such as suicide and suicidal behaviour, drunk/drug driving, physical and mental health problems, violence, and relationship and family problems. There are also huge costs to society and the state as a result of alcohol and drug use, through for example the health and criminal justice systems. More broadly there are the costs of the loss of work and study time. There do not appear to be easy solutions to the negative features of alcohol and drug use.

Box 10.1

Addressing Alcohol and Drugs in Chapter 10

In this chapter alcohol and drugs are referred to separately. This is done for ease of writing, as the policy approach to date addresses these issues separately (although this may be about to change in Irish public policy, as we shall see later). The academic literature also tends to treat the two issues in parallel rather than as one (although this was not always the case – see Hunt and Barker 2001).

One of the characteristics of the debate on alcohol and drugs policy in Ireland is the contrary policy stances taken: prohibition of many drugs (O'Mahony 2008), but liberal, market-led arguments dominate alcohol policy (Butler 2009). There is as yet no scope for taking a more liberal approach to drug use and availability in Ireland. Despite many promises by governments over decades to tackle high levels of alcohol consumption, the policy approach remains influenced by economic considerations rather than the professionally determined public health perspective. These contradictory stances (legal consumption of alcohol and illegal use of drugs) lead to the unhelpful implication that one is more of a problem than the other (Loughran 2005).

In attempting to place alcohol and drugs in a policy context, we are confronted with an enormous and complex range of interested parties, interrelated issues, government agencies, cultural beliefs and practices, legislation, policy approaches and agreements. There are also European and global dimensions which are not so apparent in other policy areas. In this chapter it is only possible to touch on some of these matters. This review begins by setting out an understanding of alcohol and drugs which emerged historically through the debate on disease or public health models of addiction. This is followed by an outline of the extent of the alcohol and drugs problems in Ireland. Two substantial sections come next. One covers key policy developments in alcohol policy in Ireland, and the second covers drugs policy. The final section explores the moral and political questions that arise from alcohol and drugs policies.

Understanding the Issues

Societal interest in controlling alcohol and drugs has a long history, with efforts to control alcohol going back to the newly forming urban areas of 'ancient Greece, Mesopotamia, Egypt and Rome' (Babor et al. 2010: 2). According to Babor and colleagues (2010), all kinds of ingenious ways were thought up by rulers and clergy to discourage alcohol-related problems, including the death penalty, the dilution of wine with water before being sold, and supervised festivities. However, it was not until the late eighteenth and early nineteenth centuries, with the emergence of temperance movements and modern medicine, that a shift developed towards a social policy approach to alcohol. Loughran (2005) also points to the temperance movement and the medical profession as being influential in how drugs policy emerged in the United States, the United Kingdom and Ireland. Walsh (1987) traces concern over drinking in Ireland back at least two and half centuries, noting reference to the seriousness of the problem by one writer in 1738. Butler (2002) says that people with alcohol problems during the nineteenth century in Great Britain and Ireland were accommodated and managed in the public lunatic asylums. It might be expected that the emergence of the temperance movement and the influence of the medical profession, with their emphasis on individual responsibility for addiction, encouraged the pursuit of policies based on a disease model. However, Butler (2002) says that this was

227

not the case, and argues that the estimated 10 per cent of admissions to asylums for alcohol-related problems by the end of the nineteenth century were not encouraged by public authorities. He concludes that public policy-makers had not 'developed a coherent ideological vision of alcoholism as a specific and treatable disease' (2002: 20). In fact the opposite occurred, when a government committee of the newly formed Irish Free State, the Intoxicating Liquor Commission of 1925:

> firmly rejected the idea that drinking problems should be conceptualised as diseases or that therapeutic institutions had a major role to play in societal management of drinking problems. Instead, the commission accepted public health arguments that the prevalence of drinking problems was a direct function of public access to alcohol and, on this basis, it recommended the retention of licensing and other control systems insofar as the electorate would tolerate controls. (Butler 2002: 20)

Box 10.2

The Disease (Curative) Versus the Public Health (Preventive) Models of Addiction

The disease model of addiction suggests that there is nothing inherently wrong with alcohol or drugs. Rather it is vulnerable individuals, with a predisposition to the disease, who become addicted, and they need to be treated and cured of their disease. The public health model believes that it is the extent of the availability of these substances that leads to addiction. The problem of addiction goes beyond the individual, it is a societal problem. Reduce the availability of alcohol and drugs, a preventive approach, and there will be less misuse of these substances and consequently less addiction.

And yet, as Walsh (1987) points out, Ireland's public policy on alcohol follows closely the trajectory of other countries, such as the United Kingdom and the United States. In the United States after prohibition ended, the 'concept of alcoholism as a discrete disease' was promoted, based on a so-called 'new scientific approach' (Butler 2002: 20, 21), and this view influenced Irish policy too. This approach also became the cornerstone of the WHO view on alcohol in the 1950s, as it too was influenced by the United States. Side by side with a shift to the disease concept of alcoholism, there was an opening up of the regulated availability of alcohol in many countries which had previously been prohibitionist, such as North America and Scandinavian countries (Babor et al. 2010). This approach follows what Babor and colleagues claim is 'the fact that most policymaking during the past century has been incremental, deliberate, and respectful of people's right to drink in moderation' (2010: 2).

Ireland's move towards the disease model of alcoholism was enshrined in legislation by the Mental Treatment Act 1945. Butler (2002) analyses the part of the 1945 Act relevant to alcoholism and drug addiction, and suggests the legislation was not initially intended to cover addiction, which was inserted at a late stage of its passage through the Oireachtas (Irish parliament). Butler argues that the references to addiction were not part of a thought-out policy, and speculates whether they would have been included if the Irish Medical Association had not intervened. One of the consequences of what Walsh (1987: 748) calls the 'medicalisation' of alcoholism was an increased number of admissions to psychiatric hospitals of people with alcohol problems.

The disease concept of alcoholism became very popular among the public, medical profession and policy-makers (Butler 2002), and it was not until the 1990s that a public health policy approach began to take precedence over it (Butler 2009). This trend was promoted by the WHO (1978) in its report of the Alma-Ata conference, *Health for All by the Year 2000*, and the *Ottawa Charter for Health Promotion* (WHO 1986), but Irish public policy was slow to follow it. Butler characterises the period from 1945 as an 'incremental drift towards an alcohol policy where the disease concept was dominant' (2002: 104), and claims that efforts to move towards a public health or health promotion model were frustrated by a lack of political will and the lack of public demand for a change in approach.

International drugs control began in 1912 with the International Opium Convention in The Hague, but it was not until the

1960s that Irish health authorities became concerned about illicit drugs (Butler 2002). Although it is a relatively new phenomenon in Ireland, drug use was seen as similar to alcohol in one respect: it was constructed 'as primarily an issue of medical concern' (Loughran 2005: 301). According to Loughran this 'was to deny the socio-cultural and socio-economic nature of the predomi- nance of drug problems in economically deprived communities' (2005: 301). However, drug use and addiction were not handled with the ambivalence that characterised alcohol policy. The primary response to drug use is prohibition (O'Mahony 2008) and exclusion (Loughran 2005). O'Mahony argues that the Irish authorities' attitude to drugs in the 1970s and 1980s 'was undoubtedly influenced by the American thinking of that era. In particular, this recognised a need to combine 'cops' and 'docs' approaches within a 'general prohibitionist framework' (2008: 82). In other words drugs usage was prohibited through the 'cops' or law enforcement, but there was also a treatment dimension, the 'docs'. The initial Irish legislation on drugs, the Misuse of Drugs Act 1977 (Government of Ireland 1977), shows this dual tendency. We will return to Irish policy developments on alcohol and drugs, but first the chapter explores the extent of alcohol and drug use in Ireland.

The Extent of Alcohol and Drug Use in Ireland

For ease of explanation we shall look first at alcohol then at drugs use.

The Extent of Alcohol Use

Box 10.3

Measuring Consumption of Alcohol

- 'Alcohol consumption is defined as annual sales of pure alcohol in litres per person aged 15 years and over' (OECD 2011: 52).
- 'Per capita [per person] consumption is a good indicator of alcohol-related harm in a country. International evidence

> indicates that the higher the average consumption of alcohol at the individual level and in a population, the higher the incidence of alcohol-related problems for both' (National Substance Misuse Strategy Steering Group 2012: 63).

Irish adults consume a lot of alcohol by international standards; in 2009 Ireland was in tenth place out of forty OECD countries (OECD 2011). The National Substance Misuse Strategy Steering Group (NSMSSG) (2012) reports that alcohol consumption in Ireland increased by 192 per cent between 1960 and 2001, from an average of 4.9 litres of pure alcohol per person to 14.3 litres. From this peak, consumption per person reduced to 11.9 litres of pure alcohol in 2010, 145 per cent higher than in 1960 (NSMSSG 2012: 63). In the large-scale SLÁN Survey (survey of lifestyle, attitude and nutrition) carried out in 2007, four in five Irish adults reported that they drank alcohol. This proportion has not changed since the first SLÁN Survey in 1998 (Morgan et al. 2009). Ireland had 19 per cent of non-drinkers, lower than the European average of 25 per cent. More women drink in Ireland than in other European countries, 77 per cent in comparison with 68 per cent, although women are more likely not to drink than men (23 per cent against 15 per cent) (Morgan et al. 2009).

One in ten drinkers reported that they drank more than recommended weekly alcohol limit, twenty-one standard drinks for men and fourteen standard drinks for women. The survey asked questions on harmful drinking patterns, and the authors concluded that 56 per cent of drinkers have habits which require attention (Morgan et al. 2009). High alcohol intake can lead to 'health and social consequences such as increased risk of heart, stroke and vascular diseases, as well as liver cirrhosis and certain cancers' (OECD 2011: 52). The possible social consequences include an increased risk of suicide, as well as greater violence, possible disability and homicide (OECD 2011).

Adult alcohol consumption is not the only matter of concern for policy-makers; much of the concern about alcohol use in Ireland is directed at children and young people. Long and Mongan (2010) review two sources of estimates on the use of alcohol among young people, ESPAD (European School Survey Project on Alcohol and Other Drugs) and Health Behaviour in

School-Aged Children (HBSC). The findings of these reports are not strictly comparable because they use different age classifications. The HBSC studies in 1998, 2002 and 2006 showed a steady decrease in lifetime use (alcohol used at least once in the lifetime of the young person) and last-month use (which indicates current usage) of alcohol among thirteen-to-sixteen-year-olds but did not report major changes in drunkenness. In comparison, 'the 2007 ESPAD survey shows a large decrease in drunkenness compared to the 1999 and 2003 figures' (Long and Mongan 2010: 7). The HBSC figures showed a consistently high level of lifetime use among seventeen-year-olds – see Table 10.1.

Table 10.1: Lifetime Use of Alcohol among 13–17-Year-Old School-Goers, from HBSC 1998, 2002 and 2006

Year of Study	13 Years	14 Years	15 Years	16 Years	17 Years
1998	65.6	72.0	83.0	87.0	85.1
2002	52.1	63.0	78.5	85.6	89.6
2006	43.1	57.0	69.9	78.0	85.6

Source: Long and Mongan (2010: 7).

The latest HBSC report for 2010 (Kelly et al. 2012) confirms the previous trends of continuing lower alcohol usage among school-aged children. The number of school-aged children who had never had an alcoholic drink increased from 47 per cent in 2006 to 54 per cent in 2010. There was also a fall in the number of children who reportedly drank in the last month, down from 26 per cent to 21 per cent (Kelly et al. 2012). On drunkenness the HBSC 2010 report found the proportion who had ever been 'really drunk' fell from 32 per cent to 28 per cent. There are age, gender and class differences, with older boys from lower social class groups more likely to have been drunk in their lifetime (Kelly et al. 2012).

Box 10.4

Binge Drinking

Binge drinking is defined by Morgan and colleagues (2009: 15) as the consumption of 'six or more standard drinks on one occasion at least once a week'.

A standard drink is 'a half pint or a glass of beer, lager or cider; a single measure of spirits; a single glass of wine, sherry or port; or a bottle of alcopop (long neck)' (Morgan et al. 2009: 3).

This definition of binge drinking is not without its critics (see Furnham 2004 for a review of the debate on this issue).

Ireland differs from most other countries in the level of 'binge' drinking. This not a neutral term, as MacLachlan and Smyth (2004) point out: it is associated particularly with the apparently uncontrollable drinking habits of young people. Yet there is evidence that a significant proportion of Irish adults binge drink too: about a quarter of all drinkers in the 30–65 age group (Morgan et al. 2009). Morgan and colleagues (2009) found that 28 per cent of the drinking behaviour of all drinkers fell into the category of binge drinking, with men (38 per cent) more likely to binge drink than women (17 per cent). Younger drinkers (40 per cent of 18- to 29-year-olds) and those from lower socio-economic groups (34 per cent) are more likely to binge drink than older people and those from higher socio-economic groups.

Research by Dooley and Fitzgerald (2012) confirmed high levels of binge drinking among young adults. They recorded 36 per cent of 18- to 19-year-olds binge drinking on a weekly basis, with the level highest for 20- to 21-year-olds at 39 per cent, and with 22- to 23-year-olds at 33 per cent (2012: 79). Binge drinking among 24- to 25-year-olds fell to 29 per cent. Morgan and colleagues (2009: 13) refer to studies which conclude that there is a relationship between the drinking habits of young people and their adult drinking behaviours. The age of onset of drinking and drinking patterns in adolescence influence later binge drinking, as well as levels of alcohol consumption in adulthood and alcohol dependence.

The Extent of Drugs Use

Ireland came late to illicit drugs use, and when drugs did arrive in the 1960s (Butler 2002), it was regarded primarily as a Dublin-centred problem. As Loughran (2005) points out, it was a very specific problem located in poorer areas of the capital city. It was not until the early 1980s that the use of heroin in Dublin reached 'epidemic' levels (Mayock 2001: 83). Over the follow-ing two decades drug use spread beyond the capital to every urban and rural area in Ireland. Although traditionally associ-ated with social and economic disadvantage, drug use became 'increasingly recognised as a widespread social phenomenon and is clearly no longer confined to marginalised communities' (Mayock 2001: 83).

The possession of all illicit drugs even for personal use is legally banned in Ireland. Therefore public policy problematises all such drug users, even those who use drugs for recreational purposes and do not have a dependence on them (Loughran 2005). The main thrust of international drugs policy is prohibi-tionist (O'Mahony 2008), and this has a profound impact on the nature of the drugs trade, production, distribution and sales. Of course, it also leads to clandestine drug use.

It is very difficult to get accurate estimates of drug usage, because of the lack of monitoring and data collection systems in some countries and the cost of large-scale surveys (see European Monitoring Centre for Drugs and Drug Addiction (EMCDDA) 2011a: 9). Ireland, as a member of the European Union, provides information on drugs use through the Reitox Irish Focal Point, which is located within the HRB, to EMCDDA. EMCDDA publishes EU data on drugs use each year (see EMCDDA 2011a, 2011b). Separately the Reitox also publishes this information annually. The annual report provides an update on the various aspects of drugs policy and developments in Ireland, as well as the most recent information on trends in drugs use, includ-ing summaries of recent research on drugs use undertaken in Ireland (Irish Focal Point 2011).

Box 10.5

Measuring Prevalence (Use) of Drugs

The standard measurement for drugs prevalence used in EU and Irish research is through the following three categories:

- Lifetime prevalence – this records use of drugs at least once in a lifetime
- Last year use – this records the use of drugs at least once in the past year, and so indicates recent use
- Last month use – this measurement is the closest we can get to measuring current use of drugs, which does not necessarily mean regular use (NACD and PHIRB 2012: 4)

References to the 'adult population' when measuring drug use mean the fifteen to sixty-four years age group, and references to young adults are those in the fifteen to thirty-four age group.
All drugs prevalence figures are estimates only.

'Cannabis remains Europe's most popular illicit drug' (EMCDDA 2011a: 16). It is estimated that 23.2 per cent or 78 million adults in Europe have used cannabis at least once in their lifetime. Last-month use for cannabis is 3.6 per cent (twelve million adults) (EMCDDA 2011a: 15). According to EMCDDA (2011a) the second most used illicit drug in Europe is cocaine, with an estimated 4.3 per cent of the adult population having used it at least once in their lifetime, and a last-month use of 0.5 per cent (1.5 million adults). The other three main categories of drugs used are amphetamines, ecstasy and opioids, with a lifetime prevalence of 3.8 per cent, 3.2 per cent and 0.4 per cent respectively. Those who use opioids, which includes heroin, make up more than 50 per cent of all requests for drugs treatment. It is also the primary drug type associated with drugs-related deaths – found in 75 per cent of the 7,600 deaths recorded. In Europe in 2009 there were also approximately 700,000 opioid users receiving substitute treatment (EMCDDA 2011a: 15). There are signs of stability in drugs use in the European Union, but during the past decade a new challenge arose with the emergence of psychoactive drugs available through head shops and online (EMCDDA 2011a).

The most recent survey on drug use in Ireland was published in 2012. The All-Ireland survey of 2010/2011 on drugs prevalence was carried out by the National Advisory Committee on Drugs (NACD) in Ireland and the Public Health Information and Research Branch (PHIRB) in Northern Ireland. It is the third survey in the series, with the first two undertaken in the years 2002/3 and 2006/7. Table 10.2 shows lifetime, last-year and last-month prevalence of illegal drugs use among adults during the three survey periods. While there was significant overall growth in lifetime illegal drugs use between 2002/3 and 2010/11, the increase in last-year and last-month use was not as great. Men are more likely to use illegal drugs than women: lifetime prevalence is 35.5 per cent for men and 19 per cent for women (NACD and PHIRB 2012).

Table 10.2: Lifetime, Last Year and Last Month Prevalence of Illegal Drug Use in Ireland among the Adult Population

Prevalence	2002/3 %	2006/7 %	2010/11 %
Lifetime	18.5	24.0	27.2
Last year	5.6	7.2	7.0
Last month	3.0	2.9	3.2

Source: NACD and PHIRB (2012: 60–2).

The trend of drugs use in Ireland reflects the general European trend. As in Europe, the Irish survey indicates that cannabis is the illicit drug most used by the adult population in Ireland, with an estimated lifetime prevalence of 25.3 per cent in 2010/11, while 2.8 per cent had used cannabis in the last month (NACD and PHIRB 2012). The overall lifetime prevalence for cannabis increased by 8 per cent in 2002/3, but the last-month use showed a smaller increase from the 2.6 per cent estimated in the previous two surveys. The lifetime prevalence of cocaine more than doubled between 2002/3 and 2010/11 from 3 per cent to 6.8 per cent (NACD and PHIRB 2012). The last month use has remained consistent over the three survey periods, and was estimated at 0.5 per cent in 2010/11, which again is very much in keeping with EU trends. Ecstasy also figures highly in the Irish surveys: 6.9 per cent of respondents in 2010/11 had used it at least once, and 0.1 per cent had used it in the last month. In comparison heroin had a lifetime prevalence of 0.8 per cent in 2010/11 and a last-month use of 0.1 per cent (NACD and PHIRB 2012). Interestingly the 2010/11 survey showed an expanded 'other opiates' category, which was heavily used. This includes a number of commonly prescribed and over-the-counter medicines, such as morphine and codeine-based medicines. The lifetime prevalence of use was 38.8 per cent, with 14.2 per cent last month use. Sedatives, tranquillisers and anti-depressants, which are legally prescribed, were also included in the survey, with significant levels of use (NACD and PHIRB 2012).

As with alcohol, policy-makers pay particular attention to young people's use of drugs. The upward trend in cannabis use in the first decade of the twenty-first century by school-aged children and young people has been reversed according to the HBSC 2010 report (Kelly et al. 2012). A reported 16 per cent of respondents had used cannabis in the twelve months prior to the study in 2006, but this figure had dropped by half to 8 per cent in 2010. Boys (10 per cent) are more likely to use cannabis than girls (6 per cent), and there is an increasing level of use as boys get older, with 1 per cent of ten- to eleven-year-olds report using cannabis compared with 17 per cent of seventeen-year-olds (Kelly et al. 2012). The *My World Study* by Dooley and Fitzgerald (2012) confirms the gender (16 per cent males to 9 per cent females) and age (2 per cent first-year students and 26 per cent sixth-year students) differences in cannabis use. The *My World Study* reported that cannabis use increases after school to 45 per cent (Dooley and Fitzgerald 2012). The authors found that '[a] shift occurs around the ages of 18–19, where for the first time young people are more likely to have smoked cannabis (34%)' and this rises to 58 per cent in the 24- to 25-year age group (Dooley and Fitzgerald 2012: 82). The All Ireland Study (NACD and PHIRB 2012) showed an increase in young adults' (15–34 years) drug use over the periods of their three reports, 2002/3, 2006/7 and 2010/11 – see Table 10.3 – although at a slower pace between the second and third surveys.

Table 10.3: Lifetime, Last Year and Last Month Prevalence of Illegal Drug Use in Ireland among the Young Adult Population

Prevalence	2002/3 %	2006/7 %	2010/11 %
Lifetime	25.9	31.4	35.7
Last year	9.8	12.2	12.3
Last month	5.2	5.0	5.3

Source: NACD and PHIRB (2012: 60–2).

If you compare Table 10.3 with Table 10.2, you will see that young adults use more drugs than the adult population as a whole. This is true for a range of drugs, so for example the adult lifetime use of cannabis was 25.3 per cent in 2010/11 in comparison with 33.4 per cent for the fifteen to thirty-four age group. The last month prevalence of cannabis use was 2.8 per cent for the adult population overall and 4.5 per cent for the young adult age group (NACD and PHIRB 2012). There are also differences between young men and young women's use of drugs.

The Development of Alcohol Policy in Ireland

As was noted earlier in this chapter, Irish alcohol policy was based on the disease concept from the mid-1940s until the early 1980s, after which it moved to a public health model. This shift in Irish policy has not been an easy one, and has continuously been confronted with resistance. The medical profession was initially slow to accept the new approach (Butler 2002). According to Cullen, they are still resistant, and 'the disease model remains substantially embedded within the public, alcohol treatment system' (2011: 259). Other resistance to the public health model comes from the drinks industry and, crucially, the cultural norms and expectations of the Irish public concerning alcohol. Finally, the complex relationship between a host of government departments and agencies adds to a less than coherent public health model (Butler 2002, 2009; Cullen 2011).

Box 10.6

Key Developments in Alcohol Policy in Ireland

- *The Psychiatric Services: Planning for the Future* 1984
- *National Alcohol Policy – Ireland* 1996
- *Strategic Task Force on Alcohol Interim Report* 2002
- *Commission on Liquor Licensing Final Report* 2003
- *Strategic Task Force on Alcohol Second Report* 2004
- *Report of the Government Alcohol Advisory Group* 2008
- Intoxicating Liquor Act 2008
- *Steering Group Report on a National Substance Misuse Strategy* 2012

Planning for the Future (Department of Health 1984) was the first policy document to challenge the understanding of alcoholism as a disease. Instead it promoted the by then widely accepted perspective of the WHO that alcohol-related problems are related to levels of consumption within the population. *Planning for the Future* concluded that prevention was the best way to address the problem of alcohol misuse in Ireland, rather than developing treatment programmes (Department of Health 1984). It took a further twelve years for Ireland's first national plan on alcohol to emerge. The *National Alcohol Policy – Ireland* was published in 1996. This was followed by a number of policy documents and related legislation in the next decade (see Box 10.6). The documents recorded the trends in alcohol consumption and its adverse health and social significance, and showed why alcohol was of serious concern to policy-makers throughout the period. They also emphasised the public health approach which, at least on paper, was the focus of public policy.

A number of documents called for a national strategy on alcohol. Other regularly occurring themes were individual awareness of alcohol use, treatment, prevention, and the relationship between alcohol and driving. 'Environmental strategies', as they are called in the 1996 *National Alcohol Policy – Ireland* strategy, such as controlling licensing, advertising, promotion, sponsorship, taxation, opening hours of pubs and off-licences, also received attention. However, despite numerous reports and this apparent concerted effort to address Ireland's alcohol problem, the sum of the parts did not quite add up to an effective policy approach. Butler says 'that for almost 30 years the ideal of a national alcohol policy ... has been presented repeatedly and with increasing coherence by public health advocates in Ireland' and yet he concludes that there is not 'any evidence of anything other than nominal political support for . . . [its] implementation' (2009: 350).

It remains to be seen if the latest policy document, the *Steering Group Report on a National Substance Misuse Strategy* (NSMSSG 2012), will significantly advance alcohol policy. It has an unusual twist: a 'substance misuse strategy', it reflects the new policy intention to develop a joint alcohol and drugs policy, which is quite distinct from international standards (EMCDDA 2011a). Otherwise, the *Steering Group Report* covers much of the familiar ground of other reports. The Group was required to review existing policies and reports as part of its brief. Its main recommendations are about alcohol control through the use of pricing strategies; separating alcohol from other goods in supermarkets and mixed retail outlets (a measure that was already in the Intoxicating Liquor Act 2008 but has never been implemented); reducing advertising's capacity to influence children and young people; and phasing out sponsorship of major events and sporting competitions by 2016 (NSMSSG 2012). The other key feature of the report is that its approach is now based on 'population health', which is a more recent version of the public health approach. Its aim is to reduce the overall consumption of alcohol in Irish society (NSMSSG 2012).

The Development of Drugs Policy in Ireland

As with alcohol policy, drugs policy in Ireland is situated within a complex web of a range of interests, governmental departments and agencies, and public opinion. But unlike alcohol, which is accepted as a legal substance, drugs are illegal in Ireland and drugs policy is located within an overall prohibitionist approach. As a result there is a much greater criminal justice element to addressing drugs issues than there is to alcohol control, which is primarily situated within a health care model. A 'war on drugs' approach is taken, which criminalises all aspects of drug involvement, from its use to manufacturing, distribution and supply (see Murphy 1996, O'Mahony 2008). This adds to the complexity, and as O'Mahony (2008) suggests, to the ambiguity of policy.

Box 10.7

Key Developments in Drugs Policy in Ireland

- *Report of the Working Party on Drug Abuse 1971*
- Misuse of Drugs Act 1977
- Special Government Task Force on Drug Abuse 1983
- Misuse of Drugs Act 1984
- Establishment of the National Coordinating Committee on Drug Abuse 1985
- *Government Strategy for the Prevention of Drug Use 1991*
- Criminal Justice (Drug Trafficking) Act 1996
- Criminal Assets Bureau Act 1996
- Proceeds of Crime Act 1996
- Housing (Miscellaneous Provisions) Act 1997
- Licensing (Combating Drug Abuse) Act 1997
- *First Report of the Ministerial Task Force on Measures to Reduce the Demand for Drugs 1996*
- *Second Report of the Ministerial Task Force on Measures to Reduce the Demand for Drugs 1997*
- Non-Fatal Offences Against the Person Act 1997
- Criminal Justice Act 1999
- *Building on Experience: National Drugs Strategy 2001–2008*
- Criminal Justice Act 2006
- *National Drugs Strategy (Interim) 2009–2016*
- Criminal Justice (Psychoactive Substances) Act 2010
- Criminal Justice (Community Service) Act 2011

In her review of drugs policy development up to the mid-2000s, Loughran (2005) questions whether the understanding of 'addiction' and the subsequent legislative course taken by the state has changed any since the 1960s. Yet, Loughran (2005) and O'Mahony (2008) concur that there has been more activity and an improvement in policy from the mid-1990s. Prior to this period the emphasis was exclusively on prohibition, and little effort was made to address the seriousness of the emerging drugs problem. From the early 1980s this affected poorer areas, particularly in Dublin city, with its grave problems of heroin use and the related conditions of HIV and AIDS (Loughran 2005).

The *Government Strategy for the Prevention of Drug Use* in 1991 was the first of its kind in Ireland, and established a central tenet of drugs policy which was to follow in the two subsequent drugs strategies in 2001 and 2009, a focus on supply and demand reduction. Efforts by the state to discourage the supply of drugs include harsher laws and longer prison sentences for suppliers. Demand reduction is aimed at trying to change individual behaviour to prevent or reduce the need for drugs. This is done, for example, through educational activities and the development of youth services (Loughran 2005).

The 1991 drugs strategy included plans for greater coordination between all interested parties and services involved in addressing the drugs problem. There were also commitments to decentralise drugs services and to develop the role of the general practitioner, as well as to give a greater role to a community-based response to drugs (Loughran 1995). However, Loughran (2005) suggests that this strategy did not work, as the number of people treated for heroin use doubled in the first half of the 1990s. On the other hand research carried out on the shift towards community-based services during this period did offer some hope of an improved treatment response to drugs users (Loughran 2005).

The hugely increased legislative and policy activity from the mid-1990s demonstrates an apparently greater willingness by the state to address the drugs issue. A number of factors contributed to this increased activity: greater public awareness and concern about drugs, increased public protest by communities devastated by drugs, and the murder of a journalist by a drugs gang in 1996 (O'Mahony 2008). The reports of the two Ministerial Task Forces in 1996 and 1997 'marked a turning point for Ireland's drugs policy, with the government recognising for the first time the link between problem drug use and socio-economic disadvantage and the need to involve local communities in tackling the problem' (Pike 2011: 3).

The local drugs task forces, which were to become a feature of the response to the drugs problem, were established as a result of the first Task Force. Improved funding was provided, which supported among other initiatives the establishment of youth projects in targeted geographical areas where drug use was at its worst (Loughran 2005). The implementation of these policy developments was accompanied by a more managerial approach to dealing with the drugs issue, and oversight structures were introduced including a Cabinet committee and other 'cross-cutting bodies' (Randall 2011: 286). It is worth noting that despite the softer elements of drugs policy geared towards harm reduction and treatment, this period also saw 'considerable focus on strengthening law enforcement' (O'Mahony 2008: 310).

The framework established as a result of the Task Force reports in the 1990s continued to provide the basis for policy into the following decade. This is evident in the new *National Drugs Strategy 2001-2008* (Department of Tourism, Sport and Recreation 2001) and its successor the *National Drugs Strategy (Interim) 2009-2016* (Department of Community, Rural and Gaeltacht Affairs 2009). A new feature of the drugs strategies was a number of core pillars for action – supply reduction, prevention, treatment and research (Department of Tourism, Sport and Recreation 2001). A review of the 2001–2008 strategy included a fifth pillar, rehabilitation (Randall 2011). These pillars provide the backbone of the current drugs strategy. The current strategy acknowledges that changes have occurred in the geography of drugs use in Ireland since the publication of the 2001–2008 strategy in 2001, where the primary concern was the heroin problem in Dublin. This has 'ameliorated' but 'this has been offset to a degree by its wider dispersal around the country' (Department of Community, Rural and Gaeltacht Affairs 2009: 5).

The current strategy also highlights concern about the 'misuse' of cocaine. The partnership approach which has already been in place for some years, in the form of drugs task forces at local and regional levels, is to continue as the primary vehicle for implementation of the strategy. To improve coordination of the national drugs strategy, it was recommended that a Ministerial Office for Drugs be established, and this position was subsequently filled. However, when the new Fine Gael–Labour government took office in March 2011 it did not reappoint a minister with responsibility for drugs. Instead it gave the Minister of State with responsibility for Primary Care the 'lead' role in relation to the national drugs strategy, and full responsibility for drugs has been relocated to the Department of Health (Irish Focal Point 2011).

The Ambiguity and Politics of Irish Alcohol and Drugs Policies

The term 'ambiguity' has been used a number of times in this chapter already, but in this section three dimensions to the meaning of ambiguity in relation to alcohol and drugs are developed and placed within broader political and policy debates. An ambiguity exists within policies on alcohol, separately ambiguity exists within policies on drugs, and thirdly there is an ambiguity between policies on alcohol and drugs. We shall deal with each of these ambiguities in turn.

Ambiguity and Alcohol Policy

Alcohol is no ordinary commodity (Babor et al. 2010), and Ireland's efforts to come to terms with this truth are evident through a long and difficult relationship with alcohol. It is a relationship replete with ambiguity. This historical ambiguity towards alcohol at all levels of society, from the general public through to the medical profession and politicians, is well documented (see for example Butler's account, 2002). Two interrelated issues are good examples of the conflictual stances in the policy-making process. First, the major policy documents on alcohol, the two successive national alcohol strategies (Department of Health 1996 and NSMSSG 2012) outline the economic benefits of alcohol consumption and production to the Irish economy. Even to mention this gives rise to ambiguity. On the one hand the documents state that drinking must be cut back, but on the other hand they point to the economic benefits of alcohol to Irish society.

The second ambiguous aspect is that representatives of the drinks industry were members of the Steering Group which produced a *National Substance Misuse Strategy*. The drinks industry disagrees with some elements of the national strategy, and two of its representative groups issued minority reports (Mature Enjoyment of Alcohol in Society (MEAS) 2011, Alcohol Beverage

Federation of Ireland (ABFI) 2012). Having the drinks industry participate in policy-making on alcohol is a trend that has emerged during the past ten years. It is part of what Butler describes as a conflict between *nannies* (promoters of public health) and *neo-liberals* (the advocates of free trade), within the social partnership model of public policy-making in Ireland (2009: 355, emphasis in original). Butler argues that alcohol policy is a political matter, with the state mediating between the public health sector and the alcohol industry, but that despite some victories for the health sector, 'the state has shown no inclination to accept in its entirety the public health perspective' (2009: 355).

Ambiguity and Drugs Policy

There is plenty of proof too of ambiguity in drugs policy in Ireland (Butler 1991, Butler and Mayock 2005, Murphy 1996, O'Mahony 2008), even if the approach to drugs in Ireland is clearly prohibitionist. One example, which Butler and Mayock describe as a 'covert style of policy making' (2005: 415), was the introduction of harm reduction practices without public debate. Needle exchange and locally based drugs services are part of this policy. But it is the provision of a methadone maintenance service which is most ambiguous. O'Mahony observes that 'the fact that methadone maintenance is in essence a form of legalisation goes completely unremarked' (2008: 114). Thousands of heroin users in Ireland take advantage of methadone maintenance, where the state effectively provides an opiate substitute to those who are addicted to heroin.

Ambiguity Between Alcohol and Drugs Policies

Ambiguity is most obvious in the difference between state and public attitudes to these two substances. Although the public and legislators alike accept alcohol is a drug, there is great ambivalence towards this idea. I have already mentioned the comment by Babor and colleagues (2010) that the development of alcohol policy at international level reflects the right of individuals to consume alcohol in moderation. Alcohol may cause problems for some in Irish society, but it is not regarded as an evil in the same moral sense that drugs are evil. State policy towards alcohol takes a primarily public health approach (including control strategies to encourage moderation), but policy towards drugs, at least formally, does not show any such tolerance of moderation, and remains strictly prohibitionist (O'Mahony 2008).

The increasing use of drugs, particularly of cannabis, suggests that despite the official rhetoric and at times the moral outrage of the public, there is a 'relative social acceptability' of certain drug use (Loughran 2005: 308). Even within the criminal justice system there is a 'softer' underbelly in evidence for some aspects of drugs offending. Some offenders can be diverted to a drug treatment court, and prison sentences are not used for first or second-time offences of possessing cannabis for personal use. The Criminal Justice (Community Service) Act 2011 should mean that even fewer drugs offenders go to prison, since those who would previously have been given a sentence of up to twelve months will instead be given community service orders, if they are thought suitable (Government of Ireland 2011b). It is worth noting that half the prison sentences given to drugs offenders in Ireland are for less than twelve months (EMCDDA 2009).

Box 10.8

A Socio-Cultural Model of Alcohol and Drugs Use

The discussion on alcohol and drugs use presented in this chapter has reflected the mainstream policy or 'common sense' (see Hunt and Barker 2001: 183) debate in Ireland. This debate can be characterised in relation to alcohol as a shift from the disease model to a public health model, while for drugs the dominant policy approach has remained prohibitionist. There is however an alternative approach which is not engaged with at a policy level in Ireland, or for that matter in other countries. This is a socio-cultural model based in the social science of anthropology.

Heath (1988) summarises the meaning of the socio-cultural model as it applies to alcohol, but it is equally valid to apply the model to drugs use. He says the socio-cultural model encompasses:

> [T]he widely accepted proposition that different beliefs and attitudes about alcohol and its effects, combined with beliefs and attitudes about how, what, where, when and with whom one should (or should not) drink, together with attitudes about the meaning of all of those, are directly related to the frequency with which problems are associated with drinking, and to differences in the nature of such problems when they occur, in various cultures.
>
> (Heath 1988: 359)

In other words, the meaning given to our views on alcohol and drugs use is socially constructed, reflecting the practices, beliefs and attitudes about these substances in different societies. This argument was first made almost twenty years earlier by Mandelbaum, who argued that 'alcohol is a cultural artefact in the sense that the drinking of alcohol is almost entirely culturally defined and exists as an entrenched part of culture'(1969, cited in Russell-Bennett, Hogan and Perks 2010: 3). According to the socio-cultural view the common sense approach to these issues ignores the cultural, political and power dimensions of alcohol and drugs use (Heath 1988, Hunt and Barker 2001). Writers from the socio-cultural perspective challenge the public health model for its view that 'alcohol and especially illicit drugs [are] inherently dangerous substances, which unless strongly controlled by enlightened social policy would create problems and entail social and physical costs for the individual and for the society as a whole' (Hunt and Barker 2001: 176).

Heath argues that on a world-wide basis not only is the phenomenon of addiction or dependence on alcohol rare, but in cultures in which alcohol is consumed few drinkers have alcohol-related problems. And where these problems do arise, the 'aspects of the cultural context in which they live often play a major role in the etiology [cause] of their problem' (1988: 398). For Hunt and Barker, 'folk devils' have been created by those who determine the dominant models of understanding alcohol and drugs use, which 'confirm the socially accepted way of viewing drug users and "problem" drinkers as demons'. Such categorisations lead to 'simplistic policy solutions to complex issues' (Hunt and Barker 2001: 183).

Conclusion

Through the first decade of this century the use of alcohol and drugs continued on an upward trend. *Trends in Treated Problem Drug Use in Ireland 2005–2010* from the Health Research Board (Bellerose, Carew and Lyons 2011) shows that that the numbers seeking treatment for harmful drug use increased by 52 per cent between 2005 and 2010. This, the authors say, demonstrates an improvement in the use and availability of drugs treatment, but it also reflects the extent of problem drug use across the country. Alcohol is identified in the data on drug treatment from 2005 to 2010 as the 'main problem substance' for over half (52.7 per cent) of those treated (Carew, Bellerose and Lyons 2011: 1). Both of these reports highlight a number of features of alcohol use in Ireland. First, they confirm the young age at which those who receive treatment began their use of alcohol and drugs. A second feature of problem alcohol and drug use is the dominance of young males. Third, there is a socio-economic dimension: people from poorer backgrounds are more likely to have problems with substance use (Bellerose et al, 2011, Carew et al. 2011; see also Haase and Pratschke 2010).

Some further challenges for policy and practice on drugs and alcohol have not been addressed in this chapter, but deserve a brief mention. The first is the increased levels of polydrug use, where users are mixing a combination of drugs. This complicates preventive and treatment strategies (Bellerose et al. 2011). Second, there was a 'moral panic' in 2010 in Ireland regarding synthetic substances that imitate psychoactive drugs. These were available through head shops and still continue to be available online, but their impact is as yet relatively unknown (EMCDDA 2011a, Kelleher et al. 2011, Ryall and Butler 2011).

There is no easy resolution to the challenges posed by the use of alcohol and drugs in Irish society, or indeed to the ambiguity in this policy area. The use of psychoactive substances is a serious problem for some in Ireland. It obviously has damaging consequences for at least some users, and it is costly for society as a whole. However, the majority of people who use alcohol and drugs do not cause harm to either themselves or others. There is also a further reality, that the use of alcohol and drugs are beneficial for many people (see Hunt and Barker 2001). Surely policy should take into account these different realities, so perhaps it is necessary to reconsider the basis on which policy is conceived. Ireland's policy approach is not unique, as it reflects international perspectives on alcohol and drugs use. This is unsurprising given Ireland's membership of the European Union, and the globalisation of the drugs issue (Jordan and Butler 2011). The 'cops and docs' approach to which O'Mahony (2008) refers still dominates Irish public policy on drugs, while there is a more obviously ambiguous policy on alcohol. We are left to wonder how the latest joint strategy on drugs and alcohol will overcome these inherent ambiguities and move Ireland towards more progressive and enlightened policies on substance use. Given the premise on which the strategy is based, change is very unlikely.

Further Reading

There is an enormous amount of reading material on alcohol and drugs. This can lead to confusion, particularly as much of it consists of rather technical reports. I give some recommendations here – which are of course not exhaustive – for useful and directly relevant material.

Essential Documents

There is no shortage of legislation in this area, particularly on the criminal justice aspects of drug use and supply. The two main Acts are mentioned below; other relevant legislation is outlined in Box 10.7.

Misuse of Drugs Act 1977: www.irishstatutebook.ie/1977/en/act/pub/0012/print.html

Misuse of Drugs Act 1984: www.irishstatutebook.ie/1984/en/act/pub/0018/print.html

Over the years a number of important policy reports, documents and strategies have been published on alcohol and drugs. The documents mentioned here outline the current policy positions on alcohol and drugs. The government has stated an intention to combine the two, but this had not been achieved at the time of writing.

National Drugs Strategy (Interim) 2009–2016: www.drugsan-dalcohol.ie/12388/1/DCRGA_Strategy_2009-2016.pdf

Steering Group Report on a National Substance Misuse Strategy 2012 (although the title is not what might be expected this is actually the national alcohol strategy): http://healthupdate.gov.ie/wp-content/uploads/2012/02/Steering-Group-Report-on-a-National-Substance-Misuse-Strategy-7-Feb-11.pdf

General Reading

Shane Butler from Trinity College Dublin is the most prolific academic writer on drugs and alcohol issues in Ireland. One of his earlier contributions was in *Administration* in 1991, on drug policies in Ireland. Other publications include the book *Alcohol, Drugs and Health Promotion in Modern Ireland* (2002), and an article with Paula Mayock on ambiguity in drug policy in the *International Journal of Drug Policy* (2005).

There are two very provocative books on prohibitionism in Irish drug policy. Tim Murphy's *Rethinking the War on Drugs in Ireland* (1996) and Paul O'Mahony's *The Irish War on Drugs: The Seductive Folly of Prohibition* (2008) argue for a different approach to addressing the drugs issue. Hilda Loughran's chapter on 'Drugs policy' in *Contemporary Irish Social Policy* (2005) gives a good overview of drugs policy up to the early 2000s. An important contribution to the literature on binge drinking in Ireland is Malcolm MacLachlan and Caroline Smyth's edited book *Binge Drinking and Youth Cultures: Alternative Perspectives* (2004).

If you are interested in up-to-date information on any aspect of alcohol and drugs policy in Ireland, the best place to find it is the National Documentation Centre on Drug Research. It is also worth looking up the publications section of the HRB website. All the materials the HRB publishes are available for down-load. Especially recommended is the quarterly bulletin *Drugnet Ireland*, which provides up-to-date articles and summaries of research and policy documents. The NACD website is also an excellent source of research materials. At European level it is important to be familiar with publications from EMCDDA.

I also recommend two relatively recent reports and a book:

NACD and PHIRB, *Drug use in Ireland and Northern Ireland: Drug Prevalence Survey 2010/11: Regional Drug Task Force (Ireland) and Health & Social Care Trust (Northern Ireland) Results* (2012): www.nacd.ie/publications/drug_use_ireland_new_2012.pdf

Irish Focal Point (2011) *2011 National Report (2010 data) to the EMCDDA by the Reitox National Focal Point*: www.drugsandalcohol.ie/16812/1/Irelandnationalreport2011r_-_Copy.pdf

Thomas Babor and colleagues' book *Alcohol No Ordinary Commodity: Research and Public Policy* (2010).

For an introduction to a socio-cultural perspective on alcohol and drugs I recommend Dwight B. Heath's chapter 'Emerging anthropological theory and models of alcohol use and alcoholism' in *Theories of Alcoholism* (1988), and Geoffrey Hunt and Judith C. Barker's (2001) article 'Socio-cultural anthropology and alcohol and drug research: towards a unified theory' in *Social Science and Medicine*.

Useful Websites

Alcohol Action Ireland – www.alcoholireland.ie
Health Research Board – www.hrb.ie
Merchants Quay Ireland Homeless & Drugs Service – www.mqi.ie
National Advisory Committee on Drugs – www.nacd.ie
National Documentation Centre on Drug Use – http://www.drugsandalcohol.ie/

11

The Neglected:
Suicide and Mental Health in Ireland?

Area of Social Care for which this Chapter Is Relevant

Suicide and mental health cut across a number of areas of social care practice as well as having resonance for many students of social care in their own lives. Few social care workers are directly employed in mental health related services. However, the chapter is also relevant for those interested in youth work, as well as in drugs and alcohol related work, and in children and family services.

Key Words in this Chapter

Suicide, Durkheim, mental health, young males, deliberate self-harm, community, neglect, suicide prevention

Key Themes in this Chapter

- Understanding suicide
- Important legislation
- The extent of suicide in Ireland
- Policy developments to address suicide
- Mental health in Ireland: a case of neglect?

Introduction

The impact of suicide is devastating for families and communities. I have attended funeral services for young adult children of people that I know and grew up with. The memory of the grief of distraught and devastated parents and other family members, as well as tearful members of the wider community, remains etched in my mind. Even priests officiating at the funeral of someone who has taken their own life admit to the difficulty of finding the right words to make sense of what has happened or to comfort the bereaved. These tragic occasions make a lasting impression. In short, suicide impacts on all of us (Smyth, MacLachlan and Clare 2003).

This chapter looks at suicide in the context of public policy. Suicide is not just an issue for individuals, families and local communities; it is rightly a matter of concern to policy-makers. Smyth and colleagues place suicide in this broader social context when they say that '[s]uicide is not just a medical or psychological problem of the individual. It is more than that – it is a problem of society' (2003: 4). We know that for centuries suicide has provoked debate, and that it raises grave and complex questions in the context of morality, religion, medicine and culture (Rogers and Pilgrim 2010). We also know that the causes of suicide are not easily found, if indeed they can be found (Walsh 2008). Finally, we know that suicide has been a taboo subject, associated with sinfulness and human failure, and thus it tends to be denied by society and in public policy. This chapter also looks at the broader issue of mental health, which is itself a controversial subject (Pritchard 1995, Rogers and Pilgrim 2010). The connection between suicide and mental health is contentious, as not all suicides can be linked to mental illness (Allen 2005, Rogers and Pilgrim 2010). Yet, suicide as a policy issue and in popular perception is firmly fixed in the field of mental health.

Understanding Suicide

Defining suicide is not an easy task (Allen 2005), but there have been many attempts to do so, including the explanation used in the Irish government's national strategy on suicide, *Reach Out*, published in 2005 (HSE 2005). *Reach Out* uses a definition from an Australian government document *LIFE Strategy* (1999): '[a] conscious or deliberate act that ends one's life when an individual is attempting to solve a problem that is perceived as unsolvable by any other means' (HSE 2005: 9). Smyth and colleagues discuss the merits of some of the many definitions of suicide, but believe that Shneidman's is the most useful, because it 'provides a more unifying, inclusive, flexible and purposive definition' (2003: 10):

> currently in the Western World, suicide is a conscious act of self-induced annihilation, best understood as a multi-dimensional malaise in a needful individual who defines an issue for which suicide is perceived as the best solution. (Shneidman 1985: 203, cited in Smyth et al. 2003: 10)

Smyth and colleagues highlight the important aspects of Shneidman's definition, which go beyond the actual act of bringing about one's own death, the central truth of any definition. The definition places suicide in a 'temporal and cultural context' by its reference to 'currently in the Western World', and this allows for different meanings of the word in diverse cultural settings and the possibility that in time a more appropriate definition may be found (Smyth et al. 2003: 10). A second, and they suggest a more important, feature of Shneidman's definition is the central role of the individual's experience in this act – 'a multi-dimensional malaise in a needful individual'. Finally they point to the phrase 'the best solution', which emphasises again the individual and their own judgement (Smyth et al. 2003: 11). For these authors, the fact that Shneidman defines suicide in human terms rather than in scientific language gives 'meaning to the word' suicide (Smyth et al. 2003: 11).

Box 11.1

Definitions of Suicide-Related Terms

Defining suicide is further complicated 'by the necessity of distinguishing between deaths which were intentionally fatal, those which were accidentally fatal (i.e. those who attempted to harm themselves but did not mean to die), those who intended to die but did not – often called "failed suicides" – and those who intended only to harm themselves – variously known as parasuicide, attempted suicide or, perhaps more accurately, deliberate self-harm' (Allen 2005: 88–9).

> *Reach Out* (the Irish Government's national suicide strategy) not only gives a definition of suicide, it also gives definitions of deliberate self-harm, parasuicide and suicidal behaviour.
>
> ### Deliberate Self-Harm (DSH)
>
> 'The various methods by which people deliberately harm themselves, including self-cutting and taking overdoses. Varying degrees of suicide intent can be present and sometimes there may not be any suicidal intent, although an increased risk of further suicidal behaviour is associated with all DSH.'
>
> ### Parasuicide
>
> 'A non-habitual act with a non-fatal outcome that is deliberately initiated and performed and is likely to cause self-harm.'
>
> ### Suicidal behaviour
>
> 'The spectrum of activities related to suicide including suicidal thinking, self-harming behaviours not aimed at causing death and suicide attempts.'
> (HSE 2005: 9)

Suicide has been part of human activity since the beginning of recorded history, and has existed in every society irrespective of its culture. The only changes that have occurred are in the 'philosophical, social and legal attitudes towards suicide' (Pritchard 1995: 9). In ancient Greece and Rome suicide was seen in a pragmatic way, without moral judgement, and considered instead on the basis of motive. For those who held high status it was an honourable thing to die by suicide, but for those who were slaves or soldiers it was thought to be an irrational and selfish act, a denial of property in the case of slaves or the denial of service to the state by a soldier (Smyth et al. 2003). The greatest influence on attitudes to suicide in the Western World has come from the Judaeo-Christian religions. There are references to suicide in the Bible, with over a dozen in the Old Testament and one in the New Testament (Pritchard 1995). Pritchard says that the Christian Church first overtly prohibited suicide in the fourth century, when Saint Augustine described it 'as a mortal sin' (1995: 10). The influence of the Christian Church's view on suicide was reflected in state laws, when even in the fifteenth century 'there were severe sanctions against suicide' (Pritchard 1995: 11). In other faiths, such as Islam and Hinduism, suicide is also taboo, with the Koran spelling out specific sanctions against suicide (Pritchard 1995).

Durkheim and Suicide

A shift from the dominant religious and moral thinking on suicide emerged from the late sixteenth century, through Western literature and philosophy, with authors such as Shakespeare, Donne, Hume and Rousseau, the last of whom 'transferred sin from man to society, thus beginning a more sociological view of the phenomenon' (Smyth et al. 2003: 7). The original and classic sociological study on suicide is Emile Durkheim's *Suicide: A Study in Sociology* (1897) Although some of his ideas 'have been overtaken by socio-historical changes' (Pritchard 1995: 24) and the data Durkheim used to develop his theory has been the subject of criticism (Sweeney 2011), his thesis remains the key work in considering the social and cultural dimensions of suicide (Smyth et al. 2003). His study entailed a shift from the psychological, where suicide was seen as an individual problem, to a societal explanation which located suicide in the realm of social relations (Morrison 2006). In the aftermath of Durkheim's study his position was opposed by those who believed that suicide was a 'psychiatric disorder', and 'many were critical of Durkheim's assertion that suicide had social causes existing outside of the individual' (Morrison 2006: 201).

The essential features of Durkheim's study were his four types of suicide, which gave a range of meanings to suicide: egotistical, altruistic, anomic, and fatalistic, based around his ideas on societal integration and regulation (Durkheim 1897/1952). Egotistical and altruistic suicide are situated as polar opposites in his consideration of social integration – 'the extent to which individuals are linked to and feel allegiance for social groups to which they are attached' (Morrison 2006: 205). These Durkheim identified as religious, family and political groups. He believed integration was declining as a result of industrialisation. Egotistical suicide then results from a process of detachment from society, where individual ends become more important than social bonds (Durkheim 1897/1952). At the other end of this polarisation is altruistic suicide, which occurs because of 'too much integration rather than too little' (Morrison 2006: 218). Altruistic suicide refers to suicide as a requirement of being selflessly over-committed to society or certain groups and their expectations (for example, suicide bombers).

Anomic and fatalistic suicides are the polar opposites in Durkheim's analysis of societal regulation. According to Durkheim, anomie occurs in industrial societies where dramatic economic change leads people to desire material things and then become disenchanted as feelings of personal failure develop, possibly leading to suicide. The lack of regulation of people's desires in these societies is at the heart of anomic suicide. Fatalistic suicide received little attention from Durkheim, but it is based on excessive control of the individual's life. This control can lead the individual to take their own life to evade that control (for example, a slave who wishes to escape from slavery might commit suicide as the only way out of their predicament). Of the four types of suicide proposed by Durkheim it is anomie that is most commonly used in efforts to explain the social dimension of suicide. For Durkheim, the problem of suicide is not so much a problem of the individual, but is 'symptomatic of the breakdown of the collective conscience, and of a basic flaw in the social fabric' (Simpson 1952: 17).

Causes of Suicide

Because of its complex nature it can be problematic to attribute specific causes to suicide, so the term 'contributory causes' of suicide is used instead (Pritchard 1995: 33). While it may be possible with almost complete certainty to establish the physical cause of death, what led an individual to take their own life may never be known (see also Begley et al. 2004 and Walsh 2008). *A Vision for Change* (the Irish mental health strategy) identifies the complexity of suicide, saying that '[s]uicide and suicidal behaviour is not simply a response to a single stress, but the outcome of a build up of stresses, which leads to a feeling of entrapment and hopelessness' (Government of Ireland 2006c: 159). The literature on suicide mentions as contributory causes mental illness, age, gender, alcohol and drugs, unemployment, single or separated status, socio-economic change, and sexual orientation.

According to Rogers and Pilgrim, '[p]sychiatric diagnosis is a weak predictor of suicide' (2010: 232). People who have been diagnosed with depression have a 15 per cent risk of suicide over their lifetime, while those with a diagnosis of schizophrenia have a 10 per cent risk, leading the authors to conclude 'that the overwhelming majority of those with a psychiatric diagnosis do not commit suicide, although more do so than in the general population' (Rogers and Pilgrim 2010: 232). In Pritchard's (1995) review of literature he identifies 'depression' as the contributory cause most often associated with suicide, but points out that the word can be problematic. There is a difference between individuals who are diagnosed as clinically depressed, and those who feel low and even consult with their GPs about their feelings, but have never sought nor have been offered psychiatric help. Walsh (2008: 51) explains that prior to suicide people might experience an 'acute onset of depression' brought about by some stressful event or events. However, he admits that this cannot be proved, and he also points out that suicidal acts cannot be attributed solely to depression. Women are much more likely to suffer from depression but yet are less likely to commit suicide than men (Allen 2005, Walsh 2008), which suggests that other factors come into play (Rogers and Pilgrim 2010).

One of the features of concern in Ireland and the Western World is the high level of young male suicides (Begley et al. 2004, Cleary 2005, HSE 2005, Smyth et al. 2003, Walker 2006). The level of suicide among young males in Ireland is higher than for any other age group. There is no single apparent reason, but a number of risk factors associated with young males are not relevant, or less relevant, to young females and other age groups. These include risk-taking behaviours, such as higher levels of alcohol and drug consumption, as well as difficulties in coping with pressures to fulfil the role of provider, changes in gender roles and the inability to value themselves (Begley et al. 2004, see also Cleary et al. 2004, Dooley and Fitzgerald 2012). Begley and colleagues set all these changes in the context of Durkheim's concept of anomie, and suggest there has been 'an unbalancing of social forces that affect individual action', as the norms of Irish society have changed and 'individual behaviour is no longer regulated by society' (2004: 4). (Some authors are more cautious about this interpretation: for example, Cleary and Brannick 2007.)

Smyth and colleagues put this in another way when they claim that Irish people have lost trust 'in those who have traditionally been our "cultural icons"' (2003: 113). Faith has been lost in individuals of cultural significance, and 'more fundamentally in the very institutions that sustained them', as many have disappointed, such as priests and politicians (Smyth et al. 2003: 113). Yet these arguments do not address the dilemma of why some men respond to these major societal and cultural changes through suicide and women apparently do not. Baudelot and Establet's observation about men and women's relationship to suicide and society is worth noting:

> Society does not shed any light on suicide, but suicide does shed some light on society. . . . In the vast majority of countries, three to four times fewer women commit suicide than men. In itself, that observation tells us nothing about suicide. But in leading us to ask why women are less vulnerable, it forces us to explore what it is about the social conditions of women and men that are so different as to produce this behavioural difference. (Baudelot and Establet 2008: 8)

Gender and age differences are not the only considerations in our attempt to understand suicide. Other factors such as lower economic status and poverty are contributory causes (Walsh 2008). Cleary and Brannick (2007) question the generalised application of 'crisis' among men. They draw attention to class differences between men, which they argue lead to differing experiences of the socio-economic transformations that have taken place in Ireland. Walsh (2008), in similar vein, acknowledges class differences too when he says that people from lower socio-economic groups experience higher levels of suicide. The potential isolation of being single or separated is another contributing factor (Rogers and Pilgrim 2010), especially for older men in rural areas (Cleary and Brannick 2007).

It is important to note the significance of alcohol (HSE 2005, National Office of Suicide Prevention 2001, Walsh 2008, Walsh and Walsh 2011). Cleary says that '[t]he combination of alcohol and the impulsive quality of suicidal behaviour is key to understanding this phenomenon' (2005: 46). Walsh and Walsh, in a study of the association of alcohol and unemployment with suicide for the period 1968 to 2009, found that '[t]he level of alcohol consumption is a significant influence on suicide among men in all age groups between 15 and 54 years' (2011: 44). Furthermore, they found some evidence that alcohol consumption is significant among young women in the fifteen to twenty-four age group. They also conclude that over time the consumption of alcohol has had a far greater influence on the suicide rate than unemployment.

Belonging to a group that is discriminated against, such as Travellers or the lesbian, gay, bisexual and transgender (LGBT) population, also increases the risk of suicide (Mayock et al. 2009, Walker 2006). According to Walker's study (2006), Travellers have a suicide rate over three times as high as the settled population, with males in the 25–29 years age group most at risk. The profile of Travellers who commit suicide is broadly similar to that of the general population (Walker 2006). Mayock and colleagues (2009), in their review of the literature on suicide and LGBT people, suggest that the stigmatisation and the stress which arises from membership of this group raises the risk of suicide much higher than for the general population (Allen 2005). Mayock and colleagues (2009) also point out that there are no specific studies of LGBT people and suicide in Ireland. There do not appear to be any Irish studies on suicide amongst immigrant or minority ethnic groups, apart from Walker's (2006) study on Travellers, already referred to. Prisoners too are at a higher risk of committing suicide than the general population (Allen 2005).

There are no easy explanations of their loved one's action for the family of many people who commit suicide. In fact there is no agreement on what causes suicide, and the best that can be said is that there are a number of contributory causes. But even these are influenced by a range of factors, which cross social, economic, cultural and psychological boundaries. This of course poses challenges to the central aim of public policy on suicide, which is prevention. We turn to this question in due course, but before that we examine key legislation in this area and the extent of suicide in Ireland.

Important Legislation

Legislation in the area of suicide is quite limited in Ireland. Only the very short Criminal Law (Suicide) Act 1993 refers specifically refers to it. This has only three sections, and its primary aim is to decriminalise suicide. It simply states in section 2(1) that '[s]uicide shall cease to be a crime'. The other significant point in the Act is that it prohibits assisted suicide, with the possibility of a prison sentence of up to fourteen years (Government of Ireland 1993b). Not everyone agrees with such a ban, and there have been calls for the decriminalisation of assisted suicide in Ireland in restricted cases of terminal illness (Hough 2012).

Suicides are recorded by coroners after an inquest which is based on information provided by the Gardaí. A coroner is an independent office of the state, with responsibility under the Coroners Act 1962 for 'the medico-legal investigations of the circumstances of sudden, unexplained, violent and unnatural deaths' (Shatter 2012). There are claims that despite the decriminalisation of suicide, not all such deaths are recorded as suicide by coroners (Keating 2012). The decriminalisation of suicide has gone some way towards comforting and giving practical assistance to the bereaved (Neville 2001), but suicide remains a very sensitive issue, and as can be observed from the claims made by Keating (2012), it may still lead to denial even by official sources. Legislation therefore can only be part of the response in addressing the difficult subject of suicide.

The Extent of Suicide in Ireland

In examining the extent of suicide in Ireland a number of factors must be taken into account. Because of the criminalisation of suicide until 1993, previous denial by the Catholic Church of full burial rights, and the stigma attached to it (Allen 2005, Neville 2001), there has been a long history of under-reporting deaths by suicide in Ireland (Walsh 2008). As has been mentioned, the under-reporting of suicide continues to be a problem, and not just because coroners decide not to record deaths as suicide (Walsh 2008).

Walsh (2008) gives a number of other reasons why deaths by suicide are not recorded correctly. Medical practitioners might certify the death as natural, either intentionally or unintentionally, or the information given to the CSO might not be sufficiently accurate for it to be categorised correctly. The CSO publishes a summary quarterly and annually, *Vital Statistics*, which records, births, deaths and marriages, including the number of suicides. However, as Walsh (2008) points out, a death might not be recorded as suicide in the year in which it occurred, and it is at least two years before final adjusted figures are published in the *Report on Vital Statistics*. It seems as if one way to try to ensure greater accuracy in reporting suicide is to add what are called 'undetermined' deaths (or deaths of undetermined intent) to deaths by suicide (Walsh 2008, Walsh and Walsh 2011). Undetermined deaths are those that cannot be decided on as intentional acts of suicide. Allen (2005) is however satisfied that the CSO figures do not underestimate the real suicide rate.

Box 11.2

Stigma, Mental Health and Suicide

Stigma is explained as follows by Pompili, Mancinelli and Tatarelli (2003: 173):

> The term stigma refers to a mark that denotes a shameful quality in the individual so marked. Mental illness is widely considered to be such a quality, an assumption supported by a number of beliefs such as the association between mental illness and irrational and unpredictable violence as portrayed by the media and the notion that mental illness is not a 'true' illness like organic disease.

> Pompili and colleagues argue that not only does the stigma associated with mental illness prevent people from seeking help, it also 'exposes them to a greater risk of suicide', as suicide may become the 'best solution for a stigmatised individual' (2003: 173).

Table 11.1 gives the suicide rates recorded by the CSO in its *Report on Vital Statistics* for the years 2001 to 2009. For 2010 the *Vital Statistics Summary* report was used as the *Report on Vital Statistics 2010* was not available at the time of writing. Between 1970 and 1998 there was a continual upward trend in suicide in Ireland. The jump from 70 suicides in 1970 to 514 in 1998 was noted as 'one of the fastest growing suicide rates in the world' (HSE 2005: 12). The figure was lower for a couple of years, before spiking again in 2001 and then decreasing until 2007. In the following two years the increase year on year has been significant, but although we do not yet have the final agreed figure for the year, it appears that 2010 showed a reduction in the number of people who committed suicide.

Table 11.1: Suicide Rates by Gender in Ireland, 2001–2010

Year	Total	Males	Females
2001	519	429	90
2002	478	387	91
2003	497	386	111
2004	493	406	87
2005	481	382	99
2006	460	379	81
2007	458	362	96
2008	506	386	120
2009	552	443	109
*2010	486	386	100

Source: CSO, *Report on Vital Statistics* for years 2001–2009; *CSO (2010a), *Vital Statistics Summary Report 2010* – on the trends of previous years the 2010 figures can be expected to increase when the *Report on Vital Statistics 2010* is published with the final adjusted figures.

Questions have been raised about the reliability of the data on suicides (HSE 2005), as the number of people who have died from 'events of undetermined intent' has increased. These are people who die from risk-taking behaviours, such as car accidents and poisonings, but it is not possible to determine whether the outcome was accidental or intentional. According to Arensman (2012) the majority of these cases are likely to have been suicides. It is evident from Table 11.1 that men are much more likely to commit suicide than women. Table 11.2 shows the significant difference in suicide levels between age groups. Men who take their lives tend to be younger than women, but in both categories younger men and women are more likely to take their lives than older persons. Walsh (2008) points out that younger men have not always been more likely to take their lives than older men. In the past older men were at a higher risk of suicide in Ireland (see also Allen 2005).

Table 11.2: Suicide Rates by Gender and Age Group in Ireland, 2001–2009

Year Gender	5–14 Years	15–24 Years	25–34 Years	35–44 Years	45–54 Years	55–64 Years	65–74 Years	75–84 Years	85+ Years
2009									
Male	1	71	104	105	74	60	20	8	—
Female	3	12	21	26	20	15	10	2	—
2008									
Male	3	69	100	75	67	46	20	5	1
Female	—	25	18	21	25	18	9	4	—
2007									
Male	7	76	91	63	56	35	26	8	—
Female	1	15	19	20	25	11	2	3	—
2006									
Male	2	89	86	67	63	43	18	9	2
Female	2	16	13	14	16	13	5	2	—
2005									
Male	2	82	92	76	66	43	19	2	—
Female	1	20	23	13	19	12	7	3	1

(Continued)

Table 11.2: (*Continued*)

Year Gender	5–14 Years	15–24 Years	25–34 Years	35–44 Years	45–54 Years	55–64 Years	65–74 Years	75–84 Years	85+ Years
2004									
Male	1	88	91	83	73	44	19	6	1
Female	—	9	17	19	19	14	7	1	1
2003									
Male	2	96	72	87	57	45	15	12	—
Female	2	16	19	20	23	18	8	4	1
2002									
Male	1	90	106	62	55	41	24	6	2
Female	2	15	21	15	19	11	4	4	—
2001									
Male	2	90	110	82	68	45	23	9	—
Female	—	16	13	19	20	18	2	2	—

Source: CSO, *Report on Vital Statistics* for years 2001–2009.

An important dimension of the discussion on suicide is what is known as deliberate self-harm (DSH). Other terms such as attempted suicide, parasuicide and non-fatal suicidal behaviour are also used to describe this (Allen 2005; see Box 11.1). Pritchard says that although 'it is an important factor associated with eventual suicide . . . [DSH] is a different phenomenon' (1995: 54). For him the difference is related to 'intent'. Motivation and intent differ between suicide, where the outcome sought is death, and DSH, where the desired outcome is non-fatal self-harm, although the DSH could unintentionally lead to death (Allen 2005, Pritchard 1995). Two features in the demographics of DSH are significantly different from suicide: there are large numbers of people who deliberately self-harm, and most are women, particularly young women. The National Suicide Research Foundation (NSRF)'s *National Registry of Deliberate Self-Harm Annual Report 2010* (2011) recorded 11,966 cases of DSH treated in hospitals in Ireland in 2010. Arensman (2012) suggests there are approximately a further 60,000 'hidden' cases.

The NSRF (2011) reports that while the female rate of DSH is higher than for males, the gap is narrowing, from 37 per cent in

2004–2005 to 13 per cent in 2009–2010. The annual report also shows a significant increase in DSH among males over the four years to 2010, up by 27 per cent and for women up by 7 per cent. The report makes a clear reference to the impact of the recession, and particularly highlights the increase in self-harm among 20- to 24-year-olds, for both males and females. Yet the peak rate for self-harm among women is in the fifteen to nineteen age group, where it is 639 per 100,000 of the population; in other words one in every 157 females in this age group attended hospital as a result of self-harm (NSRF 2011). There are also important regional variations in the level of DSH in Ireland.

Alcohol is involved in 41 per cent of cases of self-harm, although it is rare for it to be the main type of harm inflicted. The most common form of self-harm is a drug overdose, used by an average of 71 per cent of people of self-harmers. In contrast, hanging is the most common method of suicide in Ireland (Arensman 2012). Many fewer people take their own lives than deliberately cause themselves lesser harm. However, there is undoubtedly a relationship between suicide and self-harm (HSE 2005). Pritchard (1995) reported on the findings of one longitudinal study, that about 6 per cent of those who deliberately self-harm eventually die from suicide.

Policy Developments to Address Suicide

Neville (2001) sums up the change during the 1990s in public attitudes and policy approach towards suicide in his aptly titled article 'Suicide: from a crime to public health in a decade'. The first major policy document on suicide, the *Report of the National Task Force on Suicide*, referred to as a 'blueprint' by Allen (2005: 97), was published by the Department of Health and Children in 1998. The Task Force made a large number of recommendations which primarily centred on the training of relevant professional staff in the public service; education for the general public; improved coordination of services; support for voluntary groups and the provision of information on suicide and support services; the targeting of particularly vulnerable groups for educational and service intervention; the establishment of new oversight within the health services; and the appointment of regional coordinators. It also recommended change in the recording of suicide deaths by the Gardaí and the CSO. Finally, there were recommendations to reduce the availability of over-the-counter medicines such as paracetamol, and reduce the accessibility and use of alcohol, as these substances were known to be contributory causes in suicides and deliberate self-harm (Department of Health and Children 1998).

One of the outcomes of the Task Force report was the establishment of a National Suicide Review Group, which commissioned another report in 2001, *Suicide in Ireland: A National Study* (see Allen 2005). This study was asked to establish the cause of increased suicide in Ireland, particularly among young males, and the findings were to 'inform a national suicide prevention/ reduction strategy' and provide a baseline for measuring future trends (Departments of Public Health 2001: 3). In effect the study confirmed the key findings of the Task Force report, and provided some additional information on aspects of suicide in Ireland. This report was followed in 2005 with the first national policy document on suicide, *Reach Out: Irish National Strategy for Action on Suicide Prevention 2005–2014* (HSE 2005). *Reach Out* builds on the work done in the earlier reports referred to above, the work of the National Suicide Review Group and the regional Resource Officers for Suicide Prevention (HSE 2005: 15).

Box 11.3

Vision of *Reach Out: Irish National Strategy for Action on Suicide Prevention 2005–2014*

The vision of this strategy is of a society where life is valued across all age groups, where the young learn from and are strengthened by the experiences of others and where the needs of those who are going through a hard time are met in a caring way so that:

- The mental health and well-being of the whole population is valued
- Mental illness is more widely recognised and understood and those experiencing difficulties are offered the most effective and timely support possible

> • The abuse of alcohol and other drugs is reduced considerably
> • Everyone who has engaged in deliberate self-harm is offered the most effective and timely support possible
> • Those affected by a suicide death or deliberate self-harm receive the most caring and helpful response possible
>
> (HSE 2005: 8)

Reach Out establishes the context for its preventative strategy by explaining the meaning and consequences of suicide as well as by providing statistical information on suicide and deliberate self-harm in Ireland. Although they discuss the issue, the authors of the strategy decided not to set targets for suicide reduction. Instead they set as a priority improving the accuracy of the mortality rate for suicide, and left the decision on setting targets to the politicians (HSE 2005). The national strategy gives most attention to the prevention of suicide, responses to suicide, the provision of information and the carrying out of research. A key recommendation to facilitate the national strategy was the creation of the National Office for Suicide Prevention (established in 2005).

The strategy outlines four main areas for action (HSE 2005), each of which has a number of specific sub-actions. The four action areas are:

- General population approach – to improve and promote overall mental health and a positive attitude to mental health. This is to be done through supports for families, educational facilities, youth services, the workplace, sports organisations, voluntary and community groups, religious groups, media, and primary care and general practice.
- Targeted approach – to reduce the risk among groups that are known to be vulnerable to suicide
- Responding to suicide – to minimise the distress experienced by families, friends and the local community when a suicide has taken place to ensure that those bereaved 'are not left isolated and vulnerable so that the risk of any related suicidal behaviour is reduced' (HSE 2005: 45)
- Information and research – 'to improve access to information relating to suicidal behaviour and on where and how

to get help, and to encourage suicide research and improve access to research findings' (HSE 2005: 48)

Another initiative which added to policy development and improved research on suicide in Ireland was the establishment of the NSRF in Cork in 1995. The NSRF is a dedicated research organisation, which has among its aims to 'clearly determine the nature and extent of the suicide problem in Ireland' (HSE 2005: 15). Many voluntary support groups have been set up across the country over the last decade and a half to address the issue of suicide. Some operate at a national level but many of them have a local orientation, suggesting a growing public interest in and concern about the problem of suicide.

Suicide is also a concern for politicians, as the former President of Ireland Mary McAleese showed when she hosted a Presidential Forum on Suicide during her term in office and addressed public fora on this issue. The President of Ireland is also the patron of Console, one of the national support organisations for those affected by suicide. One of the political figures who promoted a suicide prevention policy was Dan Neville TD, a founder-member of the Irish Association of Suicidology who has chaired the Joint Oireachtas Sub-Committee on Suicide, a subcommittee of the Joint Oireachtas Committee on Health and Children. The Oireachtas Sub-Committee on Suicide published two reports in 2006 and 2009. The first criticised the lack of specific targets for suicide reduction in *Reach Out*. It went on to state that '[t]his report by the Joint Oireachtas Sub-Committee has, in contrast, set out recommendations, timeframes and the funding required to make inroads into our national suicide epidemic. The Government is urged to cease prevarication and to implement these' (Joint Oireachtas Committee on Health and Children 2006: 8).

In the second report in 2009 the Joint Sub-Committee tracked its own 2006 recommendations and was once again highly critical of the lack of progress on them. It also called for adequate and sustained funding for the National Office for Suicide Prevention (Joint Oireachtas Committee on Health and Children 2009). Separately, Senator Mary White (2008: 4), another member of the Oireachtas Sub-Committee on Suicide, said that it was an exceptional challenge to come up with suicide prevention policies 'since so little is scientifically proven about it'. She claimed that there is little evidence from research carried out in Ireland to demonstrate 'the effectiveness of different suicide prevention strategies' (White 2008: 4). It would seem that there is a growing interest in suicide prevention by the wider community, successive Presidents of Ireland and an ongoing personal commitment by some politicians in the Houses of the Oireachtas. But suicide prevention is part of a larger policy issue, mental health, to which we now turn.

Mental Health in Ireland: A Case of Neglect?

It is almost obligatory to begin a discussion on Irish mental health policy by stating how this issue is neglected. Historical neglect of the 'Cinderella sector' is not only a feature of Irish health policy; it is true too in many other countries (Lewis 2009: 212). Sapouna is representative of the literature when she says that '[m]ental health in Ireland is perhaps one of the most marginal and under-resourced areas in social services provision' (2006: 86). Neville (2011) demonstrates the low level of spending on mental health, stating in a Dáil debate that the budgetary allocation for mental health in 2010 was only 5.3 per cent of the overall health budget, down from 13 per cent in 1986. This is considered low compared with other countries (de Búrca, Armstrong and Brosnan 2010).

Furthermore, a study by the Irish Psychiatric Association found substantial regional differences in spending on mental health services in Ireland, and inequalities in access to them, with those from lower socio-economic groups faring worst (O'Keane, Walsh and Barry 2005). Yet it is estimated that 'about one in four' of the population experience mental health problems at some point in their lives (Government of Ireland 2006c: 17), which is close to the worldwide norm (Gould 2005). These levels of mental health problems exact a high social and economic price for individuals, families and society as a whole (Government of Ireland 2006c).

Box 11.4

Defining Mental Health

'Mental health is not just the absence of a mental disorder. It is defined as a state of well being in which every individual realises his or her abilities, can cope with normal stresses of life, can work productively and fruitfully and is able to make a contribution to his or her community'.

(*Source*: World Health Organization 2007)

The main feature of Irish mental health policy has been the shift from 'asylum based-care to community-based care as well as to a changed understanding of mental illness' (Bergin and Clarke 2005: 27). Historically mental illness was understood as a medical problem with a biological basis. However, that understanding, while still the dominant model, has altered and is becoming more inclusive of broader influences. The emphasis now is on mental health within a biopsychosocial (biological, psychological and social) model, rather than mental illness within the narrower confines of a medical model (Bergin and Clarke 2005, National Economic and Social Forum (NESF) 2007). The language used for mental illness has also been redefined, with the use of 'mental ill-health' as the general descriptor rather than what we have traditionally called 'mental illness' (NESF 2007: 9). The key legislative provision for mental health in Ireland is the Mental Health Act 2001, which is acknowledged to have advanced the rights of detained patients but is also limited in a number of respects. In particular, resources have not been made available to date for full implementation of the legislation (Kelly 2007).

Box 11.5

Key Legislative and Policy Developments in Mental Health in Ireland

- Mental Treatment Act 1945
- *The Psychiatric Services: Planning for the Future* 1984
- *Green Paper on Mental Health* 1992

- *A New Mental Health Act, White Paper* 1995
- *Guidelines on Good Practice and Quality Assurance in Mental Health Services* 1998
- Mental Health Act 2001
- Establishment of the Mental Health Commission, 2003
- *A Vision for Change: Report of the Expert Group on Mental Health Policy* 2006
- *Quality Framework for Mental Health Services in Ireland* 2007

A Vision for Change (2006) is the current strategy on mental health in Ireland. It sets out a framework for the development of mental health policy and practice. At its core is a holistic understanding of mental health, with an emphasis on an integrated multidisciplinary approach to address the biological, psychological and social factors that contribute to mental health (Government of Ireland 2006c). A 'population health' approach is advocated in the strategy, where the aim is to improve the mental health of the whole population. The strategy is person-centred, and promotes the involvement of service users and their carers at all levels in the provision of services, as well as seeking to involve communities. *A Vision for Change* stresses a recovery model of mental health. The aim is to assist those who experience mental ill-health to reach a level of independent functioning with or without psychiatric intervention. This is to be supported at local level by multidisciplinary community mental health teams, thus reducing the need for hospital admission (Government of Ireland 2006c). The strategy also aims to accelerate the closure of large psychiatric hospitals which began in the wake of *Planning for the Future* in 1984, and recommends the reinvestment of resources from the sale of properties that are no longer required, to improve the mental health service infrastructure.

Despite its enthusiastic reception from across the mental health sector, it was not long before criticisms about the implementation of the strategy began to emerge. The Expert Group on Mental Health Policy, which was responsible for bringing to fruition *A Vision for Change*, included in its recommendations the establishment of an Independent Monitoring Group to 'oversee and report on implementation' (Mental Health Commission 2009: 5). Each of the five Independent Monitoring Group's annual reports since it was established in 2006 have been critical of the slow implementation of *A Vision for Change* and the lack of action on recommendations included in its annual reports. The Mental Health Commission (2009) is quite scathing of the lack of progress, pointing to the HSE's (the agency responsible for the provision of mental health services) lack of vision for mental health services, a lack of leadership, and the lack of comprehensive implementation plans. 'Three years on there is still no leadership team and an implementation plan has been published with no resources, clear targets or defined accountability' (Mental Health Commission 2009: 31).

Box 11.6

Mental Health Policy: An International Dimension

Ireland's mental health policies are not solely a matter of national interest. As a member of the United Nations and the European Union, Ireland is a contributor to and subject of policies made on a regional and global level.

The most recent policy document on mental health by the WHO (*Draft Comprehensive Mental Health Action Plan 2013–2020*), has as its overall goal 'to promote mental well-being, prevent mental disorders, provide care, enhance recovery, promote human rights and reduce the mortality, morbidity and disability for persons with mental disorders' (WHO 2013: 6). It has a number of objectives at global, regional and national level:

1. To strengthen effective leadership and governance for mental health
2. To provide comprehensive, integrated and responsive mental health and social care services in community-based settings
3. To implement strategies for promotion and prevention in mental health
4. To strengthen information systems, evidence and research for mental health

In 2005 the European Commission published a Green Paper (policy discussion document), *Promoting the Mental Health of the Population. Towards a Mental Health Strategy for the EU.* This was followed in 2008 by the publication of the *European Pact for Mental Health and Well-Being.* The rationale for the Green Paper was to add value to existing mental health policies at member state level by creating a structure for 'exchange and cooperation between member states', 'helping to increase the coherence of actions in different policy sectors', and to open up a means by which user groups and civil society could contribute towards solutions to mental health problems (European Commission 2005: 7).

The European Pact for Mental Health and Well-Being recognises mental health as 'a human right' and identifies its human and economic costs (EU High-Level Conference 2008: 3). It calls for action in five priority areas:

1. Prevention of depression and suicide
2. Mental health in youth and education
3. Mental health in workplace settings
4. Mental health of older people
5. Combating stigma and social exclusion

(*Source*: EU High-Level Conference 2008: 3–5)

Conclusion

Mental health and particularly suicide have achieved greater prominence in the public domain in recent years. Yet there is evidence to suggest that the stigma long associated with suicide and mental health problems in Ireland has not gone away. For those affected, this stigma is a significant barrier to leading fulfilled and productive lives. In their study of discrimination against people with mental health problems, MacGabhann and colleagues (2010) found that the vast majority of people with mental health problems in Ireland feel they have suffered from unfair treatment and discrimination. The NESF (2007: 168) states that '[s]tigma and discrimination have been identified as the greatest barrier to social inclusion, quality of life and recovery for people with mental ill-health' (see also Box 11.2).

Mental health policy is not helped by its standing in public policy in Ireland. Despite some progress it continues to be treated as a less than important policy issue. This is evident in the low levels of funding, the lack of adequate specialist services for certain groups (for example children and adolescents, and those with eating disorders), inequalities in access to services, the continuing use of a small number of unsuitable institutions for the care of people with mental ill-health, the questioning of the central concept of the 'recovery' ethos within community mental health teams, and the as yet incomplete implementation of a community-based mental health service (Burke 2009, de Búrca et al. 2010, Independent Monitoring Group 2011, Mental Health Commission 2009, NESF 2007, Sapouna 2006, Tussing and Wren 2006). In an effort to overcome the barriers to poor mental health services and to advance a human rights approach to mental health provision in Ireland, Amnesty International has for ten years campaigned with only limited success for a rights-based approach to mental health. While important policy positions, such as *A Vision for Change*, use the language of citizenship and rights, there has been an almost grudging change to the fundamental direction of government policy, which continues to move along very slowly and lacks any real sense of urgency and commitment.

Irish policy on suicide is rooted within broader mental health policy, although it does have its own dynamic and has the appearance of being treated as separate or different. There is a growing public interest in the issue of suicide, and increased community support, evidenced through a growth of voluntary support groups for the bereaved and for those expressing suicidal behaviour. But just as with mental health, problems of stigma continue to be associated with suicide (HSE 2005). The extent of criticism of suicide policy also tends to be more muted. Perhaps that has to do with the realisation that suicide prevention policies are limited in what they can achieve, as was suggested by White (2008), quoted above. Walsh, in a critique of the value of suicide prevention strategies, argues that 'most of what is promulgated as prevention is nonspecific and, when specific, poorly evidence-based' (2008: 59). He points to the complexity of suicide and its roots, which he says are based in 'cultural mores' and shifts over time, and furthermore, the associated causes or 'risk factors' of suicide are common. Walsh's remarks are discouraging for those who believe that suicide can be prevented: '[f]inally although the end-point, suicide, is clear enough the diversity of causes is so great as to ensure that any search for generic solutions is futile' (2008: 59).

Further Reading

There is a lot of diverse material for further reading on suicide and mental health. In the Irish context there are some helpful sources for those who want a more in-depth and up-to-date knowledge of these areas, including some well-established texts on both mental health and suicide. Unusually in Irish social policy there is a strong and sustained critique of government policy on mental health from within official structures. Also available are up-to-date data on suicide and mental health.

Essential Documents

The legislative basis of mental health policy in Ireland is the Mental Health Act 2001: www.mhcirl.ie/Mental_Health_Act_2001/Mental_Health_Act_2001.pdf

The national strategies for mental health and suicide are essential reading for anyone who wants to familiarise themselves with Irish government policy on these issues.

Reach Out is the national suicide strategy: www.nosp.ie/reach_out.pdf

A Vision for Change is the national mental health strategy: www.dohc.ie/publications/pdf/vision_for_change.pdf?direct=1

On mental health, two other sources of essential reading are produced on an annual basis. The Mental Health Commission's Annual Report, which incorporates the report of the Inspector of Mental Health Services, is available on the Mental Health Commission's website (referred to below in useful websites). The Independent Monitoring Group's annual reports review progress on *A Vision for Change*, and are available through the Department of Health's website.

General Reading

The best book by far on the history of mental health in Ireland is Joseph Robins' *Fools and Mad: A History of the Insane in Ireland* (1986). An Irish textbook I greatly recommend is *Mental Health and Social Policy in Ireland* (2005), edited by Suzanne Quin and Bairbre Redmond, with chapters on a range of mental health issues, including one by Mary Allen on suicide. On suicide specifically I suggest Caroline Smyth, Malcolm MacLachlan and Anthony Clare's *Cultivating Suicide: Destruction of Self in a Changing Ireland* (2003), which has as its theme young male suicide. I also recommend Dermot Walsh's forthright analysis in *Suicide, Attempted Suicide and Prevention in Ireland and Elsewhere* (2008). The National Suicide Research Foundation and the National Office for Suicide Prevention produce important publications and information on suicide and related matters.

I recommend two British books. Colin Pritchard's *Suicide – The Ultimate Rejection? A Psycho-Social Study* (1995) is a little dated but still contains substantial material which is as relevant today as it was at the time of publication, and is useful even for an Irish audience. On mental health Anne Rogers and David Pilgrim's fourth edition of *A Sociology of Mental Health and Illness* (2010) is an excellent, critical book providing the reader with the full range of theoretical perspectives on mental health but with an emphasis on a sociological perspective.

Useful Websites

Amnesty International – www.amnesty.ie/mentalhealth
Central Statistics Office – www.cso.ie
Console – www.console.ie
Department of Health – www.dohc.ie
Health Research Board – www.hrb.ie
Mental Health Commission – www.mhcirl.ie
Mental Health Ireland – www.mentalhealthireland.ie
National Office for Suicide Prevention – www.nosp.ie
National Suicide Research Foundation – www.nsrf.ie
Suicide Ireland – www.suicideireland.com
World Health Organization – www.who.ie

Bibliography

Adshead, M. and Millar, M. (eds) (2008), *Public Administration and Public Policy in Ireland: Theory and Methods*, London: Routledge.

Alcock, P. (2003), 'The Subject of Social Policy' in P. Alcock, A. Erskine and M. May (eds), *The Student's Companion to Social Policy*, 2nd edn, Oxford: Blackwell, 3–10.

Alcohol Beverage Federation of Ireland (ABFI) (2012), *The National Substance Misuse Strategy: Minority Report by the Alcohol Beverage Federation of Ireland*, Dublin: ABFI.

All Ireland Traveller Health Study Team (2010), *All Ireland Traveller Health Study: Our Geels – Summary of Findings*, Dublin: School of Public Health, Physiotherapy and Population Science, UCD.

Allen, K. (2009), *Ireland's Economic Crash: A Radical Agenda for Change*, Dublin: Liffey Press.

Allen, K. (2012), 'The Model Pupil Who Faked the Test: Social Policy in the Irish Crisis', *Critical Social Policy*, 32(3): 422–39.

Allen, M. (2005), 'Mental Health and Suicide', in S. Quin and B. Redmond (eds), *Mental Health and Social Policy in Ireland*, Dublin: UCD Press, 88–103.

Amnesty International (2003), *Mental Illness: The Neglected Quarter*, Dublin: Amnesty International.

Archard, D. (2004), *Children: Rights and Childhood*, 2nd edn, London: Routledge.

Arensman, E. (2012), *Suicide and Self Harm in Ireland – An Update* , available at: www.console.ie/userfiles/file/Suicide%20and%20Self%20 harm%20in%20Ireland%20-%20An%20Update%2014-02-2012.pdf, accessed 2 June 2012.

Ariès, P. (1962), *Centuries of Childhood*, trans. R. Baldick, London: Jonathan Cape.

Arnold, S.K. (2012), 'State Sanctioned Child Poverty and Exclusion: The Case of Children in State Accommodation for Asylum Seekers', Dublin: Irish Refugee Council, available at: www. irishrefugeecouncil.ie/wp-content/uploads/2012/09/State-sanctioned-child-poverty-and-exclusion.pdf, accessed 30 September 2012.

Atkinson, A.B., Cantillon, B., Marlier, E. and Nolan, B. (2005), *Taking Forward the EU Social Inclusion Process*, Luxembourg: CEPS/INSTEAD.

Babor, T., Caetano, R., Casswell, S., Edwards, G., Giesbrecht, N., Graham, K., Grube, J., Hill, L., Holder, H., Homel, R., Livingston, M., Österberg, E., Rehm, J., Room, R. and Rossow, I. (2010), *Alcohol No Ordinary Commodity: Research and Public Policy*, 2nd edn, Oxford: Oxford University Press.

Baccaro, L. (2003), 'What is Alive and What is Dead in the Theory of Corporatism', *British Journal of Industrial Relations*, 41(4): 683–706.

Banks, S. (2008), 'The Social Work Value Base: Human Rights and Social Justice in Talk and Action, in A. Barnard, N. Horner and J. Wild (eds), *Value Base of Social Work and Social Care: An Active Learning Handbook*, Maidenhead: Open University Press, 25–36.

Barnardos (2011), *Separated Children in Foster Care*, seminar paper, available at: www.barnardos.ie/assets/files/Advocacy/Separated%20 Children/Barnardos%20Seminar_Paper_on_Fostering_Separated_ Children.pdf, accessed 19 August 2012.

Barnes, C. (2003), 'Rehabilitation for Disabled People: a "Sick" Joke?', *Scandinavian Journal of Disability Research*, 5(1): 7–23.

Barnes, C. and Mercer, G. (2003), *Disability*, Cambridge: Polity.

Barrett, A., McGuinness, S. and O'Brien, M. (2012), 'The Immigrant Earnings Disadvantage Across the Earnings and Skills Distributions: The Case of Immigrants from the EU's New Member States', *British Journal of Industrial Relations*, 50(3): 457–81.

Barron, P. (1995), 'The Child Care Act 1991: An Overview' in H. Ferguson and P. Kenny (eds), *On Behalf of the Child: Child Welfare, Child Protection and the Child Care Act 1991*, Dublin: A&A Farmar, 9–16.

Baudelot, C. and Establet, R. (2008), *Suicide: The Hidden Side of Modernity*, Cambridge: Polity Press.

Beesley, A. (2012), 'Treaty Would Bind Us Even After State Regains its Feet', *Irish Times*, 1 February, available at: www.lexisnexis. com.ezproxy.wit.ie:2048/uk/nexis/results/docview/docview. do?docLinkInd=true&risb=21_T15285131378&format=GNB FI&sort=BOOLEAN&startDocNo=301&resultsUrlKey=29_ T15285131382&cisb=22_T15285131381&treeMax=true&treeWidth= 0&csi=142626&docNo=314, accessed 8 August 2012.

Begley, M., Chambers, D., Corcoran, P. and Gallagher, J. (2004), *The Male Perspective: Young Men's Outlook on Life*, Limerick: Mid-Western Health Board.

Bellerose, D., Carew, A.M. and Lyons, S. (2011), *Trends in Treated Problem Drug Use in Ireland 2005–2010*. HRB Trends Series 12,

Dublin: Health Research Board, available at: www.drugsandalcohol.ie/16381, accessed 9 July 2012.

Bergin, M. and Clarke, J. (2005), 'Mental Health in the Community', in S. Quin and B. Redmond (eds), *Mental Health and Social Policy in Ireland*, Dublin: UCD Press, 23–38.

Bertelsmann Foundation (2011), *Social Justice in the OECD – How Do the Member States Compare: Sustainable Government Indicators 2011*, available at: www.sgi-network.org/pdf/SGI11_Social_Justice_OECD.pdf, accessed 4 February 2012.

Bloch, A. and Schuster, L. (2002), 'Asylum and Welfare: Contemporary Debates', *Critical Social Policy*, 22(3): 393–414.

Brady, H. (2008), *EU Migration Policy: An A–Z*, London: Centre for European Reform.

Brandon, D., Wells, K., Francis, C. and Ramsay, E. (1980), *The Survivors: The Study of Homeless Young Newcomers to London and the Responses Made to Them*, London: Routledge.

Browne, C. (2008), *Garda Public Attitudes Survey 2008*, Research Report No. 1/08, Tipperary: Garda Research Unit.

Brownlee, A. (2008), 'Paradise Lost or Found? The Changing Homeless Policy Landscape in Ireland', in D. Downey (ed.), *Perspectives on Irish Homelessness: Past, Present and Future*, Dublin: Homeless Agency, 34–42.

Buckley, H. (1996), 'Child Abuse Guidelines in Ireland: For Whose Protection?' in H. Ferguson and T. McNamara (eds), *Administration* (special edn), *Protecting Irish Children: Investigation, Protection and Welfare,* 44(2): 37–56.

Buckley, H. (2009), 'Reforming the Child Protection System: Why We Need to be Careful What We Wish For', *Irish Journal of Family Law*, 12(2): 27–32.

Buckley, H. (2012a), 'Radical Reform of Child Protection Services Needed', *Irish Times*, 21 June, available at: http://www.irishtimes.com/newspaper/opinion/2012/0621/1224318353631.html, accessed 21 June 2012.

Buckley, H. (2012b), 'Mandatory Reporting of Child Abuse Not a Panacea', *Irish Times*, 9 May, available at: http://www.irishtimes.com/newspaper/opinion/2012/0509/1224315800545.html, accessed 9 May 2012.

Buckley, H., Whelan, S., Carr, N. and Murphy, C. (2008), *Service Users' Perceptions of the Irish Child Protection System*, Dublin: Office of the Minister for Children and Youth Affairs, available at: www.dcya.gov.ie/documents/publications/CF_service_users.pdf, accessed 20 August 2012.

Burke, H. (1999), 'Foundation Stones of Irish Social Policy 1831–1951', in G. Kiely, A. O'Donnell, P. Kennedy and S. Quin (eds), *Irish Social Policy in Context*, Dublin: UCD Press, 11–32.

Burke, S. (2009), *Irish Apartheid: Healthcare Inequality in Ireland*, Dublin: New Island.

Burton, J. (2011), 'No Cuts to Primary Weekly Social Welfare Rates – Minister Burton', Press Office, Department of Social Protection, available at: www.welfare.ie/en/press/pressreleases/2011/Documents/pr051211.pdf, accessed 30 January 2012.

Butler, S. (1991), 'Drug Problems and Drug Policies in Ireland: A Quarter of a Century Reviewed', *Administration*, 39(3): 210–33.

Butler, S. (2002), *Alcohol, Drugs and Health Promotion in Modern Ireland*, Dublin: IPA.

Butler, S. (2009), 'Obstacles to the Implementation of an Integrated National Alcohol Policy in Ireland: Nannies, Neo-Liberals and Joined-up Government', *Journal of Social Policy*, 38(2): 343–59.

Butler, S. and Mayock, P. (2005), '"An Irish Solution to an Irish Problem": Harm Reduction and Ambiguity in the Drug Policy of the Republic of Ireland', *International Journal of Drug Policy*, 16: 415–22.

Callan, T., Nolan, B., Walsh, J.R., Whelan, C.T. and Maître, B. (2008), *Tackling Low Income and Deprivation: Developing Effective Policies*, ESRI Research Series No. 1, Dublin: ESRI.

Cameron, C. (2004), 'Social Pedagogy and Care: Danish and German Practice in Young People's Residential Care', *Journal of Social Work*, 4(2): 133–51.

Cameron, C., McQuail, S. and Petrie, P. (2007), *Implementing the Social Pedagogic Approach to Workforce Training in England: A Preliminary Study*, London: University of London.

Cameron, C., Petrie, P., Wigfall, V., Kleipoedszus, S. and Jasper, A. (2011), *Final Report of the Social Pedagogy Pilot Programme: Development and Implementation*, London: University of London.

Campbell, L. (2005), 'Garda Diversion of Young Offenders: An Unreasonable Threat to Due Process Rights?', *Irish Journal of Applied Social Studies*, 6(1): 13–26.

Carew, A.M., Bellerose, D. and Lyons, S. (2011), *Trends in Treated Problem Alcohol Use in Ireland 2005 to 2010*, HRB Trends Series 11, Dublin: Health Research Board, available online www.drugsandalcohol.ie/16037, accessed 9 July 2012.

Carey, M. (2007), 'White Collar Proletariat? Braverman, The Deskilling/Upskilling of Social Work and the Paradoxical Life of the Agency Care Manager', *Journal of Social Work*, 7(1): 93–114.

Carroll, D. (2010), 'Spectre of Cuts Eclipse Value-for-Money Question', *Irish Times*, 6 August.

Central Statistics Office (CSO) (2001–2009), *Report on Vital Statistics*, Dublin: Stationery Office.

CSO (2007), *Census 2006: Volume 5 – Ethnic or Cultural Background (Including the Irish Traveller Community)*, Dublin: Stationery Office.

CSO (2008), *National Disability Survey: First Results*, Dublin: Stationery Office, available at: www.cso.ie/releasespublications/documents/other_releases/nationaldisability/National%20Disability%20Survey%202006%20First%20Results%20full%20report.pdf, accessed 20 July 2011.

CSO (2010a), *Survey on Income and Living Conditions 2009*, Dublin: Stationery Office, available at: www.cso.ie/en/media/csoie/releasespublications/documents/silc/2010/silc_2010.pdf, accessed 19 June 2012.

CSO (2010b), *Vital Statistics Summary Report 2010*, Dublin: Stationery Office.

CSO (2011a), *Quarterly National Household Survey: Unemployment Thematic Report Quarter 1 2005–2011*, Dublin: CSO.

CSO (2011b), *Population and Migration Estimates 2011*, Dublin: CSO, available at: www.cso.ie/en/media/csoie/releasespublications/documents/population/current/Population%20and%20Migration%20Estimates%20April%202011.pdf, accessed 16 August 2012.

CSO (2012a), *Survey on Income and Living Conditions 2010*, Dublin: Stationery Office, available at: www.cso.ie/en/media/csoie/releasespublications/documents/silc/2010/silc_2010.pdf, accessed 19 June 2012.

CSO (2012b), *Profile 2; Older and Younger*, Dublin: Stationery Office, available at: www.cso.ie/en/media/csoie/census/documents/census2011profile2/Profile2_Older_and_Younger_Entire_Document.pdf, accessed 15 August 2012.

CSO (2012c), *Profile 3: At Work – Employment, Occupations and Industry in Ireland*, Dublin: Stationery Office, available at: www.cso.ie/en/media/csoie/census/documents/census2011profile3/Profile3_at_work_entire_doc.pdf, accessed 26 July 2012.

CSO (2012d), *This is Ireland: Highlights from Census 2011 Part 1*, Dublin: Stationery Office, available at: www.cso.ie/en/media/csoie/census/documents/census2011pdr/Census%202011%20Highlights%20Part%201%20web%2072dpi.pdf, accessed 26 July 2012.

CSO (2012e), *This is Ireland: Highlights from Census 2011, Part 2*, Dublin: Stationery Office, available at: http://www.cso.ie/en/media/csoie/census/documents/thisisirelandpart2census2011/This%20

is%20Ireland%20Highlights,%20P2%20Full%20doc.pdf, accessed 16 August 2012.

CSO (2012f), *Profile 7: Religion, Ethnicity and Irish Travellers*, Dublin: Stationery Office, available at: www.cso.ie/en/media/csoie/census/documents/census2011profile7/Profile%207%20Educa-tion%20Ethnicity%20and%20Irish%20Traveller%20entire%20doc.pdf, accessed 17 January 2013.

CSO (2012g), *Homeless Persons in Ireland, A Special Census Report*, Dublin: Stationery Office, available at: www.cso.ie/en/media/csoie/census/documents/homelesspersonsinireland/Homeless%20persons%20in%20Ireland%20A%20special%20Census%20report.pdf, accessed 30 September 2012.

Centre for Disability Law and Policy at NUIG (2011), *Submission on the Future of Disability Policy in Ireland*, available at: www.nuigalway.ie/cdlp/documents/future_of_disability_policy.pdf, accessed 10 August 2012.

Charleton, M. (2007), *Ethics for Social Care in Ireland: Philosophy and Practice*, Dublin: Gill & Macmillan.

Charlton, D. (2010), 'Immigration, Residence and Protection Bill 2010 Requires Significant Amendment to Achieve a Fair Immigration System: ICI', press release, 2 July, available at: http://www.immi-grantcouncil.ie/images/9175_020710_IRP.pdf, accessed 31 August 2010.

Charlton, J.J. (2006), 'The Dimensions of Disability Oppression: An Overview', in L.J. Davis (ed.), *The Disability Studies Reader*, 2nd edn, New York: Routledge, 217–27.

Christie, A. (2005), 'Social Work Education in Ireland: History and Challenges', *Portularia*, 5(1): 111–30.

Clarke, J. (2004), *Changing Welfare Changing States: New Directions in Social Policy*, London: Sage.

Clarke, J. (2005), 'New Labour's Citizens: Activated, Empowered, Responsibilized, Abandoned', *Critical Social Policy*, 25(4): 447–63.

Clarke, J., Newman, J. and Westmarland, L. (2008), 'The Antagonisms of Choice: New Labour and the Reform of the Public Services', *Social Policy and Society*, 7(2): 245–53.

Cleary, A. (2005), *Young Men on the Margins: Suicidal Behaviour Amongst Young Men*, Dublin: Katherine Howard Foundation.

Cleary, A. and Brannick, T. (2007), 'Suicide and Changing Values and Beliefs in Ireland', *Crisis*, 28(2): 82–88.

Cleary, A., Corbett, M., Galvin, M. and Wall, J. (2004), *Young Men on the Margins*, Dublin: Katherine Howard Foundation.

Coakley, A. (2004), 'Poverty and Insecurity', in B. Fanning, P. Kennedy, G. Kiely and S. Quin (eds), *Theorising Irish Social Policy*, Dublin: UCD Press, 112–27.

Coates, D., Kane, F. and Cotter, N. (2009), 'Housing the Traveller Community: From "The Problem of Itinerancy" to a Multicultural Perspective', *Administration*, 57(3): 87–107.

Cohen, B.J. (2011), 'Design-Based Practice: A New Perspective for Social Work', *Social Work*, 56(4): 337–46.

Cohen, S. (1972), *Folk Devils and Moral Panics: The Creation of the Mods and Rockers*, London: Paladin.

Coles, B. (2003), 'Young People', in P. Alcock, A. Erskine and M. May (eds), *The Student's Companion to Social Policy*, 2nd edn, Oxford: Blackwell Publishing, 296–302.

Colgan, A. (2006), 'People with Disability: Health Policy and Practice', in D. McCluskey (ed.), *Health Policy and Practice in Ireland*, Dublin: UCD Press, 171–87.

Collins, M. (1997), *Travellers in Ireland*, paper given at the Minority Ethnic Groups in Higher Education in Ireland Conference, held at St Patrick's College, Maynooth, 27 September 1996 and published by the Higher Education Unit, available at: www.ucc.ie/publications/heeu/Minority/minority.htm, accessed 25 May 2012.

Collins, M.L. (2012), *Responding to the Unemployment Crisis: What Role for Labour Market Policies?* NERI Working Paper 2012/No 5, Dublin: NERI.

Collins, S. (1998), 'Empowering Social Work Students in the College Setting', *Social Work Education*, 17(2): 203–18.

Collinson, S. (2009), *The Political Economy of Migration Processes: An Agenda for Migration Research and Analysis*, International Migration Institute, Oxford: University of Oxford, Working Paper 12, available at: www.imi.ox.ac.uk/pdfs/imi-working-papers/wp12-collinson, accessed 16 August 2012.

Commission on the Status of People with Disabilities (1996), *A Strategy for Equality: The Report of the Commission on the Status of People with Disabilities*, Dublin: Stationery Office, available at: www.nda.ie/cntmgmtnew.nsf/0/9007E317368ADA638025718D00372224/$File/strategy_for_equality_03.htm, accessed 17 July 2011.

Committee to Monitor the Effectiveness of the Diversion Programme (2010), *Annual Report of the Committee to Monitor the Effectiveness of the Diversion Programme 2010*, Dublin: Garda Office for Children and Youth Affairs.

Conroy, P. (1999), 'From the Fifties to the Nineties: Social Policy Comes Out of the Shadows', in G. Kiely, A. O'Donnell, P. Kennedy and S. Quin (eds), *Irish Social Policy in Context*, Dublin: UCD Press, 33–50.

Conroy, P. (2010), *Disability, Difference and Democracy. Some Rights and Wrongs*, Tasc Thinkpieces, available at: www.tascnet.ie/upload/file/Rights%20and%20Wrongs_PC%20%283%29.pdf, accessed 12 February 2012.

Considine, M. and Dukelow, F. (2009), *Irish Social Policy: A Critical Introduction*, Dublin: Gill & Macmillan.

Cornerstone (2009), 'News – Housing Needs Assessment', *Cornerstone*, 39: 2–3.

CORU (2010), 'Framework for a Common Code of Professional Conduct and Ethics', Dublin: CORU, available at: www.coru.ie/uploads/Framework%20Code%20of%20Professional%20Conduct%20and%20Ethics.pdf, accessed 24 July 2012.

CORU (n.d.a), 'General Frequently Asked Questions', available at: www.coru.ie/faq-section/faq/, accessed 24 July 2012.

CORU (n.d.b), 'About Us – Welcome from the CEO', available at: www.coru.ie/about-us/about-us-welcome-from-ceo/, accessed 24 July 2012.

Crosscare (2010), *Separated Children Leaving Care: The Need for Aftercare Support*, available at www.crosscare.ie/joomla/images/Crosscare_Position_Paper_on_Separated_Children_Leaving_Care_July_2010.pdf, accessed 19 August 2012.

Crossman, V. (2006), *The Poor Law in Ireland 1834–1948*, Studies in Irish Economic and Social History 10, Dundalk: Dun Dealgan Press.

Crossman, V. and Gray, P. (2011), 'Introduction: Poverty and Welfare in Ireland, 1838–1948' in V. Crossman and P. Gray (eds), *Poverty and Welfare in Ireland, 1838–1948*, Dublin: Irish Academic Press, 1–20.

Crowley, N. (2005), 'Travellers and Social Policy', in S. Quin, P. Kennedy, A. Matthews and G. Kiely (eds), *Contemporary Irish Social Policy*, Dublin: UCD Press, 231–55.

Cullen, B. (2011), 'Treating Alcohol-Related Problems Within the Irish Healthcare System, 1986–2007: An Embedded Disease Model of Treatment?', *Drugs: Education, Prevention and Policy*, 18(4): 251–60.

Cullinan, J., Gannon, B. and Lyons, S. (2008), *Estimating the Economic Cost of Disability in Ireland*, Working Paper No. 230, Dublin: ESRI.

Curry, J. (2003), *Irish Social Services*, 4th edn, Dublin: Institute of Public Administration (IPA).

Curry, J. (2011), *Irish Social Services*, 5th edn, Dublin: IPA.

Daniel, P. and Ivatts, J. (1998), *Children and Social Policy*, Basingstoke: Palgrave.

Davis, L.J. (ed.) (2006), *The Disability Studies Reader*, 2nd edn, New York: Routledge.

De Búrca, S., Armstrong, C. and Brosnan, P. (2010), *Community Mental Health Teams: Determinants of Effectiveness in an Irish Context*, Limerick: Health Systems Research Centre.

De Wispelaere, J. and Walsh, J. (2007), 'Disability Rights in Ireland: Chronicle of a Missed Opportunity', *Irish Political Studies*, 22(4): 517–43.

Delaney, E. (2002), *Irish Emigration since 1921*, Studies in Irish Economic and Social History 8, Dundalk: Dundalgan Press.

Dellepiane, S. and Hardiman, N. (2012), 'Governing the Irish Economy: A Triple Crisis', in N. Hardiman (ed.) *Irish Governance in Crisis*, Manchester: Manchester University Press, 83–109.

Department of Children and Youth Affairs (DCYA) (2011), *Children First: National Guidance for the Protection and Welfare of Children*, Dublin: DCYA, available at: www.dcya.gov.ie/documents/child_welfare_protection/ChildrenFirst.pdf, accessed 11 June 2012.

DCYA (2012a), *Report of the Independent Child Death Review Group: Dr Geoffrey Shannon and Norah Gibbons*, Dublin: Stationery Office, available at: www.dcya.gov.ie/documents/publications/Report_ICDRG.pdf, accessed 23 August 2012.

DCYA (2012b), *Report of the Task Force on the Child and Family Support Agency*, Dublin: Stationery Office, available at: www.dcya.gov.ie/documents/ChidFamilySupportAgency/TaskForceReport.pdf, accessed 23 August 2012.

DCYA (n.d.), *Policies and Legislation*, DCYA, available at: www.dcya.gov.ie/viewdoc.asp?fn=%2Fdocuments%2Fyouthaffairs%2Fpolicies.htm&mn=youd&nID=4, accessed 11 June 2012.

Department of Community, Rural and Gaeltacht Affairs (2009), *National Drugs Strategy Interim 2009–2016*, Dublin: Department of Community, Rural and Gaeltacht Affairs, available at: www.drugsandalcohol.ie/12388/1/DCRGA_Strategy_2009–2016.pdf, accessed 5 July 2012.

Department of Education and Science (DES) (2003a), *National Youth Work Development Plan 2003–2007*, Dublin: Stationery Office.

DES (2003b), *Pre-School for Travellers: National Evaluation Report*, Dublin: DES.

DES (2006), *A Report and Recommendations for a Traveller Education Strategy*, Dublin: Stationery Office.

Department of Education and Skills (2012), *Key Statistics 2010/2011: Number of Full-Time Students in Institutions Aided by the Department of Education & Skills, 2010–2011*, available at: www.education.ie/

servlet/blobservlet/stat_web_stats_10_11.pdf, accessed 19 June 2012.

Department of Education and Skills and Office of the Minister for Integration (2010), *Intercultural Education Strategy, 2010–2015*, Dublin: Department of Education and Skills and Office of the Minister for Integration.

Department of Environment (1991), *A Plan for Social Housing*, Dublin: Stationery Office.

Department of Environment, Community and Local Government (DECLG) (2011a), *National Housing Strategy for People with a Disability 2011–2016*, Dublin: DECLG, available at: www.environ.ie/en/DevelopmentHousing/Housing/PublicationsDocuments/FileDownLoad,28016,en.pdf, accessed 9 August 2012.

DECLG (2011b), *Housing Policy Statement*, available at: www.environ.ie/en/DevelopmentHousing/Housing/PublicationsDocuments/FileDownLoad,26867,en.pdf, accessed 30 January 2013.

DECLG (2012), *Annual Count of Traveller Families 2011*, available at: www.environ.ie/en/Publications/StatisticsandRegularPublications/TravellerAccommodation/, accessed 18 May 2012.

Department of Environment, Heritage and Local Government (DEHLG) (2008), *The Way Home: A Strategy to Address Adult Homelessness in Ireland 2008–2013*, Dublin: DEHLG, available at: www.environ.ie/en/Publications/DevelopmentandHousing/Housing/FileDownLoad,18192,en.pdf, accessed 6 October 2012.

DEHLG (2010), *Rental Accommodation Scheme*, Dublin: DEHLG, available at: www.environ.ie/en/DevelopmentandHousing/Housing/SocialHousingSupport/RentalAccomodationScheme/, accessed 6 October 2010.

DEHLG (various years), *Annual Housing Statistics Bulletin*, Dublin: DEHLG.

DEHLG (n.d.), *Rental Accommodation Scheme (RAS): Information for Landlords (Accommodation Providers and Agents)*, available at: www.environ.ie/en/DevelopmentHousing/Housing/SocialHousingSupport/RentalAccomodationScheme/PublicationsDocuments/FileDownLoad,2460,en.pdf, accessed 15 September 2012.

Department of Environment and Local Government (2000), *Homelessness an Integrated Strategy*, Dublin: Stationery Office.

Department of Environment and Local Government, Department of Health and Children, DES, and Department of Justice, Equality and Law Reform (2002), *Homelessness Preventative Strategy*, Dublin: Stationery Office.

Department of Health (1980), *Task Force on Child Care Services Final Report*, Dublin: Stationery Office.

Department of Health (1984), *The Psychiatric Service: Planning for the Future*, Dublin: Stationery Office.

Department of Health (1996), *National Alcohol Policy – Ireland*, Dublin: Stationery Office.

Department of Health (2012), *Value for Money and Policy Review of Disability Services in Ireland*, Dublin: Department of Health, available at: www.dohc.ie/publications/pdf/VFM_Disability_Services_Programme_2012.pdf?direct=1, accessed 8 August 2012.

Department of Health and Children (DHC) (1998), *Report of the National task Force on Suicide*, available at: www.dohc.ie/publications/pdf/taskforce_suicide_1998.pdf?direct=1, accessed 2 June 2012.

DHC (1999), *Children First: National Guidelines for the Protection and Welfare of Children*, Dublin: Stationery Office.

DHC (2000), *The National Children's Strategy – Our Children, Their Lives*, Dublin: Stationery Office, available at: www.dcya.gov.ie/documents/Aboutus/stratfullenglishversion.pdf, accessed 18 August 2012.

DHC (2001a), *Quality and Fairness: A Health System for You – Health Strategy*, Dublin: Stationery Office, available at: www.lenus.ie/hse/bitstream/10147/46392/1/1317.pdf, accessed 24 July 2012.

DHC (2001b), *Youth Homeless Strategy*, Dublin: Stationery Office, available at: www.dohc.ie/publications/pdf/ythhmlss.pdf?direct=1, accessed 20 October 2010.

DHC (2002), *Traveller Health: A National Strategy 2002–2005*, Dublin: DHC, available at: www.dohc.ie/publications/pdf/Traveller_health.pdf?direct=1, accessed 19 May 2012.

Department of Justice, Equality and Law Reform (DJELR) (2003), *Commission on Liquor Licensing – Final Report*, Dublin: DJELR.

DJELR (2004), 'National Disability Strategy', press release, 21 September 2004, available at: www.justice.ie/en/JELR/NDS.pdf/files/NDS.pdf, accessed 17 July 2011.

DJELR (2005), *Guide to the Disability Act 2005*, Dublin: DJELR, available at: www.justice.ie/en/JELR/DisabilityAct05Guide.pdf/Files/DisabilityAct05Guide.pdf accessed 18 July 2011.

DJELR (2008), *Report of the Alcohol Advisory Group*, Dublin: DJELR.

Department of Tourism, Sport and Recreation (2001), *Building on Experience: National Drugs Strategy 2001–2008*, Dublin: Stationery Office.

Departments of Public Health (2001), *Suicide in Ireland: A National Study*, Departments of Public Health on Behalf of the Chief Executive

Officers of the Health Boards, available at: www.nosp.ie/suicide_ in_ireland.pdf, accessed 3 June 2012.

Devlin, M. (2006), *Inequality and the Stereotyping of Young People*, Dublin: Equality Authority.

Devlin, M. (2009), 'Theorising "Youth"', in C. Forde, E. Kiely and R. Meade (eds), *Youth and Community Work in Ireland: Critical Perspectives*, Dublin: Blackhall, 33–56.

Devlin, M. (2010), 'Youth Work in Ireland – Some Historical Reflections', in P. Coussée, G. Verschelden, T. Van de Walle, M. Mędlińska and H. Williamson (eds), *The History of Youth Work in Europe – Vol. 2. Relevance for Today's Youth Work Policy*, Strasbourg: Council of Europe, 93–104.

Devlin, M. (2012), 'Youth Work in the Republic of Ireland', in Youthnet (ed.), *Youth Work Policy and Delivery in Ireland: A North South Context*, Belfast: Youthnet, 33–45.

Devlin, M. and Gunning, A. (2009), *The Purpose and Outcomes of Youth Work: Report to the Youth Services Interagency Group*, Dublin: Irish Youth Work Press.

Dickens, J. (2008), 'Welfare, Law and Managerialism: Inter-Discursivity and Inter-Professional Practice in Child-Care Social Work', *Journal of Social Work*, 81(1): 45–64.

Disability Federation of Ireland (2012), *Value for Money & Policy Review of the HSE's Disability Programme: DFI's Initial Response*, available at: www.disability-federation.ie/userfiles/file/DFIiniti- alanalysis.07.12.pdf, accessed 10 August 2012.

Donnison, D. (1975), 'An Approach to Social Policy', in National Economic and Social Council, *An Approach to Social Policy*, Dublin: Stationery Office, 7–68.

Dooley, B. and Fitzgerald, A. (2012), *My World Study: National Study of Youth Mental Health in Ireland*, Dublin: UCD School of Psychology/ Headstrong.

Dostal, J.M. (2007), 'The Workfare Illusion: Re-Examining the Concept and the British Case', *Social Policy and Administration*, 42(1): 19–42.

Downey, D. (ed.) (2008), *Perspectives on Irish Homelessness: Past, Present and Future*, Dublin: Homeless Agency.

Doyle, A. (2003), 'Disability Policy in Ireland', in S. Quin and B. Redmond (eds), *Disability and Social Policy in Ireland*, Dublin: UCD Press, 10–27.

Doyle, P. (1990), *The God Squad*, London: Corgi.

Drudy, P.J. (2005), 'Housing: The Case for a New Philosophy' in B. Reynolds and S. Healy (eds), *Securing Fairness and Wellbeing in a Land of Plenty*, Dublin: CORI Justice Commission, 36–49.

Drudy, P.J. and Punch, M. (2005), *Out of Reach: Inequalities in the Irish Housing System*, Dublin: TASC/New Island.

Dublin Regional Homeless Executive (2011), *Homelessness and the Housing Needs Assessment: The Revised report for Dublin*, available at: www.homelessagency.ie/Uploaded-Files/Homelessness-and-Housing-Need-2011.aspx, accessed 30 January 2013.

Dublin Regional Homeless Executive (2013), 'Delivering the Pathway to Home', available at: www.homelessagency.ie/Dublin-Homeless-Action-Plan/Delivering-Pathway-to-Home.aspx, accessed 30 January 2013.

Durkheim, E. (1897/1952) *Suicide: A Study in Sociology*, trans. J.A. Spaulding and G. Simpson, London: Routledge.

Duvell, F. and Jordan, B. (2002), 'Immigration, Asylum and Welfare: The European Context', *Critical Social Policy*, 22(3): 498–517.

Erskine, A. (2003), 'The Approaches and Methods of Social Policy', in P. Alcock, A. Erskine and M. May (eds), *The Student's Companion to Social Policy*, 2nd edn, Oxford: Blackwell, 4–16.

European Commission (2005), *Green Paper – Improving the Mental Health of the Population: Towards a Strategy on Mental Health of the European Union*, Brussels: Health and Consumer Protection Directorate-General, available at: http://ec.europa.eu/health/ph_determinants/life_style/mental/green_paper/mental_gp_en.pdf, accessed 17 January 2013.

European Commission (2007), *Communication from the Commission to the Council, the European Parliament, the European Economic and Social Committee and the Committee of the Regions: Third Annual Report on Migration and Integration*, Official Journal of the European Union, available at: http://ec.europa.eu/home-affairs/policies/immigra-tion/docs/com_2007_512_en.pdf, accessed 22 January 2011.

European Monitoring Centre for Drugs and Drug Addiction (EMCDDA) (2009), *Drug Offences – Sentencing and Other Outcomes: Online Annex: Results by Country*, available at: www.emcdda.europa.eu/attachements.cfm/att_92889_EN_onlineannex_SIsentencing.pdf, accessed 7 July 2012.

EMCDDA (2011a), *Statistical Bulletin 2011*, available at: www.emcdda.europa.eu/stats11/gps, accessed 30 June 2012.

EMCDDA (2011b), *Annual Report 2011: The State of the Drugs Problem in Europe*, Luxembourg: Publications Office of the European Union, available at: www.emcdda.europa.eu/publications/annual-report/2011, accessed 30 June 2012.

European Union (2007), 'Council Decision of 25 June 2007 Establishing the European Fund for the Integration of Third-Country Nationals for the Period 2007 to 2013 as Part of the General Programme 'Solidarity and Management of Migration Flows' (2007/435/EC), *Official Journal of the European Union*, available at: http://eur-lex.europa.eu/LexUriServ/LexUriServ.do?uri=OJ:L:2007:168:0018:0036:EN:PDF, accessed 22 January 2011.

European Union High-Level Conference (2008), *European Pact for Mental Health and Well-Being*, Brussels: European Union, available at: http://ec.europa.eu/health/mental_health/docs/mhpact_en.pdf, accessed 17 January 2013.

Eurostat (2007), *Eurostat Yearbook 2006–2007*, available at: http://epp.eurostat.ec.europa.eu/portal/page?_pageid=1073,46587259&_dad=portal&_schema=PORTAL&p_product_code=KS-CD-06-001-04, accessed 17 February 2009.

Eurostat (2011), *Asylum Applicants and First Instance Decisions on Asylum Applications in 2010*, available at http://epp.eurostat.ec.europa.eu/cache/ITY_OFFPUB/KS-QA-11-005/EN/KS-QA-11-005-EN.PDF, accessed 19 August 2012.

Eurostat (2012), *Asylum Applicants and First Instance Decisions on Asylum Applications: First Quarter 2012*, available at: http://epp.eurostat.ec.europa.eu/cache/ITY_OFFPUB/KS-QA-12-008/EN/KS-QA-12-008-EN.PDF, accessed 19 August 2012.

Evans, E.J. (ed.) (1978), *Social Policy 1830–1914: Individualism, Collectivism and the Origins of the Welfare State*, London: Routledge & Kegan Paul.

Expert Reference Group on Disability Policy (2011), *Report of Disability Policy Review*, Department of Health, available at: www.dohc.ie/publications/pdf/ERG_Disability_Policy_Review_Final.pdf?direct=1, accessed 10 August 2012.

Fahey, T. (2004), 'Housing Affordability: Is the Real Problem in the Private Rented Sector?', in *ESRI Quarterly Economic Commentary*, Dublin: ESRI, 79–96.

Fahmy, E. (2006), 'Youth, Poverty and Social Exclusion', in C. Pantazis, D. Gordon and R. Levitas (eds), *Poverty and Social Exclusion in Britain: The Millennium Survey*, Bristol: Policy Press, 347–73.

Fanning, B. (1999), 'The Mixed Economy of Welfare', in G. Kiely, A. O'Donnell, P. Kennedy and S. Quin (eds), *Irish Social Policy in Context*, Dublin: UCD Press, 51–69.

Fanning, B. (2002), *Racism and Social Change in the Republic of Ireland*, Manchester: Manchester University Press.

Fanning, B. (2006), 'Immigration, Racism and Social Exclusion' in B. Fanning and M. Rush (eds), *Care and Social Change in the Irish Welfare Economy*, Dublin: UCD Press, 80–92.

Fanning, B. (2011), *Immigration and Social Cohesion in the Republic of Ireland*, Manchester: Manchester University Press.

Fanning, B. (2012), *Racism and Social Change in the Republic of Ireland* , 2nd edn, Manchester: Manchester University Press.

Farrell, C., McEvoy, H. and Wilde, J. (2008), *Tackling Health Inequalities: An All-Ireland Approach to Social Determinants*, Dublin: Institute of Public Health/Combat Poverty Agency.

Farrelly, T. and O'Doherty, C. (2005), 'The Health and Social Care Professionals Bill (2004): Implications and Opportunities for the Social Professions in Ireland', *Administration,* 53(1): 80–90.

Farrelly, T. and O'Doherty, C. (2011), 'Social Care, After the Act – Reflections Five Years On After the Passing of the Health and Social Care Professionals Act 2005', *Administration*, 59(2): 73–83.

Ferguson, H. (1996), 'Protecting Irish Children in Time', in H. Ferguson and T. McNamara (eds), *Administration* (special edition), *Protecting Irish Children: Investigation, Protection & Welfare*, 44(2): 5–36.

Ferguson, H. (2004), *Protecting Children in Time: Child Abuse, Child Protection and the Consequences of Modernity*, Basingstoke: Palgrave Macmillan.

Ferguson, H. and Kenny, P. (1995), 'Introduction', in H. Ferguson and P. Kenny (eds), *On Behalf of the Child: Child Welfare, Child Protection and the Child Care Act 1991*, Dublin: A&A Farmar, 1–6.

Ferguson, H. and McNamara, T. (eds) (1996), *Administration* (special edition), *Protecting Irish Children: Investigation, Protection & Welfare*, 44(2).

FESET (n.d.), *List of Members*, available at: www.feset.org/en/home/membership/list-of-members.html, accessed 29 July 2012.

Finnerty, J. (2010), 'A New Model of Social Housing?' *CornerStone*, 42: 11–13.

Finney, N. and Simpson, L. (2009), *'Sleepwalking to Segregation': Challenging Myths About Race and Migration*, Bristol: Policy Press.

Fitzgerald, E. and Winston, N. (2005), 'Housing, Equality and Inequality', in M. Norris and D. Redmond (eds), *Housing Contemporary Ireland: Policy, Society and Shelter*, Dublin: IPA, 224–44.

Fitzgerald, F. (2012a), 'Using the Law to Achieve Better Outcomes for Children', Speech by Minister for Children and Youth Affairs, Frances Fitzgerald TD, to the conference Making Children Visible – The Principles of Best Interests and Hearing the Voice of the Child in Irish Law, Children's Rights Alliance, Dublin, 6 July, available at: www.dcya.gov.ie/viewdoc.asp?Docid=2206&CatID=12&mn=&StartDate=1+January+2012, accessed 20 August 2012.

Fitzgerald, F. (2012b), 'Priority Questions: Children in Care', *Dáil Éireann Debate*, 755(2), 5, 14 February, available at: http://debates.

oireachtas.ie/dail/2012/02/14/00005.asp, accessed 20 August 2012.

Fitzpatrick Associates (2006), *Review of the Implementation of the Government's Integrated and Preventative Homeless Strategies*, Dublin: DEHLG.

France, A. (2007), *Understanding Youth in Late Modernity*, Buckingham: Open University Press.

France, A. (2008), 'From Being to Becoming: The Importance of Tackling Youth Poverty in Transitions to Adulthood', *Social Policy and Society*, 7(4): 495–505.

Fraser, D. (ed.) (1984), *The New Poor Law in the Nineteenth Century*, London: Macmillan.

Fraser, U. (2003), 'The Asylum Procedure', in U. Fraser and C. Harvey (eds), *Sanctuary in Ireland: Perspectives on Asylum Law and Policy*, Dublin: IPA.

Fredrickson, G.M. (2002), *Racism: A Short History*, Princeton, N.J.: Princeton University Press.

Free Legal Advice Centres (FLAC) (2009), *One Size Doesn't Fit All: A Legal Analysis of the Direct Provision and Dispersal System, 10 Years On*, Dublin: FLAC, available at: www.flac.ie/download/pdf/one_size_doesnt_fit_all_full_report_final.pdf, accessed 17 August 2012.

Furlong, A. and Cartmel, F. (2007), *Young People and Social Change: New Perspectives*, 2nd edn, Maidenhead: McGraw Hill/Oxford University Press.

Furnham, A. (2004), 'Binge Drinking: Causes, Consequences and Cures', in M. MacLachlan and C. Smyth (eds), *Binge Drinking and Youth Cultures: Alternative Perspectives*, Dublin: Liffey Press, 21–47.

Gambrill, E. (1999), 'Evidence-Based Practice: An Alternative to Authority-Based Practice', *Families in Society*, 80: 341–50.

Gannon, B. and Nolan, B. (2006), *The Dynamics of Disability and Social Inclusion*, Dublin: Equality Authority, available at: www.equality.ie/index.asp?locID=105&docID=624, accessed 20 July 2011.

Garrett, P.M. (2009), 'The Republic of Ireland: A "Syndrome of Permanent Temporary Posts" and Crises in Child Protection', *European Journal of Social Work*, 12(2): 273–75.

Garrett, P.M. (2010), 'Examining the "Conservative Revolution": Neoliberalism and Social Work Education', *Social Work Education*, 29(4): 340–55.

Geddes, M. (2000), 'Tackling Social Exclusion in the European Union? The Limits to the New Orthodoxy of Social Partnership', *International Journal of Urban and Regional Research*, 24(4): 782–800.

Gibbons, J. and Gray, M. (2005), 'Teaching Social Work Students About Social Policy', *Australian Social Work*, 58(1): 58–75.

Glendinning, C. (2008), 'Increasing Choice for Older and Disabled People: A Critical Review of New Developments in England', *Social Policy and Administration*, 42(5): 451–69.

Glennester, H., Hills, J., Piachaud, D. and Webb, J. (2004), *One Hundred Years of Poverty and Policy*, York: Joseph Rowntree Foundation.

Goldson, B. (2001), 'The Demonization of Children: From the Symbolic to the Institutional', in P. Foley, J. Roche and S. Tucker (eds), *Children in Society: Contemporary Theory, Policy and Practice*, Basingstoke: Palgrave, 34–41.

Gould, N. (2005), 'International Trends in Mental Health Policy', in S. Quin and B. Redmond (eds), *Mental Health and Social Policy in Ireland*, Dublin: UCD Press, 7–22.

Government of Ireland (1958), *Programme for Economic Expansion*, Dublin: Stationery Office.

Government of Ireland (1962), Coroners Act 1962, Dublin: Stationery Office.

Government of Ireland (1977), Misuse of Drugs Act 1977, Dublin: Stationery Office.

Government of Ireland (1988), Housing Act 1988, Dublin: Stationery Office.

Government of Ireland (1989), Prohibition of Incitement to Hatred Act 1989, Dublin: Stationery Office.

Government of Ireland (1991), Child Care Act 1991, Dublin: Stationery Office.

Government of Ireland (1993a), Unfair Dismissals Act 1993, Dublin: Stationery Office.

Government of Ireland (1993b), Criminal Law Suicide Act 1993, Dublin: Stationery Office.

Government of Ireland (1995), *Charting Our Education Future*, White Paper, Dublin: Stationery Office.

Government of Ireland (1996), Refugee Act 1996, Dublin: Stationery Office.

Government of Ireland (1997), *Sharing in Progress: National Anti-Poverty Strategy*, Dublin: Stationery Office, available at: www.socialinclusion.ie/NationalAnti-PovertyStrategy-SharinginProgress1997.pdf.pdf, accessed 16 August 2012.

Government of Ireland (1998), Housing (Traveller Accommodation) Act 1998, Dublin: Stationery Office.

Government of Ireland (1999), Immigration Act 1999, Dublin: Stationery Office.

Government of Ireland (2000a), Equal Status Act 2000, Dublin: Stationery Office.

Government of Ireland (2000b), Illegal Immigrants (Trafficking) Act 2000, Dublin: Stationery Office.

Government of Ireland, (2001a), Children Act 2001, Dublin: Stationery Office.

Government of Ireland (2001b), Youth Work Act 2001, Dublin: Stationery Office.

Government of Ireland (2002a), *Building an Inclusive Society: Review of the National Anti-Poverty Strategy Under the Programme for Prosperity and Fairness*, Dublin: Stationery Office.

Government of Ireland (2002b), Housing (Miscellaneous Provisions) Act 2002, Dublin: Stationery Office.

Government of Ireland (2003), Immigration Act 2003, Dublin: Stationery Office.

Government of Ireland (2004), Immigration Act 2004, Dublin: Stationery Office.

Government of Ireland (2005a), Health and Social Care Professionals Act 2005, Dublin: Stationery Office, available at: www.irishstatutebook.ie/pdf/2005/en.act.2005.0027.pdf, accessed 24 July 2012.

Government of Ireland (2005b), *The Ferns Report*, Dublin: Stationery Office.

Government of Ireland (2005c), Disability Act 2005, Dublin: Stationery Office, available at: www.oireachtas.ie/documents/bills28/acts/2005/a1405.pdf, accessed 17 July 2011.

Government of Ireland (2006a), Criminal Justice Act 2006, Dublin: Stationery Office.

Government of Ireland (2006b), *Towards 2016: Ten-Year Framework Social Partnership Agreement 2006–2015*, Dublin: Stationery Office, available at: www.taoiseach.gov.ie/attached_files/Pdf%20files/Towards2016PartnershipAgreement.pdf, accessed 20 July 2011.

Government of Ireland (2006c), *A Vision for Change: Report of the Expert Group on Mental Health Policy*, Dublin: Stationery Office, available at: www.hse.ie/eng/services/Publications/services/Mentalhealth/Mental_Health_-_A_Vision_for_Change.pdf, accessed 23 May 2012.

Government of Ireland (2007a), *National Action Plan for Social Inclusion 2007–2016*, Dublin: Stationery Office.

Government of Ireland (2007b), Health Act 2007, Dublin: Stationery Office.

Government of Ireland (2007c), Citizens Information Act 2007, Dublin: Stationery Office.

Government of Ireland (2007d), *Ireland National Development Plan 2007–2013: Transforming Ireland – A Better Quality of Life for All*, Dublin: Stationery Office, available at: www.ndp.ie/documents/ndp2007-2013/NDP-2007-2013-English.pdf, accessed 17 July 2011.

Government of Ireland (2007e), *National Action Plan for Social Inclusion 2007–2016*, Dublin: Stationery Office, available at: www.socialinclusion.ie/documents/NAPinclusionReportPDF.pdf,accessed 20 July 2011.

Government of Ireland (2008), Intoxicating Liquor Act 2008, Dublin: Stationery Office.

Government of Ireland (2009a), *Report of the Commission to Inquire into Child Abuse*, Dublin: Stationery Office.

Government of Ireland (2009b), *Report into the Catholic Archdiocese of Dublin*, Dublin: Stationery Office.

Government of Ireland (2009c), Housing Miscellaneous Provisions Act 2009, Dublin: Stationery Office.

Government of Ireland (2010a), *Announcement of Joint EU–IMF Programme for Ireland*, Government Statement 28/11/2008, available at: www.finance.gov.ie/viewdoc.asp?DocID=6600&CatID=1&StartDate=01+January+2010, accessed 8 August 2012.

Government of Ireland (2010b), *The National Recovery Plan 2011–2014*, Dublin: Stationery Office, available at: www.budget.gov.ie/The%20National%20Recovery%20Plan%202011-2014.pdf, accessed 8 August 2012.

Government of Ireland (2010c), Immigration, Residence and Protection Bill 2010, Dublin: Stationery Office.

Government of Ireland (2011a), Code of Professional Conduct and Ethics for Social Workers Bye-Law 2011, Statutory Instrument No. 143 of 2011, Dublin: Stationery Office.

Government of Ireland (2011b), Criminal Justice (Community Service) Act 2011, Dublin: Stationery Office.

Government of Ireland (2012a), *Action Plan for Jobs 2012*, Dublin: Stationery Office.

Government of Ireland, (2012b), *Pathways to Work*, Dublin: Stationery Office.

Gray, A. (2004), *Unsocial Europe: Social Protection or Flexploitation*, London: Pluto Press.

Griffiths, P. (1996), *Youth and Authority: Formative Experiences in England, 1560–1640*, Oxford: Clarendon Press.

Haase, T. and Pratschke, J. (2010), *Risk and Protection Factors for Substance Use Among Young People: A Comparative Study of Early-School Leavers and School-Attending Students*, Dublin: Stationery Office, available at:

www.nacd.ie/publications/RiskYoungPeopleSchool.pdf, accessed 28 June 2012.

Hanlon, N. (2009), 'Valuing Equality in Irish Social Care', *Irish Journal of Applied Social Studies*, 9(1): 6–14, available at http://arrow.dit.ie/ijass/vol9/iss1/3/, accessed 23 July 2012.

Hardiman, N. (2006), 'Politics and Social Partnership: Flexible Network Governance', *Economic and Social Review*, 37(3): 343–74.

Harney, M. (2004), 'Health and Social Care Professionals Bill 2004: Second Stage', Seanad Éireann Debate, 178(13).

Harvey, B. (2007), *Evolution of Health Services and Health Policy in Ireland*, Dublin: Combat Poverty Agency.

Health Information and Quality Authority (HIQA) (2012), *National Standards for the Protection and Welfare of Children for Health Service Executive Children and Family Services*, Dublin: HIQA, available at: www.hiqa.ie/system/files/Child-Protection-Welfare-Standards.pdf, accessed 20 August 2012.

Health Promotion Unit (2004), *Strategic Task Force on Alcohol – 2nd Report*, Dublin: DHC.

Health Service Executive (HSE) (2005), *Reach Out: National Strategy for Action on Suicide Prevention*, Dublin: HSE, available at: www.nosp.ie/reach_out.pdf, accessed 30 May 2012.

HSE (2009), *The Education and Development of Health and Social Care Professionals in the Health Services*, Dublin: HSE.

HSE (2010), *Roscommon Child Care Case: Report of the Inquiry Team to the Health Service Executive*, Dublin: HSE, available at: www.hse.ie/eng/services/Publications/services/Children/RoscommonChild-CareCase.pdf, accessed 28 October 2010.

HSE (2011), *Time to Move on from Congregated Settings: A Strategy for Community Inclusion*, Report of the Working Group on Congregated Settings, available at: www.hse.ie/eng/services/Publications/services/Disability/timetomoveonfromcongregatedsettings.pdf, accessed 9 August 2012.

Healy, S., Mallon, S., Murphy, M. and Reynolds, B. (2012), *Socio-Economic Review 2012: Shaping Ireland's Future – Securing Economic Development, Social Equity and Sustainability*, Dublin: Social Justice Ireland.

Heath, D.B. (1988), 'Emerging Anthropological Theory and Models of Alcohol Use and Alcoholism', in C.D. Chaudron and D.A. Wilkinson (eds), *Theories of Alcoholism*, Toronto: Addiction Research Foundation, 353–410.

Helleiner, J. (2000), *Irish Travellers: Racism and the Politics of Culture*, Toronto: University of Toronto Press.

Henman, P. (2012), 'Making Social Policy "Sexy": Evaluating a Teaching Innovation', *Australian Social Work*, iFirst article, DOI:10.1080/0 312407X.2011.652139, 1–14.

Higher Education and Training Awards Council (2010), *Awards Standards – Social Care Work*, available at: www.hetac.ie/docs/B.2.9-5.5_Awards_Standards_Social_Care_Work_2010.pdf, accessed 26 July 2012.

Hirst, P. and Thompson, G. (1999), *Globalization in Question*, 2nd edn, Cambridge: Polity Press.

Homeless Agency (2007), *A Key to the Door: The Homeless Agency Partnership Action Plan on Homelessness in Dublin 2007–2010*, Dublin: Homeless Agency.

Homeless Agency (2009), *Pathway to Home*, Dublin: Homeless Agency, available at: http://www.homelessagency.ie/getdoc/f1f3f07f-0845-4011-be50-189ffae0cee4/pathway-to-home-model.aspx, accessed 18 September 2010.

Honahon, P. (2010), *The Irish Banking Crisis: Regulatory and Financial Stability Policy 2003–2008*, Dublin: Department of Finance, available at: www.bankinginquiry.gov.ie/The%20Irish%20Banking%20 Crisis%20Regulatory%20and%20Financial%20Stability%20 Policy%202003-2008.pdf, accessed 11 June 2010.

Hough, J. (2012), 'Review Urged of Assisted Suicide Law', *Irish Examiner*, 6 January, available at: http://www.irishexaminer.com/ireland/kfqlsncwmhql/rss2/, accessed 1 June 2012.

Hourigan, N. and Campbell, M. (2010), *The TEACH Report – Traveller Education and Adults: Crisis, Challenge and Change*, Dublin: Directors of the National Association of Travellers' Centres.

Howard, N. (n.d.), *The Irish Association of Social Care Workers*, available at: www.iascw.ie/History.html, accessed 23 July 2012.

Hunt, G. and Barker, J.C. (2001), 'Socio-Cultural Anthropology and Alcohol and Drug Research: Towards a Unified Theory', *Social Science and Medicine*, 53: 165–88.

Hutson, S. and Liddiard, M. (1994), *Youth Homelessness: The Construction of a Social Issue*, Basingstoke: Macmillan.

Huysmans, J. (2000), 'The European Union and the Securitization of Migration', *Journal of Common Market Studies*, 38(5): 751–77.

Hyslop, I. (2011), 'Social Work as a Practice of Freedom', *Journal of Social Work*, 12(4): 404–22.

Immigrant Council of Ireland (ICI) (2010), *Information and Referral Service 2010: Review of Trends and Statistics*, Dublin: ICI, available at www.immigrantcouncil.ie/images/stories/241_Information_and_ Referral_Service_20102.pdf, accessed 25 October 2010.

ICI (2011), *Celebrating Diversity and Rights: 10 Years of the Immigrant Council of Ireland*, Dublin: ICI, available at: www.immigrantcouncil.ie/images/stories/pdfs/161211_ICIAnnualReview2011.pdf, accessed 16 August 2012.

Inclusion Ireland (2010), *Budget 2011: Inclusion Ireland Submission to Government*, Dublin: Inclusion Ireland, available at: www.inclusion-ireland.ie/documents/Budget2011.pdf, accessed 20 July 2011.

Independent Monitoring Group (2011), *A Vision for Change – The Report of the Expert Group on Mental Health Policy, 5th Annual Report on Implementation*, available at www.dohc.ie/publications/vision_for_change_5th/hse_nat_reg/final_5th_annual_report, accessed 6 June 2012.

Inglis, T. (1998), *Moral Monopoly: The Rise and Fall of the Catholic Church in Modern Ireland*, Dublin: UCD Press.

International Federation of Social Work (2011), 'Statement of Ethical Principles', available at: http://ifsw.org/policies/statement-of-ethical-principles/, accessed 26 July 2012.

IMPACT (2012), *Statutory Registration for Health and Social Care Professionals*, available at: www.impact.ie/Your-Sector/Public-Sector/Health/Issues/Statutory-registration.htm, accessed 25 July 2012.

Irish Association of Social Care Educators (2011), *Minutes of IASCE Meeting 9th December 2011*, available at: http://staffweb.itsligo.ie/staff/pshare/iasce/minutes/Minutes%20from%20Meeting%209th%20of%20December.pdf, accessed 25 July 2012.

Irish Association of Social Care Educators (n.d.), IASCE home page, available at: http://staffweb.itsligo.ie/staff/pshare/iasce/, accessed 23 July 2012.

Irish Association of Social Care Workers (n.d.), 'Ethical Guidelines', available at: www.iascw.ie/Ethical%20Guidelines.html, accessed 23 July 2012.

Irish Council for Social Housing (2012), *Social Housing: Newsletter of the Irish Council for Social Housing*, Summer 2012, available at: www.icsh.ie/eng/. . ./ICSH%20Newsletter%20Summer%202012.pdf, accessed 30 January 2013.

Irish Focal Point (2011), *2011 National Report (2010 data) to the EMCDDA by the Reitox National Focal Point. Ireland: New Developments, Trends and In-depth Information on Selected Issues*, Dublin: Health Research Board.

Irish Times (2005), 'Noonan's Views on Hoodies', Letters to the Editor, p. 17, 14 November, available at: http://www.lexis-nexis.com.ezproxy.wit.ie:2048/uk/nexis/results/docview/docview.do?docLinkInd=true&risb=21_T14889348437&format

=GNBFI&sort=BOOLEAN&startDocNo=1&resultsUrlKey=29_
T14889348441&cisb=22_T14889348440&treeMax=true&treeWidth=
0&csi=142626&docNo=3, accessed 10 June 2012.

Irish Traveller Movement (2011), *Cuts to Traveller Education: Position Paper*, available at: www.itmtrav.ie/uploads/Position_Paper_Traveller_Education_Cuts_April_2011.pdf, accessed 18 May 2012.

Irish Vocational Education Association (IVEA) (2009), *2009 Summary Report on Youth Work Provision in Ireland*, Dublin: IVEA.

Irish Youth Justice Service (2008a), *National Youth Justice Strategy 2008–2010*, Dublin: Irish Youth Justice Service.

Irish Youth Justice Service (2008b), *Designing Effective Local Responses to Youth Crime*, Dublin: Department of Justice, Equality and Law Reform.

Jenkinson, H. (2000), 'Youth Work in Ireland: The Struggle for Identity', *Irish Journal of Applied Social Studies*, 2(2): 106–24.

Joint Committee on Constitutional Amendment on Children (2010), *Final Report of the Joint Committee on Constitutional Amendment on Children*, Dublin: Houses of the Oireachtas, available at: www.oireachtas.ie/documents/committees30thdail/j-conamendchildren/reports_2008/FinalReport2010.pdf, accessed 21 August 2012.

Joint Oireachtas Committee on Health and Children (2006), *The High Level of Suicide in Ireland*, Seventh Report, available at: www.nosp.ie/oireachtas_report.pdf, accessed 4 June 2012.

Joint Oireachtas Committee on Health and Children (2009), *The High Level of Suicide in Ireland*, First Report, available at: www.oireachtas.ie/documents/committees30thdail/j-healthchildren/reports_2009/FirstReport.pdf, accessed 5 June 2012.

Jones, D.N. (1999), 'Regulating Social Work: Key Questions', *Practice: Social Work in Practice*, 11(3): 55–63.

Jordan, T. and Butler, S. (2011), 'The Globalization of Addiction: A Study in the Poverty of Spirit', *Drugs: Education, Prevention and Policy*, 18(4): 270–5.

Joyce, C. (2012), *Annual Policy Report on Migration and Asylum 2011*: Ireland, Dublin: ESRI, available at: http://emn.ie/files/p_201212201232142011_Annual%20Policy%20Report%20on%20Migration%20and%20Asylum_Dec2012.pdf, accessed 10 December 2012.

Joyce, C. and Quinn, E. (2009), *European Migration Network: Policies on Unaccompanied Minors in Ireland*, Dublin: ESRI, available at: www.esri.ie/UserFiles/publications/20090902092430/BKMNEXT145.pdf, accessed 19 August 2012.

Bibliography

Kate, M.-A. (2005), *The Provision of Protection to Asylum-Seekers in Destination Countries*, UNHCR Evaluation and Policy Unit, available at: www.unhcr.org/42846e7f2.pdf, accessed 19 August 2012.

Kearns, K. (1997), 'Social Democratic Perspectives on the Welfare State' in M. Lavalette and A. Pratt (eds), *Social Policy: A Conceptual and Theoretical Introduction*, London: Sage, 11–30.

Keating, D. (2012), 'Other Questions – Coroners Service', *Oireachtas Debates*, 7 February, available at: http://debates.oireachtas.ie/dail/2012/02/07/00014.asp, accessed 1 June 2012.

Kelleher, C., Christie, R., Lalor, K., Fox, J., Bowden, M. and O'Donnell, C. (2011), *An Overview of New Psychoactive Substances and the Outlets Supplying Them*, Dublin: NACD, available at: http://www.nacd.ie/publications/Head_Report2011_overview.pdf, accessed 26 June 2012.

Kelly, B.D. (2007), 'The Irish Mental Health Act 2001', *Psychiatric Bulletin*, 31: 21–24, available at: http://pb.rcpsych.org/content/31/1/21.full.pdf+html, accessed 8 June 2012.

Kelly, C., Kelly, F. and Craig, S. (2010), *Annual Report of the National Intellectual Disability Database Committee 2009*, Dublin: Health Research Board, available at: www.hrb.ie/uploads/tx_hrbpublications/Annual_Report_of_the_National_Intellectual_Disability_Database_Committee_2009_01.pdf, accessed 14 July 2011.

Kelly, C., Gavin, A., Molcho, M. and Nic Gabhainn, S. (2012), *The Irish Health Behaviour in School-Aged Children (HBSC) Study 2010*, Dublin and Galway: Department of Health and National University of Ireland, Galway, available at: www.nuigalway.ie/hbsc/documents/nat_rep_hbsc_2010.pdf, accessed 30 June 2012.

Kelly, F. and Kelly, C. (2011), *Annual Report of the National Intellectual Disability Database Committee 2010*, Dublin: HRB, available at: www.hrb.ie/uploads/tx_hrbpublications/NIDD_Committee_Annual_Report_2010_-_HRB_Statistics_Series_13.pdf, accessed 9 August 2012.

Kelly, O. (2010), 'Failure to End Long-Term Homelessness "A Disgrace"', *Irish Times*, available at: www.irishtimes.com/newspaper/ireland/2010/0913/1224278757070.html accessed 18 September 2010.

Kenna, P. (2006), *Housing Law and Policy in Ireland*, Dublin: Clarus Press.

Kennedy, E. (1970) *Reformatory and Industrial Schools System Report*, Dublin: Stationery Office.

Kenny, M. and Lodge, A. (2004), 'Traveller Community', in A. Lodge and K. Lynch (eds), *Diversity at School*, Dublin: IPA/Equality Authority, 92–101.

Kenny, M. and McNeela, E. (2006), *Assimilation Policies and Outcomes: Travellers' Experience*, Dublin: Pavee Point.

Kidd, A.J. (1999), *State, Society and the Poor in Nineteenth-Century England*, Basingstoke: Macmillan.

Kiely, E. (2009), 'Irish Youth Work Values: A Critical Appraisal', in C. Forde, E. Kiely and R. Meade (eds), *Youth and Community Work in Ireland: Critical Perspectives*, Dublin: Blackhall, 11–32.

Kiely, E. and Kennedy, P. (2005), 'Youth Policy', in S. Quin, P. Kennedy, A. Matthews and G. Kiely (eds), *Contemporary Irish Social Policy*, 2nd edn, Dublin: UCD Press, 186–205.

Kilkelly, U. (2006), *Youth Justice in Ireland: Tough Lives, Rough Justice*, Dublin: Irish Academic Press.

Kilkelly, U. (2007), *Barriers to the Realisation of Children's Rights in Ireland*, Dublin: Ombudsman for Children's Office.

Kilkelly, U. (2011), 'Policing, Young People, Diversion and Accountability in Ireland', *Crime, Law and Social Change*, 55: 133–51.

Kirby, P. (2001), 'Inequality and Poverty in Ireland: Clarifying Objectives', in S. Cantillon, C. Corrigan, P. Kirby and J. O'Flynn (eds), *Rich and Poor: Perspectives on Tackling Inequality in Ireland*, Dublin: Oak Tree Press/Combat Poverty Agency, 1–35.

Kirby, P. (2010), *Celtic Tiger in Collapse: Explaining the Weaknesses of the Irish Model*, 2nd edn, Basingstoke: Palgrave Macmillan.

Kirby, P. and Murphy, M. (2008), *A Better Ireland is Possible: Towards an Alternative Vision for Ireland*, Dublin: Community Platform.

Kirby, P. and Murphy, M.P. (2011), *Towards a Second Republic: Irish Politics after the Celtic Tiger*, London: Pluto Press.

Krugman, P. (2010a), 'Needless Suffering Will Result If Policymakers Meddle', *Irish Times*, 14 June, available at: www. lexisnexis.com.ezproxy.wit.ie:2048/uk/nexis/results/docview/ docview.do?docLinkInd=true&risb=21_T15280647120&format =GNBFI&sort=BOOLEAN&startDocNo=1&resultsUrlKey=29_ T15280647124&cisb=22_T15280647123&treeMax=true&treeWidth= 0&csi=142626&docNo=18, accessed 7 August 2012.

Krugman, P. (2010b), 'Myths of Austerity', *New York Times*, 1 July, available at: www.nytimes.com/2010/07/02/opinion/02krugman. html, accessed 7 August 2012.

Lalor, K. (2009), *Audit of Social Care Student Numbers and Programme Providers in Ireland*, available at http://arrow.dit.ie/cgi/viewcontent.cgi?article=1008&context=aaschsslcon, accessed 28 June 2012.

Lalor, K., de Róiste, Á. and Devlin, M. (2007), *Young People in Contemporary Ireland*, Dublin: Gill & Macmillan.

Lalor, K. and Share, P. (2009), 'Understanding Social Care', in P. Share and K. Lalor (eds), *Applied Social Care: An Introduction for Students in Ireland*, 2nd edn, Dublin: Gill & Macmillan, 3–20.

Langford, S. (1999), 'The Impact of the European Union on Irish Social Policy Development in Relation to Social Exclusion', in G. Kiely, A. O'Donnell, P. Kennedy and S. Quin (eds), *Irish Social Policy in Context*, Dublin: UCD Press, 90–113.

Lavalette, M. (1997), 'Marx and the Marxist Critique', in M. Lavalette and A. Pratt (eds), *Social Policy: A Conceptual and Theoretical Introduction*, London: Sage, 51–79.

Lavan, A. (2010), review of 'Social Care Practice in Ireland: An Integrated Perspective', by C. McCann James, Á. de Róiste and J. McHugh, Dublin: Gill & Macmillan, *Critical Social Policy*, 30(1): 147–49.

Layte, R. (2011), 'Should We Be Worried About Income Inequality in Ireland?' *ESRI Research Bulletin*, available at: www.esri.ie/UserFiles/publications/RB20110203.pdf, accessed 4 February 2012.

Levitas, R. (2005), *The Inclusive Society? Social Exclusion and New Labour*, 2nd edn, Basingstoke: Palgrave Macmillan.

Lewis, L. (2009), 'Introduction: Mental Health and Human Rights: Social Policy and Sociological Perspectives', *Social Policy and Society*, 8(2): 211–14.

Lister, R. (2004), *Poverty*, Cambridge: Polity.

Loftus, C. (2012), *Decent Work? The Impact of the Recession on Low Paid Workers*, Dublin: Mandate Trade Union.

Lolich, L. (2011), '… And the Market Created the Student to Its Image and Likening. Neo-Liberal Governmentality and its Effects on Higher Education in Ireland, *Irish Educational Studies*, 30(2): 271–84.

Long, J. and Mongan, D. (2010), 'Alcohol and Drug Use Among Young People in Ireland', *Drugnet Ireland*, 33: 3–7, available at: www.drugsandalcohol.ie/13279/1/Drugnet_33.pdf, accessed 29 June 2012.

Lorenz, W. (2005), 'Social Work and a New Social Order: Challenging Neo-liberalism's Erosion of Solidarity, *Social Work and Society*, 3(1): 93–101.

Lorenz, W. (2008), 'Paradigms and Politics: Understanding Methods Paradigms in an Historical Context: The Case of Social Pedagogy', *British Journal of Social Work*, 38: 625–44.

Loughnan, J. (2008), 'The Way Home: Ending Homelessness by 2010?', *Cornerstone*, 35: 10–11.

Loughran, H. (2005), 'Drugs Policy', in S. Quin, P. Kennedy, A. Matthews and G. Kiely (eds), *Contemporary Irish Social Policy*, 2nd edn, Dublin: UCD Press, 299–322.

Lynch, K. (2005), 'Neo-Liberalism and Marketization: The Implications for Higher Education', *European Educational Research Journal*, 5(1): 1–17.

MacGabhann, L., Lakeman, R., McGown, P., Parkinson, M., Redmond, M., Sibitz, I., Stevenson, C. and Walsh, J. (2010), *Hear My Voices: The Experience of Discrimination of People with Mental Health Problems in Ireland*, Dublin: Dublin City University.

Mac Gréil, M. (2010), *Emancipation of the Travelling People*, Dublin: Columba Press.

MacLachlan, M. and Smyth, C. (2004), 'Binge Drinking: Towards Constructive Action', in M. MacLachlan and C. Smyth (eds), *Binge Drinking and Youth Cultures: Alternative Perspectives*, Dublin: Liffey Press, 3–17.

Mac Laughlin, J. (1995), *Travellers and Ireland: Whose Country, Whose History?* Cork: Cork University Press.

MakeRoom (2009), 'MakeRoom Welcomes Passing of Housing Bill', press release, 2 July, available at: www.makeroom.ie/blog/archive/2009/07/02/make-room-welcomes-passing-of-housing-bill/, accessed 17 September 2010.

Martin, F. (2000), *The Politics of Children's Rights* , Cork: Cork University Press.

Mature Enjoyment of Alcohol in Society (MEAS) (2011), *National Substance Misuse Strategy 2009–2016 Minority Report by Mature Enjoyment of Alcohol in Society*, Dublin: MEAS.

Mayock, P. (2001), 'Cocaine Use in Ireland: An Exploratory Study', in R. Moran, L. Dillon, M. O'Brien, P. Mayock and E. Farrell, with B. Pike, *A Collection of Papers on Drug Issues in Ireland*, Dublin: Health Research Board, 83–152.

Mayock, P., Bryan, A., Carr, N. and Kitching, K. (2009), *Supporting LGBT Lives: A Study of the Mental Health and Well-Being of Lesbian, Gay, BiSexual and Transgender People*, Dublin: GLEN and BeLonG to Youth Service.

Mayock, P., Corr, M.L. and O'Sullivan, E. (2008), *Young People's Homeless Pathways*, Dublin: Homeless Agency.

Mayock, P. and O'Sullivan, E. (2007), *Lives in Crisis: Homeless Young People in Dublin*, Dublin: Liffey Press.

Mayock, P. and Vekić, K. (2006), *Understanding Youth Homelessness in Dublin City*, Dublin: Stationery Office.

McCann, M., O'Síocháin, S. and Ruane, J. (1994), *Irish Travellers: Culture and Ethnicity*, Belfast: Institute of Irish Studies, Queen's University Belfast.

McCann James, C., de Róiste, Á. and McHugh, J. (2009), *Social Care Practice in Ireland: An Integrated Perspective*, Dublin: Gill & Macmillan.

McCrystal, P. and Wilson, G. (2009), 'Research Training and Professional Social Work Education: Developing Research-Minded Practice', *Social Work Education*, 28(8): 856–72.

McCullagh, C. (2006), 'Juvenile Justice in Ireland: Rhetoric and Reality', in T. O'Connor and M. Murphy (eds), *Social Care in Ireland*, Cork: CIT Press, 161–76.

McDonnell, P. (2007), *Disability and Society: Ideological and Historical Dimensions*, Dublin: Blackhall.

McGuinness, C. (1993), *Kilkenny Incest Investigation by South Eastern Health Board*, Dublin: Stationery Office.

McLaughlin, K. (2007), 'Regulation and Risk in Social Work: The General Social Care Council and the Social Care Register in Context', *British Journal of Social Work*, 37(7): 1263–1277.

McMahon, S. (2009), 'The Voluntary Youth Work Sector's Engagement with the State: Implications for Policy and Practice', in C. Forde, E. Kiely and R. Meade (eds), *Youth and Community Work in Ireland: Critical Perspectives*, Dublin: Blackhall, 105–126.

McVeigh, R. (2007), '"Ethnicity Denial" and Racism: The Case of the Government of Ireland Against Irish Travellers', *Translocations*, 2(1): 90–133, available at: www.imrstr.dcu.ie/volume1issue2/volume1issue2-6.pdf, accessed 14 May 2012.

McVeigh, R. (2008), 'The 'Final Solution': Reformism, Ethnicity Denial and the Politics of Anti-Travellerism in Ireland', *Social Policy and Society*, 7(1): 91–102.

Meade, R. (2009), 'Community Development: A Critical Analysis of its "Keywords" and Values', in C. Forde, E. Kiely and R. Meade (eds), *Youth and Community Work in Ireland: Critical Perspectives*, Dublin: Blackhall, 57–80.

Meehan, N. (2010), 'Church and State Bear Responsibility for Bethany Home', *History Ireland*, 18(5): 10–11.

Mental Health Commission (2009), *From Vision to Action? An Analysis of the Implementation of A Vision for Change*, Dublin: Mental Health Commission, available at: www.mhcirl.ie/Publications/From_Vision_to_Action_An_Analysis_of_the_Implementation_of_A_Vision_for_Change.pdf, accessed 4 June 2012.

Migrant Rights Centre Ireland (2005), *Social Protection Denied: The Impact of the Habitual Residency Condition on Migrant Workers*, Dublin: MRCI, available at: www.mrci.ie/media/File/Social%20Protection%20Denied%20-%20Impact%20of%20HRC.pdf, accessed 16 August 2012.

Moran, J. (2005), 'Refugees and Social Policy', in S. Quin, P. Kennedy, A. Matthews and G. Kiely (eds), *Contemporary Irish Social Policy*, 2nd edn, Dublin: UCD Press, 256–76.

Moran, J. (2009), 'Containment and Asylum Seekers: Locking Up the Poor and Vulnerable as a Welfare Response in Ireland', paper presented at the Sociological Association of Ireland Conference, Waterford Institute of Technology, Waterford, 9 May 2009.

Morgan, K., McGee, H., Dicker, P., Brugha, R., Ward, M., Shelley, E., Van Lente, E., Harrington, J., Barry, M., Perry, I. and Watson, D. (2009) *SLÁN 2007: Survey of Lifestyle, Attitudes and Nutrition in Ireland. Alcohol Use in Ireland: A Profile of Drinking Patterns and Alcohol-Related Harm from SLÁN 2007*, Dublin: DHC, available at: www.dohc.ie/publications/pdf/slan_alcohol_report.pdf?direct=1, accessed 30 June 2012.

Morrison, K. (2006), *Marx, Durkheim, Weber: Formations of Modern Social Thought*, 2nd edn, London: Sage.

Mulkeen, M. (2009a), 'Equality: A Challenge to Social Care', in P. Share and K. Lalor (eds), *Applied Social Care: An Introduction for Students in Ireland*, Dublin: Gill & Macmillan, 110–21.

Mulkeen, M. (2009b), 'Anti-Discriminatory Practice: A New Direction for Social Care', in P. Share and K. Lalor (eds), *Applied Social Care: An Introduction for Students in Ireland*, Dublin: Gill & Macmillan, 276–87.

Mullally, S. (2011), 'Separated Children in Ireland: Responding to "Terrible Wrongs"', *International Journal of Refugee Law*, 23(4): 632–55.

Muncie, J. and Hughes, G. (2002), 'Modes of Youth Governance: Political Rationalities, Criminalization and Resistance', in J. Muncie, G. Hughes and E. McLaughlin (eds), *Youth Justice: Critical Readings*, London: Sage, 1–18.

Murphy, T. (1996), *Rethinking the War on Drugs in Ireland*, Cork: Cork University Press.

National Advisory Committee on Drugs (NACD) and Public Health Information and Research Branch (PHIRB) (2012), *Drug Use in Ireland and Northern Ireland: Drug Prevalence Survey 2010/11: Regional Drug Task Force (Ireland) and Health & Social Care Trust (Northern Ireland) Results*, Dublin and Belfast, available at: www.nacd.ie/publications/drug_use_ireland_new_2012.pdf, accessed 26 June 2012.

National Council for Curriculum and Assessment (2005), *Guidelines on Intercultural Education in the Primary School*, Dublin: NCCA.

National Disability Authority (2006), *Mainstreaming Position Paper*, Dublin: National Disability Authority.

National Economic and Social Council (NESC) (2005), *The Developmental Welfare State*, Report No. 113, Dublin: NESC.

National Economic and Social Forum (2007), *Mental Health and Social Inclusion*, Report 36, Dublin: National Economic and Social Forum.

National Office of Suicide Prevention (2001), *Suicide in Ireland: A National Study*, Dublin: Departments of Public Health on behalf of the Chief Executive Offices of the Health Boards.

National Social Work Qualification Board (NSWQB) (2006), *Social Work Posts in Ireland*, Dublin: NSWQB.

National Substance Misuse Strategy Steering Group (2012), *Steering Group Report on a National Substance Misuse Strategy*, Dublin: Department of Health, available at: http://healthupdate.gov. ie/wp-content/uploads/2012/02/Steering-Group-Report-on-a-National-Substance-Misuse-Strategy-7-Feb-11.pdf, accessed 10 February 2012.

National Suicide Research Foundation (2011), *National Registry of Deliberate Self-Harm Annual Report 2010*, Cork: National Suicide Research Foundation.

Neumayer, E. (2005), *Asylum Recognition Rates in Western Europe: Their Determinants, Variation and Lack of Convergence*, London: LSE Research Online, available at: http://eprints.lse.ac.uk/613/1/JournalofConflictResolution_49%281%29.pdf, accessed 16 August 2012.

Neville, D. (2001), 'Suicide: From a Crime to Public Health in a Decade', *The Furrow*, 52(7/8): 387–94.

Neville, D. (2011), 'Suicide Incidence', *Parliamentary Debates Dáil Éireann: Official Report (Unrevised)*, 74(1), 14 September, available at: http://debates.oireachtas.ie/dail/2011/09/14/unrevised1.pdf, accessed 5 June 2012.

Ni Shuinéar, S. (2002), 'Othering the Irish (Travellers)', in R. Lentin and R. McVeigh (eds), *Racism and Anti-Racism in Ireland*, Belfast: Beyond the Pale, 177–92.

Nolan, B. (2009), 'Income Inequality and Public Policy', *Economic and Social Review*, 40(4): 489–510.

Nolan, B. and Maître, B. (2008), *A Social Portrait of Communities in Ireland*, Dublin: Office for Social Inclusion, available at: www. socialinclusion.ie/publications/documents/SocialPortraitOfCommunities.pdf, accessed 16 August 2012.

Nolan, B. and Whelan, C.T. (1996), *Resources, Deprivation, and Poverty*, Oxford: Clarendon.

Norris, M. and Redmond, D. (eds) (2005), *Housing Contemporary Ireland: Policy, Society and Shelter*, Dublin: IPA.

Norris, M. and Winston, N. (2005), 'Housing and Accommodation of Irish Travellers: From Assimilationism to Multiculturalism and Back Again', *Social Policy and Administration*, 39(7): 802–21.

Ó'Cinnéide, S. (2010), 'From Poverty to Social Inclusion: The EU and Ireland', in European Anti Poverty Network Ireland (ed.), *Ireland and the European Social Inclusion Strategy: Lessons Learned and the Road Ahead*, Dublin: EAPN Ireland, 18–33.

O'Connell, J. (2002), 'Travellers in Ireland: An Examination of Discrimination and Racism', in R. Lentin and R. McVeigh (eds), *Racism and Anti-Racism in Ireland*, Belfast: Beyond the Pale, 49–62.

O'Connell, P.J., Joyce, C. and Finn, M. (2012), *International Migration in Ireland, 2011*, Working Paper No. 434, Dublin: ESRI.

O'Connor, H. (2010), *Youth Unemployment in Ireland: The Forgotten Generation*, Dublin: National Youth Council of Ireland.

O'Connor, N. (2008), 'Can We Agree the Number of People Who are Homeless (and Does it Really Matter?)', in D. Downey (ed.), *Perspectives on Irish Homelessness: Past, Present and Future*, Dublin: Homeless Agency, 58–63.

O'Connor, T. (2006), 'Social-Care Practice: Bringing Structure and Ideology in from the Cold', in T. O'Connor and M. Murphy (eds), *Social Care in Ireland: Theory, Policy and Practice*, Cork, CIT Press, 85–100.

O'Connor, T. (2009), 'Social Care and Social Change: Future Direction or Lost Opportunity', in P. Share and K. Lalor (eds), *Applied Social Care: An Introduction for Students in Ireland*, 2nd edn, Dublin: Gill & Macmillan, 99–109.

O'Doherty, C. (2003), 'The Future of Social Care: Providing Services and Creating Social Capital', *Irish Journal of Applied Social Studies*, 4(2): 59–63, available at: http://arrow.dit.ie/ijass/vol4/iss2/6, accessed 17 January 2013.

O'Doherty, C. (2006), 'Social Care and Social Capital', in T. O'Connor and M. Murphy (eds), *Social Care in Ireland: Theory, Policy and Practice*, Cork, CIT Press, 25–41.

O'Donnell, R. and O'Reardon, C. (2000), 'Social Partnership in Ireland's Economic Transformation', in G. Fajertag and P. Pochet (eds), *Social Pacts in Europe – New Dynamics*, Brussels: European Trade Union Institute/Observatoire Social Europeen, 1–17.

O'Donovan, M-A. (2011), *Annual Report of the National Physical and Sensory Disability Database Committee 2010*, Dublin; Health Research Board, available at: www.hrb.ie/uploads/tx_hrbpublications/Annual_Report_of_the_National_Physical_and_Sensory_Disability_Database_Committee_2010.pdf, accessed 9 August 2012.

O'Donovan, M.-A., Doyle, A. and Craig, S. (2010), *Annual Report of the National Physical and Sensory Disability Database Committee 2009*, Dublin; HRB, available at: www.hrb.ie/uploads/tx_hrbpublications/NPSDDC_annual_report_2009_statistics_series_11.pdf, accessed 14 July 2011.

O'Keane, V., Walsh, D. and Barry, S. (2005), *'The Black Hole': The Irish Psychiatric Association Report on the Funding Allocated to Adult Mental Health Services: Where is it Actually Going?* available at: http://www.irishpsychiatry.ie/Libraries/External_Affairs/IPA_The_Black_Hole_Report.sflb.ashx, accessed 6 June 2012.

O'Mahony, P. (2008), *The Irish War on Drugs: The Seductive Folly of Prohibition*, Manchester: Manchester University Press.

Ó Riain, S. (2008), 'Competing State Projects in the Contemporary Irish Political Economy', in M. Adshead, P. Kirby and M. Millar (eds), *Contesting the State: Lessons from the Irish Case*, Manchester: Manchester University Press, 165–85.

O'Sullivan, E. (2003), 'Marxism, the State and the Homelessness in Ireland', in M. Adshead and M. Millar (eds), *Public Administration and Public Policy in Ireland: Theory and Methods*, London: Routledge, 37–53.

O'Sullivan, E. (2005), 'Homelessness' in M. Norris and D. Redmond (eds), *Housing Contemporary Ireland: Policy, Society and Shelter*, Dublin: IPA, 245–67.

O'Sullivan, E. (2008), 'Pathways Through Homelessness: Theoretical Constructions and Policy Implications', in J. Doherty and B. Edgar (eds), *In My Caravan I Feel Like Superman: Essays in Honour of Henk Meert 1963–2006*, St Andrews: FEANTSA/Centre for Housing Research, University of St Andrews, 71–100.

O'Sullivan, E. (2009), 'Residential Child Welfare in Ireland, 1965–2008: An Outline of Policy, Legislation and Practice: A Paper Prepared for the Commission to Inquire into Child Abuse', Dublin: *CICA Report* 4, 245–430.

O'Toole, J. (2009), 'Gender and Social Care: Mapping a Structural Analysis', in P. Share and K. Lalor (eds), *Applied Social Care: An Introduction for Students in Ireland*, Dublin: Gill & Macmillan, 137–49.

Office of the Children's Ombudsman (2010), *A Report Based on an Investigation Into Children First: National Guidelines for the Protection and Welfare of Children*, Dublin: OCO, available at: www.oco.ie/assets/files/PressReleases/Children%20First/OCOinvestigationintoimplementatofChildrenFirst.pdf, accessed 24 May 2010.

Office of the Children's Ombudsman (2012), *Advice of the Ombudsman for Children on the Heads of the Children First Bill 2012 and The Criminal*

Justice (Withholding of Information on Offences Against Children and Vulnerable Persons) Bill 2012, Dublin: OCO, available at: www.oco.ie/assets/files/publications/advice_to_government/Adviceon-WithholdingandChildrenFirstJun12.pdf, accessed 21 August 2012.

Office of the Minister for Children (2007), *The Agenda for Children's Services*, Dublin: Stationery Office.

Office of the Minister for Children and Youth Affairs (2008), *National Review of Compliance with Children First: National Guidelines for the Protection and Welfare of Children*, Dublin: Stationery Office.

Office of the Minister for Children and Youth Affairs (2009), *Report of the Commission to Inquire into Child Abuse, 2009 – Implementation Plan*, Dublin: Stationery Office, available at: www.dcya.gov.ie/documents/publications/Implementation_Plan_from_Ryan_Commission_Report.pdf, accessed 20 August 2012.

Office of the Minister for Integration (2008), *Migration Nation: Statement on Integration Plan and Diversity Management*, Dublin: Office of the Minister for Integration, available at: www.integration.ie/website/omi/omiwebv6.nsf/page/AXBN-7SQDF91044205-en/$File/Migration%20Nation.pdf, accessed 1 August 2012.

Office of the Refugee Applications Commissioner (2012), *Annual Report 2011*, available at: www.orac.ie/pdf/PDFCustService/AnnualReports/Office%20of%20the%20Refugee%20Applications%20Commissioner%20-%20Annual%20Report%20-%202011.pdf, accessed 17 August 2012.

Oliver, M. (1990), *The Politics of Disablement*, Basingstoke: Macmillan.

Organisation for Economic Co-Operation and Development (2011), *Health at a Glance 2011: OECD Indicators*, Paris: OECD, available at: http://dx.doi.org/10.1787/health_glance-2011-en, accessed 29 June 2012.

Organisation for Economic Co-Operation and Development (2012), 'G20 Labour Ministers Must Focus on Young Jobseekers', press release, 15 May, available at: www.oecd.org/document/39/0,3746,en_21571361_44315115_50323559_1_1_1_1,00.html, accessed 21 June 2012.

PA Consulting (2009), *Inspiring Confidence in Children and Family Services: Putting Children First and Meaning It*, Dublin: Health Service Executive.

Pavee Point (2011), *Briefing: Why Recognise Travellers as an Ethnic Group?* available at http://paveepoint.ie/2011/10/briefing-why-recognise-Travellers-as-an-ethnic-group/, accessed 25 May 2012.

Pearson, C. (2000), 'Money Talks? Competing Discourses in the Implementation of Direct Payments', *Critical Social Policy*, 20(4): 459–77.

Penketh, L. (2006), 'Racism and Social Policy', in M. Lavalette and A. Pratt (eds), *Social Policy: Theories, Concepts and Issues*, 3rd edn, London: Sage, 87–104.

Peyton, L. and Wilson, K. (2006), *Mid-Term Review of the National Children's Strategy 2000–2010*, Dublin: National Children's Advisory Council.

Phelan, E. and Norris, M. (2008), 'Neo-Corporatist Governance of Homeless Services in Dublin: Reconceptualization, Incorporation and Exclusion', *Critical Social Policy* 28(1): 51–73.

Pike, B. (2011), 'Where Do Drugs Fit In?', *Drugnet Ireland*, 37: 3–4.

Pillinger, J. (2008), 'Pathways Into, Through and Out of Homelessness', in D. Downey (ed.), *Perspectives on Irish Homelessness: Past, Present and Future*, Dublin: Homeless Agency, 64–73.

Pompili, M., Mancinelli, I. and Tatarelli, R. (2003), 'Stigma as a Cause of Suicide', *British Journal of Psychiatry*, 183: 173–74.

Powell, F. (1981), 'Dean Swift and the Dublin Foundling Hospital', *Studies*, 70(278/279): 162–70.

Powell, F. (1992), *The Politics of Irish Social Policy 1600–1990*, Lewiston: Edwin Mellen Press.

Powell, F., Geoghegan, M., Scanlon, M. and Swirak, K. (2010), *Working With Young People: A National Study of Youth Work Provision and Policy in Contemporary Ireland*, Cork: University College Cork.

Pratt, A. (1997), 'Neo-Liberalism and Social Policy', in M. Lavalette and A. Pratt (eds), *Social Policy: A Conceptual and Theoretical Introduction*, London: Sage, 31–49.

Pritchard, C. (1995), *Suicide – The Ultimate Rejection? A Psycho-Social Study*, Buckingham: Open University Press.

Quin, S. and Redmond, B. (2003), 'Introduction', in S. Quin and B. Redmond (eds), *Disability and Social Policy in Ireland*, Dublin: UCD Press, 1–9.

Quin, S. and Redmond, B. (2005), 'Disability and Social Policy' in S. Quin, P. Kennedy, A. Matthews and G. Kiely (eds), *Contemporary Irish Social Policy*, 2nd edn, Dublin: UCD Press, 138–56.

Quinn, E., Stanley, J., Joyce, C. and O'Connell, P.J. (2008), *Handbook on Immigration and Asylum in Ireland 2007*, Research Series No. 5, Dublin: ESRI.

Raftery, M. and O'Sullivan, E. (1999), *Suffer the Little Children: The Inside Story of Ireland's Industrial Schools*, Dublin: New Island.

Randall, N. (2011), 'Drug Policy and Rationality: An Exploration of the Research–Policy Interface in Ireland', *Drugs: Education, Prevention and Policy*, 18(4): 285–94.

Reception and Integration Agency (RIA) (2005), 'Code of Practice for Persons Working in Accommodation Centres', available at: www. ria.gov.ie/en/RIA/Code%20of%20Practice%20Doc%20Sept%20 2005.pdf/Files/Code%20of%20Practice%20Doc%20Sept%202005. pdf, accessed 19 August 2012.

RIA (2012), *Monthly Statistics Report: May 2012*, available at: www.ria.gov.ie/en/RIA/RIAMay%28A4%292012.pdf/Files/ RIAMay%28A4%292012.pdf, accessed 17 August 2012.

Referendum Commission (2012), *The Children Referendum – The Referendum Commission's Independent Guide*, Dublin: Referendum Commission.

Resident Managers Association (n.d.), 'About', available at: http:// residentmanagersassociation.com/?page_id=2, accessed 23 July 2012.

Richardson, V. (2005), 'Children and Social Policy', in S. Quin, P. Kennedy, A. Matthews and G. Kiely (eds), *Contemporary Irish Social Policy*, 2nd edn, Dublin: UCD Press, 157–85.

Robins, J. (1986), *Fools and Mad: A History of the Insane in Ireland*, Dublin: IPA.

Robins, J. (1987), *Lost Children: History of the Charity Child in Ireland, 1700–1900*, Dublin: IPA.

Rogers, A. and Pilgrim, D. (2010), *A Sociology of Mental Health and Illness*, 4th edn, Buckingham: Open University Press.

Round Table Solutions/Pathfinder (2010), *Evaluation of the Programme of Advocacy Services for People with Disabilities in the Community and Voluntary Sector*, Dublin: Citizens Information Board, available at: www.citizensinformationboard.ie/publications/advocacy/evalua- tion_of_advocacy_services_for_people_with_disabilities_2010.pdf, accessed 21 July 2012.

RTE (2012), 'As It Happened – Children's Referendum Count', 13 November, available at: http://www.rte.ie/news/2012/1111/live- childrens-referendum.html, accessed 13 November 2012.

Russell, H., Maître, B. and Nolan, B. (2010), *Monitoring Poverty Trends in Ireland 2004–2007: Key Issues for Children, People of Working Age and Older People*, ESRI Research Series, No. 17, available at: www.esri. ie/UserFiles/publications/RS17.pdf, accessed 4 February 2012.

Russell-Bennett, R., Hogan, S. and Perks, K. (2010), 'A Qualitative Investigation of Socio-Cultural Factors Influencing Binge-drinking: A Multi-Country Study', in Australian and New Zealand Market- ing Conference: Doing More With Less (ANZMAC 2010), 29 November–1 December 2010, Christchurch, New Zealand, available at: http://eprints.qut.edu.au/40863/1/c40863.pdf, accessed 17 January 2013.

Ryall, G. and Butler, S. (2011), 'The Great Irish Head Shop Controversy', *Drugs: Education, Prevention and Policy*, 18(4): 303–11.

Sales, R. (2007), *Understanding Immigration and Refugee Policy: Contradictions and Continuities*, Bristol: Policy Press.

Sapouna, L. (2006), 'Tracing Evidence of Institutionalisation in the Process of Deinstitutionalisation – the Irish Case', in P. Herman and L. Sapouna (eds), *Knowledge in Mental Health: Reclaiming the Social*, New York: Nova Science, 85–99.

Scholte, J.A. (2005), *Globalization: A Critical Introduction*, 2nd edn, Basingstoke: Palgrave Macmillan.

Sedghi, A. (2012), 'Youth Unemployment Across the OECD: How Does the UK Compare?' *Guardian*, 16 May, available at: www.guardian.co.uk/news/datablog/2012/may/16/youth-unemployment-europe-oecd, accessed 21 June 2012.

Seefeldt, K., Abner, G., Bolinger, J.A., Xu, L. and Graham, J.D. (2012), *At Risk: America's Poor During and After the Great Recession*, Bloomington, Ind.: School of Public and Environmental Affairs, Indiana University.

Separated Children in Europe Programme (2004), *Statement of Good Practice*, 3rd edn. Copenhagen/Geneva: Save the Children/UNHCR.

Shakespeare, T. (2003), 'The Social Model of Disability', in L.J. Davis (ed.), *The Disability Studies Reader*, 2nd edn, New York: Routledge, 197–204.

Shakespeare, T. (2006), *Disability Rights and Wrongs*, Abingdon: Routledge.

Shannon, G. (2009), *Third Report of the Special Rapporteur on Child Protection: A Report Submitted to the Oireachtas*, available at: www.omc.gov.ie/documents/publications/Child_Protection_Rapporteur_Report.pdf, accessed 2 May 2010.

Share, P. (2009), 'Social Care and the Professional Development Project', in P. Share and K. Lalor (eds), *Applied Social Care: An Introduction for Students in Ireland*, 2nd edn, Dublin: Gill & Macmillan, 58–73.

Share, P. and Lalor, K. (eds) (2009) *Applied Social Care: An Introduction for Students in Ireland*, 2nd edn, Dublin: Gill & Macmillan.

Share, P. and McElwee, N. (eds) (2005), *Applied Social Care: An Introduction for Students in Ireland*, Dublin: Gill & Macmillan.

Shatter, A. (2012), 'Other Questions – Coroners Service', Oireachtas Debates, 7 February, available at: http://debates.oireachtas.ie/dail/2012/02/07/00014.asp, accessed 1 June 2012.

Shneidman, E. (1985), *The Definition of Suicide*, New York: John Wiley.

Silke, D. (2005a), 'Accommodating the Traveller Community', in M. Norris and D. Redmond (eds), *Housing Contemporary Ireland: Policy Society and Shelter*, Dublin: IPA, 268–88.

Silke, D. (2005b), 'Housing Policy', in S. Quin, P. Kennedy, A. Matthews and G. Kiely (eds), *Contemporary Irish Social Policy*, 2nd edn, Dublin: UCD Press, 51–79.

Simpson, G. (1952), 'Editor's Preface', in E. Durkheim (1897/1952), *Suicide: A Study in Sociology*, trans. J.A. Spaulding and G. Simpson, London: Routledge.

Smith, M. and Whyte, B. (2008), 'Social Education and Social Pedagogy: Reclaiming a Scottish Tradition in Social Work', *European Journal of Social Work*, 11(1): 15–28.

Smyth, C., MacLachlan, M. and Clare, A. (2003), *Cultivating Suicide: Destruction of Self in a Changing Ireland*, Dublin: Liffey Press.

Smyth, E. (2008), 'Just a Phase? Youth Unemployment in the Republic of Ireland', *Journal of Youth Studies*, 11(3): 313–29.

Smyth, E., McCoy, S. and Darmody, M. (2004), *Moving Up: The Experiences of First Year Students in Post-Primary Schools*, Dublin: Liffey Press.

Social Care Ireland (2011), 'What is Social Care Work?' available at: http://socialcareireland.ie/index.php/faq/, accessed 24 July 2012.

Social Inclusion Division (n.d.), 'What is Poverty?' available at: www.socialinclusion.ie/poverty.html, accessed 28 January 2012.

Social Justice Ireland (2010), *Policy Briefing: Poverty*, Dublin: SJI, available at: www.socialjustice.ie/sites/default/files/file/SJI%20Briefing%20Docs/2010-02-01%20-%20Policy%20Briefing%20Poverty%20Feb%202010%20FINAL.pdf, accessed 28 January 2012.

Social Justice Ireland (2011), *Socio-Economic Review 2011*, Dublin: Social Justice Ireland.

Somers, J. and Bradford, S. (2006), 'Discourses of Partnership in Multi-Agency Working in the Community and Voluntary Sectors in Ireland', *Irish Journal of Sociology*, 15(2): 67–85.

SONAS DP (2005), *Final Report*, Dublin: SONAS DP.

Squires, P. (1990), *Anti-Social Policy: Welfare, Ideology and the Disciplinary State*, Hemel Hempstead: Harvester-Wheatsheaf.

Standing, G. (2011), *The Precariat: The New Dangerous Class*, London: Bloomsbury Academic.

Staniforth, B., Fouché, C. and O'Brien, M. (2011), 'Still Doing What We Do: Defining Social Work in the 21st Century', *Journal of Social Work*, 11(2): 191–208.

Stewart, K. (2005), 'Changes in Poverty and Inequality in the UK in International Context', in J. Hills and K. Stewart (eds), *A More Equal*

Society? New Labour, Poverty, Inequality and Exclusion, Bristol: Policy Press, 297–321.

Sweeney, L. (2011), *Young Irish Male Perspectives on Depression and Peer Suicide*, unpublished PhD thesis, College of Health Sciences, University College Dublin.

Sweeney, P. (2012), 'The Advocates of Austerity Are Now Calling for Growth', available at http://www.progressive-economy. ie/2012/06/advocates-of-austerity-are-now-calling.html, accessed 10 November 2012.

Task Force on the Travelling Community (1995), *Report of the Task Force on the Travelling Community: Executive Summary*, available at: www. lenus.ie/hse/bitstream/10147/45449/1/7868.pdf, accessed 17 May 2012.

Tomlinson, M. and Walker, R. (2012), 'Labour Market Disadvantage and the Experience of Recurrent Poverty', in P. Emmenegger, S. Häusermann, B. Palier and M. Seeleib-Kaiser (eds), *The Age of Dualization: The Changing Face of Inequality in Deindustrializing Societies*, Oxford: Oxford University Press, 52–70.

Toolan, D. (2003), 'An Emerging Rights Perspective for Disabled People in Ireland: An Activist's View', in S. Quin and B. Redmond (eds), *Disability and Social Policy in Ireland*, Dublin: UCD Press, 171–81.

Townsend, P. (1979), *Poverty in the United Kingdom: A Survey of Household Resources and Standards of Living*, Berkeley, Calif.: University of California Press.

Treacy, D. (2009), 'Irish Youth Work: Exploring Potential for Social Change', in C. Forde, E. Kiely and R. Meade (eds), *Youth and Community Work in Ireland: Critical Perspectives*, Dublin: Blackhall, 177–98.

Tussing, D. and Wren, M-A. (2006), *How Ireland Cares: The Case for Health Care Reform*, Dublin: New Island.

United Nations (1989), *Convention on the Rights of the Child*, Geneva: United Nations.

United Nations (2000), *Protocol to Prevent, Suppress and Punish Trafficking in Persons, Especially Women and Children*, available at: www. uncjin.org/Documents/Conventions/dcatoc/final_documents_2/ convention_%20traff_eng.pdf, accessed 20 August 2012.

United Nations (2006), *UN Convention on the Rights of Persons with Disabilities*, available at: www.un.org/disabilities/documents/ convention/convention_accessible_pdf.pdf, accessed 9 August 2012.

United Nations Committee on the Rights of the Child (2006), *Concluding Observations Ireland*, Geneva: United Nations.

United Nations High Commissioner for Refugees (UNHCR) (2000), *The State of the World's Refugees*, Oxford: Clarendon.

UNHCR (2011), *Asylum Levels and Trends in Industrialised Countries 2010*, available at: www.unhcr.org/4d8c5b109.pdf, accessed 18 August 2012.

Van Heugten, K. (2011), 'Registration and Social Work Education: A Golden Opportunity or a Trojan Horse', *Journal of Social Work*, 11(2): 174–90.

Vertovec, S. (2007), *Circular Migration: The Way Forward in Global Policy*, Oxford: University of Oxford International Migration Institute, Working Paper 4, available at: www.imi.ox.ac.uk/pdfs/imi-working-papers/wp4-circular-migration-policy.pdf, accessed 22 January 2011.

Wade, R.H. (2007), 'Should We Worry About Income Inequality?', in D. Held and A. Kaya (eds), *Global Inequality*, Cambridge: Polity Press, 104–31.

Walker, M.R. (2006), *Suicide Among the Irish Traveller Community 2000–2006*, Wicklow: Wicklow County Council.

Wallace, J. and Pease, B. (2011), 'Neoliberalism and Australian Social Work: Accommodation or Resistance?', *Journal of Social Work*, 11(2): 132–142.

Walsh, B. (1987), 'Alcohol and Alcohol Problems Research 15. Ireland', International Review Series, *British Journal of Addiction*, 82(7): 747–51, available at: http://ehis.ebscohost.com.ezproxy.wit.ie:2048/ehost/pdfviewer/pdfviewer?vid=3&hid=115&sid=d80b9738-28f4-4362-b406-f6c261534027%40sessionmgr111, accessed 28 June 2012.

Walsh, B. and Walsh, D. (2011), 'Suicide in Ireland: The Influence of Alcohol and Unemployment', *Economic and Social Review*, 42(1): 27–47.

Walsh, D. (2005), *Juvenile Justice*, Dublin: Thompson Round Hall.

Walsh, D. (2008), *Suicide, Attempted Suicide and Prevention in Ireland and Elsewhere*, Dublin, Health Research Board.

Ward, E. (1996), 'Ireland's Refugee Policies and the Case of the Hungarians', *Irish Studies in International Affairs*, 7: 131–41.

Watson, D. and Nolan, B. (2011), *A Social Portrait of People with Disabilities in Ireland*, Dublin: Department of Social Protection and ESRI, available at: www.socialinclusion.ie/documents/2011-09-21_SocPortraitPWDReportforWebsite.pdf, accessed 18 July 2012.

Watson, D., Lunn, P., Quinn, E. and Russell, H. (2011), *Multiple Disadvantage in Ireland: An Equality Analysis of Census 2006*, Dublin: Equality Authority/ESRI.

Weiss, I., Gal, J. and Katan, J. (2006), 'Social Policy for Social Work: A Teaching Agenda', *British Journal of Social Work*, 36: 789–806.

White, M. (2008), *What We Can Do About Suicide in the New Ireland*, available at: www.senatormarywhite.ie/uploads/What_We_Can_Do_About_Suicide_In_The_New_Ireland.pdf, accessed 5 June 2012.

Wilberforce, M., Glendinning, C., Challis, D., Fernandez, J-L., Jacob, S., Jones, K., Knapp, M., Manthorpe, J., Moran, N., Netten, A. and Stevens, M. (2011), 'Implementing Consumer Choice in Long-term Care: The Impact of Individual Budgets on Social Care Providers in England', *Social Policy and Administration*, 45(5): 593–612.

Wilkinson, R. and Pickett, K. (2010), *The Spirit Level: Why Equality Is Better for Everyone*, 2nd edn, London: Penguin.

Williams, D. and Lalor, K. (2001), 'Obstacles to the Professionalisation of Residential Child Care Work, *Irish Journal of Applied Social Studies*, 2(3): 73–90.

Wilson, A., Riddle, S. and Barron, S. (2000), 'Welfare for Those Who Can? The Impact of the Quasi-Market on the Lives of People with Learning Difficulties', *Critical Social Policy*, 20(4): 479–502.

Woods, M. (2006), 'The Contours of Learning/Intellectual Disability', in D. McCluskey (ed.), *Health Policy and Practice in Ireland*, Dublin: UCD Press, 188–206.

World Bank (2012), *World Development Indicators 2012*, Washington D.C.: World Bank, available at: http://data.worldbank.org/sites/default/files/wdi-2012-ebook.pdf, accessed 16 August 2012.

World Health Organization (WHO) (1978), *Primary Health Care: Report of the International Conference on Primary Health*, Alma-Ata, USSR, 6–12 September, available at: whqlibdoc.who.int/publications/9241800011.pdf, accessed 29 June 2012.

WHO (1986), *Ottawa Charter for Health Promotion*, available at: www.who.int/healthpromotion/conferences/previous/ottawa/en/index.html, accessed 29 June 2012.

WHO (2007), 'What is Mental Health?' Online Q&A 3 September, available at: www.who.int/features/qa/62/en/index.html, accessed 6 June 2012.

WHO (2013), *Draft Comprehensive Mental Health Action Plan 2013–2020*, Geneva: WHO, available at: http://apps.who.int/gb/ebwha/pdf_files/EB132/B132_8-en.pdf, accessed 17 January 2013.

Wren, M.-A. (2006), *How Ireland Cares: The Case for Health Care Reform*, Dublin: New Island.

Yeates, N. (2008), 'Global Migration Policy', in N. Yeates (ed.), *Understanding Global Social Policy*, Bristol: Policy Press, 229–52.

Index

Note: Tables are indicated by page numbers in bold

Index

Index

Index

Index

Index

Index

Index

Index